THE
INDEPENDENT
MAN

W. O. Saunders, the Independent Man

THE
INDEPENDENT
MAN

by KEITH SAUNDERS

The Story of W. O. Saunders
and His Delightfully
Different Newspaper

Library of Congress Catalog Card Number: 62-16359

N.C.
B
Saunders

PRINTED AND BOUND IN THE UNITED STATES OF AMERICA

BY EDWARDS & BROUGHTON COMPANY, RALEIGH, N. C.

CONTENTS

CONTENTS

PREFACE

For more years than I care to admit, I procrastinated in the matter of setting down for posterity the story of my father, the late W. O. Saunders, and his newspaper, *The Independent*, published at Elizabeth City, North Carolina, from June 1908 to September 1937.

Finally, when I realized that I could put it off no longer, I set about the writing of this volume, using as source materials the bound files (from 1918 on) of *The Independent* in the University of North Carolina Library, some earlier incomplete volumes loaned by a friend, portions of an unfinished and unpublished autobiography, other selected writings, and my personal recollections of W. O. Saunders as a father and as my mentor during the eight years (1929-1937) in which I served my journalistic apprenticeship under him.

Whether the decision was a wise one or not is now moot, but I decided at the outset that I would not attempt a serious biography of my father, because I doubted that I could be sufficiently objective to bring it off. I chose, instead, to write a book that was more *by* W. O. Saunders than *about* W. O. Saunders, making extensive use of his newspaper writings with introductions, interpolations and comments of my own. It was my feeling that what he did and said (and in my opinion he was utterly incapable of guile or dissembling) would more effectively tell what kind of a man he was than would my own words alone.

There is little continuity in this book beyond the first few chapters. After that, each chapter pretty much stands by itself as dealing with some aspect of *The Independent's* editorial policy, some illuminating episode in Dad's newspaper career, some particular facet of The Independent Man's character, or some crusade which he carried on. I think that, collectively, they tell the reader what kind of a man was W. O. Saunders.

In the early years of his free-swinging, name-calling, rough-and-ready newspaper, "W.O." succeeded in getting himself shot at once, assaulted from ambush several times, threatened with a tar-and-feather party and sued for libel some 50 or 60 times. Only the circumstances that he had a tough hide, a sense of humor, was right most of the time and published his weekly in a state with a liberal libel law kept this brash young editor from being incarcerated or assassinated.

Dad's main trouble was that he felt privileged to say that Citizen Jones was stealing the county blind, even though Jones had not been placed under indictment and the only evidence available to the editor was of a circumstantial nature. He generally knew what he was talking about but would have had a helluva time proving it at the time he wrote his news story or editorial.

My Dad was many things—fearless, forthright, audacious, witty, kind, compassionate—but if I had to characterize him briefly, I'd have to say something like this: W. O. Saunders was a common man, and because he was such a man he was ever ready to do battle with anyone who would essay to cheat, lie to, deceive, defraud, bamboozle, take advantage of, trample, or otherwise wrong or abuse a fellow common man. That, in my opinion, was basically what made W. O. Saunders tick.

So look not in these pages for a penetrating or profound character study; look, instead, for an entertaining tale of a highly personal journalist—one of the last and greatest of that rare breed—and his delightfully, daringly different small town weekly newspaper. The title is a name by which Editor Saunders liked to refer to himself in the early days of his career as an editor.

I gratefully acknowledge the helpful advice given me by James C. Derieux, a former editor of *The American Magazine* and of *Collier's* and a friend and admirer of my father; the kindness of Harry Golden in taking time out from a busy lecture and writing schedule to do the foreword for this book; to Mrs. Carson Davis for furnishing me with early copies of *The Independent* which I otherwise might not have seen; to those whose financial assistance made publication of this book possible; and finally, to my devoted wife, Mary, whose patience and forebearance enabled me to prepare the manuscript of THE INDEPENDENT MAN at times when I should have been helping her with the dishes or yard work.

THE AUTHOR

THE LOCALE

W. O. Saunders published his controversial, hide-peeling, iconoclastic, but never dull weekly newspaper—*The Independent*—in the town of Elizabeth City, North Carolina, for a period of nearly thirty years. For one fully to appreciate the story of Editor Saunders and his newspaper, one should know something about its locale.

Despite many drawbacks, Elizabeth City wasn't a bad little town at all. There were hundreds scattered around America that differed from it in few respects.

The town is situated on a horseshoe bend in the placid and picturesque Pasquotank River, on the Inland Waterway. Like most small towns it has its Main Street, which starts at the river's edge and runs west for a little more than a mile to the Norfolk Southern Railroad tracks and depot. Crossing Main Street at right angles in the center of the town is the principal north-south thoroughfare, Road Street, which begins at Knobb's Creek and ends at the gates of the Hollywood Cemetery. The usual Confederate monument stands in the center of the square between the county courthouse and the U.S. District Court building and Post Office.

Located about fifty miles south and west of the seaport city of Norfolk, Va., Elizabeth City is the gateway to

Roanoke Island, site of the first English settlement in America (1584) and birthplace of Virginia Dare, and to Kitty Hawk, where the Wright Brothers in 1903 had made man's first successful flight in a power-driven, heavier-than-air machine.

Lumber manufacturing was the town's principal industry half a century ago and remains so even today, there being several sizable lumber, millwork and plyboard plants located on waterways just outside the city limits. Elizabeth City's lumber industry was started back about the turn of the century by enterprising Northerners attracted there by a fortuitous (for them) combination of vast stands of timber, waterways over which rafts and barges could move freely, and, above all else, an abundance of cheap labor.

This labor, mostly colored, drew less than ten cents an hour and worked a 60-hour week when *The Independent* first started publishing. Their lot improved within Dad's day to where they were earning $12 to $14 a week and working a 48-hour week, which was still not much better than starvation wages.

Dad once commented in a philosophy/humor column in *The Independent* that: "It's been my observation that mills that call their hands to work with a whistle pay such durn poor wages that the poor devils who work in 'em can't afford to own a watch or clock by which they could tell the time for themselves."

In addition to its lumber industry, Elizabeth City had— and still has—a cotton mill, several hosiery mills, candy factory and marine railways and piers at which yachts of wealthy Northerners could tie up in fresh water at a reasonable cost when not on cruise. And it had a wholesale fish house which processed and shipped to northern markets tons of fresh and salt water fish caught in nearby Albemarle, Currituck, Croatan and Pamlico sounds.

But Elizabeth City essentially was a rural town, the trading center for half a dozen rural counties where thousands of carloads of Irish potatoes and hundreds of carloads of May peas and other truck crops were grown. The farmers of this section were for the most part a hardworking, decent, churchgoing lot. They worked in the fields all week and came to Elizabeth City on Saturday to have their horses shod, to have corn ground into meal, to buy such farming essentials as harness, barbed wire and plowshares, and to stock up on flour, sugar, lard and other commodities which they could not produce on their farms. While the menfolk were about their business, the good farm women peddled eggs, butter and other produce and then went to the Bee Hive, McCabe & Grice's or Rucker & Sheely's to buy thread, yard goods, shoes or women's wear.

In short, Elizabeth City was a typical Baptist-Methodist-Democratic small town when Dad cast his lot there in 1908. The town at that time had no paved streets; one bogged down on Main Street on rainy days and kicked up a cloud of dust in dry weather. The public utilities were privately owned, including the sewerage system. Electric lights and power were undependable, the water was hardly fit for human consumption, and more than half the town was not served by sewers. There were 1,700 smelly, fly-breeding ground privies in the town proper.

Most of the town's physical shortcomings could be traced to graft and greed in City Hall and in the County Courthouse, and when Dad cleaned the rascals out of those institutions he paved the way for progress to come to Elizabeth City. He lived to see the town acquire a well groomed look, with municipally owned electric light, water and sewerage systems; a fireproof hotel; a fine public library; a first-rate hospital owned jointly by the city and county; fire and street cleaning departments with the most modern equipment, and just about everything that makes for modern living. Details of *The Independent's* fight on graft and corruption as well as its fight for sanitation are related in ensuing chapters.

Dad's newspaper played an important part in the material and civic progress of the town and region. I feel certain, though, that he would have much preferred that an objective history of Elizabeth City and the Albemarle region should record that his newspaper played a greater role as a torch-bearer among an inherently fine and upstanding people who were, nevertheless, hidebound by more than two centuries of isolation, lack of education and much poverty.

He jolted a rural region out of its smug conceit that all was well with its best of all possible worlds. And as he progressed in emancipating the minds of his local public and in creating a provincial respect for freedom of thought and freedom of speech he got a good many jolts in return, and had a lot of youthful conceit ironed out of him.

Although it came to be widely circulated throughout North Carolina and some thirty other states in its heyday, *The Independent* was essentially a newspaper serving six or eight rural counties in Northeastern North Carolina. As such, it waged campaign after campaign for the uplift or betterment of the section and its people. It gave birth to the idea of a handsome memorial to the Wright Brothers on Kill Devil Hills, birthplace of aviation, and the project was brought to fruition largely through the combined efforts of W. O. Saunders and his good friend, Lindsay Warren, then rising to eminence in Congress.

Concurrently, *The Independent* advocated construction of a highway and a bridge over Currituck Sound, linking the mainland with the Wright Memorial, Nags Head and Roanoke Island. And these, too, were built. Starting in

1928 and continuing for several years thereafter, *The Independent* advocated that Lake Mattamuskeet in Northeastern North Carolina be taken over by the Federal Government and made into a wildlife refuge, and this finally came about in 1934.

Also in 1934, Dad wrote an editorial suggesting that a symphonic drama be written around the story of Virginia Dare and Sir Walter Raleigh's ill-fated Lost Colony, and that this be produced each summer in an amphitheater on Roanoke Island. This vision of an American Oberammergau captured the imagination of Prof. Frederick Koch, then head of the drama department and the Carolina Playmakers at the University of North Carolina, and of the brilliant young playwright, Paul Green, also of Chapel Hill. Dad visited Koch and Green at Chapel Hill, they visited him in Elizabeth City, and they went together to the actual site where the colonists landed and built a fort in 1584.

The result was that Paul Green wrote "The Lost Colony," a stirring outdoor drama which, except for a wartime blackout, has been produced each summer since 1937.

The Wright Memorial and "The Lost Colony" are the outstanding monuments to Dad's vision and drive, but there were other improvements in the way of health and sanitation, conservation measures, roads and bridges which might not have come about at all or would most certainly have been delayed for years but for the persistent prodding of *The Independent*.

I go back to Elizabeth City about once a year. It is a nice little town. And I like to think that it is nicer because Dad published his newspaper there for close to thirty years.

FOREWORD

H. L. Mencken once wrote that if the South only had forty editors like W. O. Saunders, it could be rid of most of its problems in five years.

And indeed it would. But if you can't have forty editors like W. O. Saunders it was still good to have had one. Saunders takes his place beside Marion Reedy, E. W. Howe, Oscar Ameringer and William Allen White, as one of the truly great personal journalists of our times.

In his newspaper days, W. O. Saunders did all things that make some newspapermen colorful. During a particularly interesting murder case, he succeeded in tieing up the only telephone wire out of Elizabeth City (N.C.), and thereby insured that his scoop was his and his alone.

But W. O. Saunders also did the things that make a few newspapermen great.

Saunders was the editor of *The Independent* which was published in Elizabeth City, a rural provincial area in the eastern part of North Carolina. It was an area one might say was not quick to adopt enlightened views.

In some ways, therefore, W. O. Saunders was a greater editor than those noble men I've mentioned because daily he put his honor—and his livelihood—on the line. He lived through a crisis when one-half of his six thousand subscrib-

2

ers cancelled their subscriptions and eighty per cent of his
advertisers cancelled out. W. O. Saunders survived because
he would not back water. He was a great man.

The crisis arose out of the anti-Semitic attacks launched
by a bigoted evangelist named Mordecai Ham who used the
name of Jesus for hate-mongering.

Mordecai Ham was once a powerful and influential figure
in the backwoods. I personally had some experience with
him. There were small towns where the few Jewish businessmen collected a ransom from themselves and sent an
emissary to Ham, offering him the money if he promised
not to visit their town.

But W. O. Saunders was not frightened by Ham. Nor
was he persuaded by him. He ran front page editorials
denouncing his message of hate and castigating Ham's
desecration of Christianity. When the folks advised him
to lay off, Saunders increased the intensity of his attacks.

Now why would Saunders take up this cause at such
a cost to himself? For the same reason I suspect that
Thomas Jefferson fought for religious freedom for all,
though there were few "Jews, Turks, and heathens" in
Virginia at the time. Both Saunders and Jefferson were
not only patriots but essentially American gentlemen.

When Saunders went after Ham, there were no social-
action societies in the South to protect a beleagured minor-
ity. The Federal laws were hard to invoke and the state had
not passed the laws it one day would. Indeed, there weren't
enough Jews to mount a barricade, for there were no more
than six Jewish families in the whole area. But W. O.
Saunders fought for a principle—for America—and he
won! He kept hammering away, telling his subscribers
about the meaning of America, and the American Dream,
and eventually Elizabeth City, North Carolina, sent Mordecai Ham packing.

It is true that Ham still hopped here and there about the South, but he never fully recovered from the editorial blows of W. O. Saunders.

Let us stand up, therefore, and salute the memory of this noble American.

—HARRY GOLDEN

Charlotte, North Carolina
February 1, 1962

A REBEL
1.   IS BORN

Some individuals are born with a rebellious streak in their makeups. One such individual was my father. I'm not at all sure that he ever knew just where this "orneriness" came from—whether through heredity, or environment, or some pronounced incident in his early life. But it was there.

In fact, Dad may have rebelled against being born at all. His parents in later years told him that his delivery was prolonged, and was accomplished only with the aid of a pair of plow lines against which my grandmother pulled while bracing her feet against the foot of the bedstead.

And well he might have rebelled, for it was no soft environment into which young William Oscar Saunders was born on May 24, 1886.

The environment into which Dad was born will not ring a bell with many who are living today, but many of our fathers and mothers knew some such life from firsthand experience or had neighbors or relatives who did.

His father was a Southern Baptist; his mother was a Southern Methodist. She had come from a House of Plenty, where there were big barns overflowing with wheat and corn and housing fine, sleek cattle; a huge smokehouse filled with hams and bacon; and a pantry bountifully stocked with homemade mince meat, prepared pumpkin, lard, molasses, honey, flour and meal from wheat and corn grown on the plantation and ground at the old water mill on Goodman's mill pond. All this plus almost limitless quantities of dried and preserved fruits, jellies, jams, pickles and condiments. Those oldtimers in the House of Plenty did not neglect the flesh pots.

Dad's father, on the other hand, came from a House of Want, of a once fairly proud family that had imported its house furnishings from England—heavy, cumbersome mahogany and walnut stuff that was later traded off for shiny quartered-oak factory-built makeshifts.

John Saunders had brought Ella Byrd to the House of Want. There were holes in the roof of the old homestead, great cracks in the floors, and many a windowpane that was stuffed with rags to keep out the cold of winter. The Civil War had left Dad's paternal ancestors impoverished. The grandmother had died while John, the youngest of several children, was a mere slip of a boy. The old home place had grown up with black gum and yaupon. Grandmother cooked in a big open fireplace, her only cooking utensils an iron pot hung from a crane and a large iron frying pan, called a creeper.

The first year my grandfather and grandmother were married little was grown on the farm. Grandpa had first to clear the land of its growth of small timber and shrubs, and then he had to lime and sour the land to bring it back into productivity. Of course, he had no money with which to buy lime, so he felled trees, split them into stove length pieces and hauled the wood to town, trading a load of wood for a load of oyster shells. Then he burned the oyster shells so as to make lime with which to sweeten his soil.

Grandma wrestled with her one pot and pan, washed the children's too-seldom clothes, scrubbed floors, tended pigs and chickens, worked a garden, made clothing for the family when she had the makings, patched and darned and quilted—and bore children.

Grandpa, undernourished in youth, was never a strong man. After a few years he turned the farm over to a Negro tenant and moved to town (Hertford, North Carolina, county seat of Perquimans County), where life appeared easy to his rustic eyes. But it wasn't easy. He earned a precarious livlihood as a jack-leg carpenter, a machinist's helper, a huckster—anything that offered him an opportunity to turn an honest penny.

He succeeded better at huckstering than at anything else. Grandpa was a religious, God-fearing man. Afraid of the devil, too. He respected an obligation and farmers, discovering this, would trust him with their chickens, eggs, hides, bees-wax and other produce, which he would retail or sell to wholesale produce dealers for a profit. In time he opened a small store stocked with a modest line of staples, meats and country produce. It fell to young Will's lot at the age of ten, going on eleven, to look after the little shop while his father scoured the countryside for his produce, or was buying and slaughtering meat animals.

Dad didn't like keeping store, cutting meats, haggling with penny-pinching customers. But the work had its compensations. There were many hours in the store during which no customer appeared. Dad devoted those slack hours to reading. He had little opportunity to go to school. There wasn't much of a school to go to, anyway, and at school they kept you in one book for months when Dad could read and assimilate everything of interest to him in a book in a few hours, or in a few days at the most.

He read pretty much everything he could get his hands on, especially the five-cent blood-and-thunder weeklies such as Nick Carter, Old King Brady, and the James Brothers. He avidly read the editorials of a promising new writer named Arthur Brisbane. The one intellectual in the town, Dr. Tom Cox, subscribed to the late Elbert Hubbard's "Philistine," and Dad read everything he could buy or borrow that was attributed to that writer. In fact, he formed such an admiration for Elbert Hubbard that some years later when his first child turned out to be a girl he named her Elizabeth Elberta Saunders.

And then one day Dr. Tom Cox told Dad that there was nothing really new under the sun; that Hubbard and Brisbane and Brann, the iconoclast, who was raising the devil in Texas, all got their style and their ideas from Emerson, Hugo, Carlyle, Macauley and Voltaire. Dad made a resolution to read the works of these great thinkers and writers.

About that time, Dad received a mental jolt that profoundly influenced his life. He later wrote of this episode in these words:

"It was a Sunday morning and the Sabbath School class which I attended in the Baptist church was concerned with the lesson of the covenant of God with Noah. The teacher expounded from the Book of Genesis, wherein it is related that God placed a rainbow in the heavens after the flood, as a covenant with Noah that he would never again destroy the earth by flood.

"Now it happened that this Sabbath School teacher was the principal of the public school which I sometimes attended, and only a short while before this teacher had explained the rainbow as a simple phenomenon of an arc or circle consisting of the prismatic colors, formed by the refraction and reflection of rays of light from drops of water or vapor suspended in the part of the heavens opposite the sun.

"And so I timidly raised a question: Had not drops of water or vapor been suspended in the heavens from the

beginning of time? Had not the same sun shone upon them
and produced the same color effects even before Noah and
the ark? Would we not have had the same rainbow if there
had never been a Noah?

" 'Shut up!' barked the purveyor of divine wisdom. 'You
are an infidel.'

"Me an infidel! I quailed before the hateful word, for an
infidel was anathema in the sight of man and God in the
little town in which I lived.

"I left the Sabbath School that morning with the word
infidel ringing in my ears. Presently my shame and humil-
iation turned to anger and defiance. And so an infidel is
one who seeks the truth? was the thought that formed in
my mind. I determined to know more about infidels. I had
dared to think, and for thinking I had been publicly
damned.

"What had those famous infidels like Thomas Paine and
Robert G. Ingersoll thought, that they had been forever
damned? I would find out. I sought and read Paine's 'Age
of Reason' and the Lectures of Robert Ingersoll. And so,
early in life, in spite of a religious ancestry and family
prayers, I was shunted off into agnosticism. If I was not
born a rebel, I was early in life made one.

"But for that rainbow episode, I might have become an
evangelical preacher or a patent medicine fakir. The possibilities of both of these professions had profoundly interested me in my boyhood. . . .

"I am sure I might have continued to aspire to one or
the other of these ignoble professions had not my contempt
for ignorance, gullibility and hypocrisy been aroused by
the cruel and thoughtless rebuke of a teacher. What men
needed was frankness, sincerity and truth. Instead of catering to ignorance, superstition and fear, the leaders of men
should have a passion for truth and righteousness. I would

rather be a writer and expose shams, hypocrisies and lies, exalt truth, defy the enemies of right and reason. At the age of seventeen I had determined to become an editor."

The fact that he had almost no education other than self-education, and precious little of that, did not deter Dad from applying for a job on the staff of a newspaper in nearby Norfolk, Virginia. He didn't get it, of course, but he did talk the paper into letting him handle its circulation in Hertford and Perquimans County.

He had no inkling at the time, but this lowly job was destined in a scant few months to catapult him into the journalistic sphere to which he so fervently aspired.

A BACKWARDS
2. BEGINNING

Dad began his journalistic career all topsy-turvy. A great murder trial was getting under way in Elizabeth City, N. C., eighteen miles from Hertford, and the struggling daily newspaper in Norfolk, fifty miles from the scene of the crime, had no reporter to spare to cover the most sensational case in local history. Dad, who was doing circulation work for the paper, offered his reporting services on a space rate basis, and a news editor whose mind that day was befuddled with too much drink gave him the assignment without questioning his experience—or lack of same.

The body of an attractive girl by the name of Nellie Cropsey had been found floating in the Pasquotank River, and a suitor with whom she was known to have quarreled was indicted on suspicion of murder.

It was Dad's first job of reporting, and he found himself at a press table with star reporters from Baltimore, Washington, Philadelphia and New York, for the case was a national sensation.

The trial lasted for nearly two weeks. The Norfolk paper printed Dad's stuff, and lawyers on both sides of the case commended his reporting of the trial. He was too green, too earnest, to color or distort the facts for the sake of making his stories more interesting or lurid. The reporters from the big metropolitan newspapers paid no attention to him and he remained shy of them. But the experience of covering the Nellie Cropsey murder trial cast the die in so far as Dad's career was concerned.

At the conclusion of the trial the owner of *The Tar Heel*, a weekly newspaper in Elizabeth City, offered Dad the editorship of his paper at a starting salary of six dollars a week. At six it started and there it stuck.

The Tar Heel, like most rural weeklies of the period, and like some even of the present day, was edited largely with paste pot and shears. The editor faithfully clipped from other newspapers and magazine articles that interested him and which, he assumed, would interest his readers. He made the rounds of the stores on Main Street, loafed much around the courthouse, met the incoming trains each day and jotted down trivial items of personal mention.

He had no opinions, wrote no editorials and never bothered to play up any big news. If a house burned down, a ship was wrecked or somebody got his head shot off, the editor assumed that his public knew the facts from personal knowledge and writing a piece about it was a sheer waste of time. After all, what people were interested in was seeing their own names in the paper. If Mrs. Smith Sundayed with Mrs. Jones at South Mills or Will Raper went to Norfolk on business, such was news and was faithfully recorded. Old Man Pastorfield cancelled his subscription because he hadn't seen his name in the paper for close to twelve months. Such was the nature of *The Tar Heel* when young Saunders arrived on the scene and assumed the editorship.

Meanwhile, Dad had been reading Pulitzer's *World* and Hearst's *Evening Journal* and studying their methods and their makeup. In short order he had the Elizabeth City *Tar Heel* looking what it was, an amateurish imitation of

New York yellow journalism. He printed all the news that was fit to print, and then some. And he wasn't long in discovering that the most unpopular role a man can possibly essay is to go among his fellow men taking notes and ruthlessly printing them.

Everybody likes sensational journalism until it turns the spotlight on themselves, their kin or their very dear friends. Messrs. Pulitzer and Hearst could print the most awful things about Boss Tweed and John D. Rockefeller and get away with it, because if either Boss Tweed or Mr. Rockefellow had gone a-gunning for either Mr. Pulitzer or Mr. Hearst he couldn't have found either of them. But the chief of the Elizabeth City fire department who took $80 graft in a purchase of fire hose and the town alderman who got his house lights free from the private public utilities company had no difficulty whatever in finding the editor of the local paper. A one-man newspaper in a small town where everybody knows everybody else is expected to be a good little newspaper.

So Dad's premiere as editor was short-lived. He was getting the owner of the paper in a lot of hot water, and a number of key men in the town were telling him to drop his brash young editor—or else. So Dad pulled up stakes and went to a neighboring town, Edenton, where there was an idle newspaper plant owned by leading citizens. They leased him the plant at a nominal rental for the sake of having some sort of a newspaper in their town. But Edenton, rich in history, proud of its traditions, and respectful of the high order of its old fashioned citizenship, was no field for a sensational personal journalist. Dad's newspaper venture there lasted but three months, but he departed with the confidence and good will of an honorable and understanding citizenry who never reminded him that he owed them three months' rent. His income as "owner, editor and publisher" of *The Edenton Transcript* was probably less than a dollar a day. But at least he was learning.

Back to Norfolk he went, with two rich experiences as editor behind him, and begged for work in the news rooms of Norfolk newspapers. James M. Thomson, who later became publisher of the *New Orleans Item*, was hammering his way into the political control of Norfolk with a tawdry little sheet that was daily exposing graft and corruption in the city administration. Thomson, it developed, had been greatly amused by Dad's swan song in the *Transcript*, an editorial in which he had asserted without malice that Edenton's colonial history was impressive but made "damn poor belly timber." Thomson took Dad on as a rewrite man— at a dollar a day.

At that time, a fellow could somehow live on a dollar a day, even in a city. For if certain expenses were higher in the city than in the small towns, the city had its bar rooms and the bar rooms had free lunches. Dad later reminisced about those days and said he would always remember the old-time bar rooms with a feeling of appreciation and gratitude, for he was thirsty and they gave him a big schooner of beer for a nickel; and he was hungry, and they threw in a free lunch with the beer. This enabled him to carry on. He soon learned every bar room in Norfolk and what it served on its free lunch counter each day.

He paid twenty-five cents a night for a bed in a cheap lodging house. For a dime he had rolls and coffee for breakfast at a dairy lunch counter. Lunch and supper cost him a nickel each, thanks to the saloons. He laundered his underwear, socks and handkerchiefs, shined his shoes with banana peels, made a collar last a week by cleaning it with bread crumbs. He kept himself in cheap clothes of a sort, and had two dollars left over for a visit to a brothel every fourth Saturday night.

"Dollar days! Good old days they were," Dad recalled some years later. "I had less and desired less than at any other time in my life. National advertising and high pressure salesmanship had not created the discontent of these modern times. Many working men supported families and held their heads up on a dollar wage in those days. We had no auto license tags or gasoline, no radios or movie tickets to buy; buying on the installment plan was almost unknown.

"True, I couldn't buy a suit of clothes at one time; I bought a coat at one time, a pair of pants at another. And those odd coats were odd indeed!—always two or three inches too short and forever riding up and exposing the shiny seat of my trousers."

One day Managing Editor Jim Thomson said to Dad: "Saunders, why don't you wear a longer coat?" Dad hadn't thought much about it. It took him a full minute to frame a reply, and then he said: "I'll put an inch on my coat for every dollar raise in salary you'll give me." That week he was raised to seven dollars a week and his troubles began.

Until he got that dollar raise he had thought little about money. He was working for the sheer love of work and through an obsession of pride in his chosen profession; the salary didn't matter. He had never had occasion to question its adequacy, had taken the inconveniences and hardships of poverty as a matter of course. He had been schooled to poverty.

But that dollar raise gave him a new outlook on life. He began to plan what to do with that extra dollar, and he soon found that he could do so many different things with that extra dollar that he wished there were more extra dollars to do more things with. He began to take more pride in his personal appearance and began to pay attention to a pretty girl. The more things he found to do with an extra dollar, the more extra dollars he yearned to do with.

Now it so happened that one of the owners of *The Norfolk Dispatch* was a devout religious man who taught one of the largest men's Bible classes in the city. One day he said to Will Saunders: "Young man, I wish you would become a member of my Bible class."

Dad asked him casually if membership in the class would hasten another raise in his salary. The prompt reply was that it would. Dad had heard that the success of many mediocre country come-ons in the city was achieved by joining a rich man's Bible class and selling their souls to the rich man; now his suspicions were confirmed. He thought less of one of the newspaper's owners. He later told in these words how his budding, tinseled journalistic career soon began to show tarnish:

"I thought still less of these owners when, after a long and bitter fight for lower electric light and gas rates for the people of Norfolk, *The Dispatch* announced that its fight had been won. Rates for certain large consumers had been reduced; rates for the home owner and small business man were undisturbed.

"I read the headlines in *The Dispatch* proclaiming its great victory. I went to Jim Thomson and asked him if he hadn't read the new rate schedule wrong? 'Why,' said I, naively, 'this is no victory for the people; it benefits only the privileged class.'

" 'That is what we were fighting for, Saunders,' replied Thomson. He tried to explain to me that the paper's chief concern was for the economic welfare of the business interests upon whom it depended for its advertising patronage and without which no paper could meet its payroll.

"A feeling of shame and nausea came over me. Thomson had been one of my idols, a towering, fiery-headed, brave and honest demi-god, waging relentless war against graft and pillage and greed in behalf of the masses who could not help themselves. And now I beheld him as but the mouthpiece of business interests who gave him their advertising accounts so long as he wrote and published to suit them.

"And what of his war against the entrenched political machine in Norfolk? Was it but to drive out one set of rascals, who were friendly to the rival newspaper, only to let in another set of rascals who would pay tribute to *The Dispatch?* I wondered."

Dad was still in the cub reporter class, but he was having his eyes opened. He had no idea of the further enlightenment he was in for in the years just ahead.

Dad stayed with the *Dispatch* for a while because a gruff but kindly city editor named Marshall Ballard saw potentialities in the spunky young Saunders and guided and assisted him until he became a pretty good reporter. Then the *Norfolk Ledger* and the *Dispatch* merged and became the *Ledger-Dispatch*, headed by one S. J. Slover.

Some twenty-five years later, Dad told in *The Independent* how he came to part ways with the Norfolk newspapers. He wrote:

"I had no use for Sam Slover and could never work under a man of his type. Slover was a newspaper man for the money he could get out of it; I was a newspaper man for the love of it. We could never understand each other."

Dad next got a job as chief clerk for the North Carolina Pine Association in Norfolk, but his itch to write bothered him, and there were so many things in Norfolk that were crying to be written about. While working for the Pine Association, he published at intervals a little pamphlet called the *Muck Rake*, in which he tore the hide off predatory business interests and thieving politicians in Norfolk, an activity which inevitably caused him to lose his job. He then went to New Orleans as staff correspondent for the *Lumber Trade Journal* published in that city. In the panic of 1907-08 he lost his job with the *Journal* and found himself stranded in Norfolk with a wife and two babies (he had married in March 1905). There wasn't a job in sight, so he went to Elizabeth City, where his wife and babies could find a haven in the humble home of her people.

And thus, via a circuitous routing that had taken him to Norfolk, to Edenton, back to Norfolk, down to New Orleans, and back again to Norfolk, W. O. Saunders finally came back in the winter of 1908 to the little town where he had begun his journalistic career as an eager but green young reporter covering a major criminal trial.

THE COURTHOUSE
3. RING

Big cities are not alone in having their political bosses.
Nearly every county seat has its courthouse ring or clique.
And some of these bosses in small-town America are every
bit as shrewd, quite as ruthless, and in many cases more intelligent than a Tweed, a Hague or a De Sapio.

W. O. Saunders collided head-on with Boss Rule when
he moved to Elizabeth City in 1908 and took over the editorship of a small and struggling newspaper, *The Daily Star*,
owned by Walter L. Cohoon and his father, F. F. Cohoon.
A wealthy, intelligent and belligerent attorney by the name
of E. F. Aydlett was running things in Elizabeth City in
those days, and woe be unto the newspaper that dared print
anything that displeased him.

Aydlett had the largest law practice in town and commanded a following in every county in the First Congressional District. His word was law. They called him the
Grand Wizard. No political move was made, no public
enterprise projected, no public improvements undertaken, no
political candidacy announced without the sanction and
approval of the Grand Wizard. From his law offices on
Main Street he made and unmade politicians, and no business could prosper that thwarted his will.

And then there was a minor boss or contact man who

always held some public office and carried out the orders of the Grand Wizard. His name was Mac Sawyer, commonly called Boss Mac.

Dad had worked on the paper only a week or two before he received a telephone call from the Grand Wizard asking him if he expected to publish anything concerning a certain criminal assault case. Dad answered in the affirmative. "Well, you mustn't publish it," Aydlett said, "and I trust you understand that my wishes must be respected."

With considerable satisfaction, Dad played up the assault case on the front page of the newspaper that very afternoon. The paper had not been long on the streets when Cohoon dashed into the shop, red in the face, and demanded to know why Dad had disregarded the Grand Wizard's request. Cohoon then served notice that if Dad ever printed anything else with which Mr. Aydlett was concerned without first submitting it to Mr. Aydlett, Dad would be fired. Whereupon Dad wanted to know who the hell Cohoon wanted to be editor of his newspaper—W. O. Saunders or E. F. Aydlett? For this impertinence, he was fired. But before clearing out he served notice on Cohoon that he intended to publish a free-speaking newspaper of his own in Elizabeth City and write what he damn well pleased about Aydlett, Boss Mac, Cohoon or anyone else in the town. He was soon to learn that this threat was easier made than implemented.

In *The Independent's* 25th anniversary edition in 1933, Dad told publicly for the first time just how acute were the labor pains that preceded the birth of his newspaper.

"For weeks I walked the streets of Elizabeth City without employment, without money and without a substantial friend. In this desperate plight something had to be done, for I was married now and had two babies and a wife to support. I learned that printers' supply houses sold their goods on terms of one-fourth cash and the balance in monthly installments running over a period of two years. I was 24 years old and full of energy and optimism. I figured out a modest printing equipment costing $1,200. I needed $300 to make the first payment on it. I went out into the town to organize a stock company offering 30 shares of stock at $10 a share. It looked so simple. But nobody was interested.

"But there was a lawyer in the town who had a bee in his bonnet, Roscoe W. Turner. Turner wanted to be a Trial Judge of the county and he was in disfavor with E. F. Aydlett and M. N. Sawyer, without whose favor no man could succeed to any office. Turner conceived a great scheme.

"He knew that I didn't like Aydlett and that I had no use for Aydlett's key man, Mac Sawyer. Turner also knew that there were many citizens in the town, both Republicans and Democrats, who had no use for either Aydlett or Sawyer. Turner passed the hat among these men and collected a fund of $300, telling them that he was going to turn me loose on Aydlett and Sawyer for a period of three months, which is as long as he thought I would last.

"And then Turner sent for me. He didn't tell me the truth at all. He told me of his great fatherly interest in any young man who was trying to get a foothold in life. He told me what a poor boy he had been himself.

" 'I have a little spare money lying idle and I'm going to lend you $300 with no strings tied to it. Just give me a bill of sale on your printing plant,' he said.

"The deal was made and I innocently launched a newspaper that Turner confidently expected to use to achieve his personal ambition. Without knowing what Turner had up his sleeve, I did exactly what he shrewdly expected me to do. The first issue of my paper, published on June 8, 1908, had something in it that offended Mr. Aydlett. Mr. Aydlett met me on the street and bawled me out, telling me that I could not publish a newspaper in this town with his name in it. And that was all he needed to say to get my dander up and make me resolve not to publish an issue of *The Independent* without his name in it."

Dad had published but a few issues of his newspaper in Elizabeth City before every advertiser in the town had deserted him. Some openly told him that they could not advertise with him because *The Independent* had offended the Grand Wizard, and they valued his trade and that of his family and friends. Another said apologetically that the Grand Wizard was his lawyer and was in possession of many of his business secrets. Others who dropped their advertising said they would come back when Dad's fight on the Grand Wizard was over. Then came the squeeze play, as described in *The Independent* twenty-five years later. Dad wrote:

"A few weeks later Roscoe Turner sauntered into my office in an upstairs room at the corner of Main and Water streets and confidently announced that the war on Aydlett and Sawyer should cease.

" 'It has only begun,' I said quietly.

" 'It has ended,' said Turner. 'I have got what I wanted. I knew that I could drive old Mac Sawyer to terms. I am going to be the next Trial Judge of Pasquotank County, and your attacks on Mr. Aydlett and Mr. Sawyer must cease.'

" 'Like hell,' I replied.

" 'But I hold a bill of sale on your plant, and I will close you out if you don't obey my orders,' said Turner.

" 'Close me out,' I cried, "and I will go to this town with a handbill and tell them just what a dirty scamp you are! I don't believe the decent people of this town will let a debt

of $300 stand between them and the publication of a news-
paper that dares to tell the truth about the graft, greed
and cussedness existing in Elizabeth City.'

"Turner saw that I had him cornered, and he went back
to Mr. Sawyer and told him he was only bluffing when he
had represented himself as controlling *The Independent*.

" 'Well, the only way you can clear your skirts is to make
a public denial that you are in any way responsible for the
dirty sheet,' said Mac Sawyer.

"And that afternoon Turner came out in a signed statement in Cohoon's *Daily Star* branding as false and defamatory statements that he had any connection with *The Independent* or was in any way responsible for it. Whereupon
the next issue of *The Independent* printed a copy of the
bill of sale held by Roscoe Turner and invited him to be
a good sport as well as a cheerful liar and relinquish that
bill of sale, since he had repudiated it."

Turner didn't relinquish the bill of sale, and the document several years later got into the hands of another
ambitious politician named Dack Newbury, who used it to
contrive a deal with Boss Mac. Newbury obligated to
deliver *The Independent* to its enemies if he failed over a
period of twelve months in silencing the newspaper with
respect to Grand Wizard Aydlett, Boss Mac Sawyer and
certain of their henchmen. What then happened might have
come straight out of a whodunit novel. Here's the amazing
story as Dad told it:

"A contract between Newbury and Boss Mac was drawn
up and witnessed. Boss Mac and his crowd were to pay
to Newbury the sum of one thousand dollars if for a period
of one year *The Independent* had made no adverse mention
of any of the several parties named. It was a holograph
contract and it was thought best to make a typewritten and
carbon copy of it, one for each of the signatories. Later

it was decided that it was a dangerous document and that only the one holograph should be preserved. It was entrusted to a respected elderly attorney, a friend of both parties, who agreed to lock it in his private safe and never let it be seen until called for by the contracting parties jointly. The typewritten copies were burned.

"When the contract was signed and delivered, Newbury sent for me and behind the closed doors of his office said something like this:

" 'Sonny, you have been having a hard time of it. I'm your friend and want to see you succeed. You have a nice wife and fine little children; you owe them a better living than you're giving 'em. Your wife and children would be a great deal happier if you were not always in trouble and if you were making money.

" 'I'm going to fix for you to make some money, and I am going to make you the most powerful influence in this town and county. From now on, Boss Mac and myself are going to run this town. I am going to get a thousand dollars cold cash if you will keep off the necks of the gang for the next twelve months. I don't want this money. I'm going to give it to *you*. And I'm going to give you that $300 note and bill of sale against your print shop. I'm also going to see that every business house controlled by Mac Sawyer advertises in your paper.

" 'You're going to make a lot of money. You'll be happy, your wife and children will be happy, and nobody will think any less of you. In fact, they'll think more of you, because nobody has any respect for a billygoat that stands on a railroad track and invites a locomotive to hit him. You're a billygoat on the track, and you're going to be run over and smashed, sure as hell. Now let's be sensible about this.'

"I was hurt and stunned. And so it was for this that

I had dared and labored! I told Newbury No, emphatically No!

" 'I expected you to say that,' said Newbury. 'It is the most natural thing for you to say right off the bat, but if you will think it over for an hour I believe you will change your mind. No more libel suits, nobody shooting at you any more, money for your payroll and for your family every Saturday, and a thousand dollars for a new press or what you like at the end of the year. I'm going to leave you here to think it over. I'll be back in an hour for your answer.'

"Dack Newbury put on his hat, strode out of his office, closed the door behind him and left me alone. I buried my head on a typewriter desk in his office and cried. And then I got mad all over and reached for paper to write him a blazing answer to his nefarious proposal. Right on top in the first drawer of the typewriter desk lay a freshly used sheet of carbon paper. I was about to lay it aside when my eye, accustomed to reading type upside down and backwards, fell upon the words in reverse beginning with the first line.

"I jumped to my feet, laid the sheet of carbon paper against one of the windows in the office, and read the contract between Dack Newbury and Boss Mac, et al. They had destroyed the typewritten sheets but had not thought about the telltale carbon paper.

"When Newbury returned, I told him my answer was No. The very next day I printed the contract between the Republican and Democratic bosses on the front page of *The Independent* and exposed their collusion and attempt to bribe me. They were dumbfounded. I suppose they thought I had jimmied the safe of their lawyer for the one and only copy of the contract supposed to be in existence.

The poor old lawyer in whose safe the holograph safely reposed must have had a lot of tall explaining to do. I did not divulge the simple fact of how the exact wording of the contract had come into my hands."

And then the war was on in earnest between Elizabeth City's ruling clique and The Independent Man.

LIBEL SUITS
4. GALORE

The Independent Man and his little newspaper suffered through some rough times in those early years.

The paper was handset and printed on a hand press. Its four small pages were printed two pages at a time, and they had to throw in the type from the first two pages to get enough characters to set up the other two.

Dad was never quite sure where he would get the money to meet his next payroll or buy his next ream of newsprint, but this hapless circumstance did not deter him at all from going after the Grand Wizard and his cronies with relentless vigor and determination. He showed how the city and county administrations were honeycombed with corruption, exposed certain political chicanery of the local public utilities company, showed up graft in the fire, street and police departments, and raised hell generally in the columns of *The Independent*.

This sort of journalistic activity literally invited legal reprisals or attempted reprisals, and Dad was hounded and harassed by countless libel suits. Grand Wizard Aydlett and his henchmen dragged Editor Saunders all over the First Congressional District, prosecuting him in any jurisdiction where they could find a copy of *The Independent* in circulation. He had to defend himself in Camden, Washington, Dare and Beaufort counties, among others. In every instance, Aydlett, being a senior member of the district bar and a political power to boot, retained top-notch legal talent, leaving Dad dependent on what he could muster with his meager financial resources. Luckily, a fair-minded citizenry was quick to resent the Grand Wizard's highhandedness and to side with the scrappy underdog of a newspaperman who dared to do battle with the formidable E. F. Aydlett. Also in Dad's favor was a circumstance of geography.

It sometimes makes a whale of a difference which side of a state line a person lives on. There isn't a lot of difference, really, between a citizen who lives in the southeastern corner of the Commonwealth of Virginia and one who resides a few miles or a few yards away in the northeastern corner of the State of North Carolina. But, for the editor of a newspaper, there is a tremendous difference.

That difference, without which a hell-raising, spade-calling newspaper such as *The Independent* could never have flourished nor long existed, is a difference in the laws of libel as they apply on opposite sides of the Virginia-North Carolina state line.

The criminal libel laws of Virginia were written in the days of dueling and were designed to discourage such "affairs of honor." In Virginia law it is an axiom that "the greater the truth, the greater the libel." If you call an honest man a crook, his reputation for honesty and probity would turn your libel against you. But if you call a crook a crook, he has no recourse to the law or to the court of public opinion; his only recourse is to fight or shoot. And so Virginia makes it extremely libelous for a publisher to tell the truth about its crooks, lest some good publisher should be bumped off by the first trigger-happy crook he told the truth about. The result is that crooks and grafters in politics could flourish in Virginia, where a newspaperman understandably would be reluctant to tell the truth about them.

North Carolina has a different sort of libel law. In the Old North State, the publication of the truth is privileged if in the interest of the public good. And North Carolina publishers are protected by a law that enables them to satisfy a complainant in a criminal libel action by retraction and apology.

Before a suit for criminal libel may be brought against the editor and publisher of a newspaper in North Carolina, the complainant must serve notice upon the publisher, specifying the libelous language and demanding a full and ample retraction and apology to be published as conspicuously as the alleged libel. If the retraction and apology is made in ten days from the date of notice, no criminal action can lie against the publisher, and only nominal damages are obtainable in a civil action.

In Norfolk, Va., back in 1907, Dad did a little free lance publishing. He was hot and eager to reform everything and everybody. In one issue of his little sheet called *The Muck Rake* he offended the Hon. W. W. Dey, one of the political bosses of that city. Mr. Dey met Dad on the street and threatened that the first time he caught Dad in front of the Burrow-Martin Drug Store he would publicly kick Dad's backsides. The Burrow-Martin store was the favorite loafing place for coke guzzlers and skirt chasers in Norfolk in those days. Every town has such a rendezvous.

Dad pondered for some minutes over Mr. Dey's threats and then hastily dashed off an open letter in which he invited Mr. Dey to meet him in front of Burrow-Martin's at 4 o'clock that afternoon and execute his threat, stating that he (Dad) preferred having it over with at once rather than wait around indefinitely under the threat of an unexpected swift kick from behind.

Young Saunders then had 2,000 handbills printed, conveying that invitation to the big political boss. It was against the law for unlicensed individuals to distribute handbills in Norfolk, but a fair wind was blowing over the business district of the city that day, and from the roof of Norfolk's one skyscraper he released those 2,000 handbills and let the winds handle the distribution. Those "invitation" fluttered over a good half of the business section of the city. By four o'clock that afternoon two platoons of police were required to disperse the curious crowds gathered on the public square in front of that drug store to see the prominent townsman kick the behind of the young journalist.

Dad never kept the appointed rendezvous. Three policemen arrested him early in the afternoon, marched him to the city jail, locked him in a cell and held him incommunicado for several hours, Finally, some friends learned of his incarceration and put up a bond for his release, which was conditioned upon his keeping off Main Street and going straight home.

It inevitably followed that the young editor was indicted on a charge of criminal libel, accused of violating the anti-dueling laws of Virginia, and was convicted in the city court. The verdict of the lower tribunal was reversed only after a long, hard fight in which the higher court was persuaded that there was nothing in the evidence to show that Dad had intended to kick Mr. Dey's backsides, too. The higher court accepted the logic that it takes two to fight a duel, even with boots.

Had the same incident occurred in North Carolina, Dad probably would have been indicted for provoking a breach of the peace and there would have been no expensive legal battle. And if he had actually libeled Mr. Dey, he could have been prosecuted only after failure to heed a prescribed notice to retract and apologize.

So many criminal libel actions were brought against Dad in the early days of *The Independent* that he completely lost count of them. He once recalled that there were 40 demands for retractions and apologies in a matter of 40 days.

Next to E. F. Aydlett, the Grand Wizard, the individual who made the most trouble for Editor Saunders was Walter L. Cohoon, an attorney and co-owner, with his father, of *The Independent's* competition. Cohoon was troubesome because he not only sued Dad for libel on numerous occasions but assaulted him several times and once threatened his life.

Cohoon's lifelong enmity for my father had its genesis in a series of events that took place in 1908, when *The Independent* was but a few months old.

Dad desperately needed advertising revenues and explored every legitimate avenue of obtaining same. Learning that nearby Currituck County, which had no newspaper of its own, was about to place some legal advertising, Dad went after the business. But Cohoon wanted it, too, and he told the County Commissioners they shouldn't support *The Independent* because it was owned and controlled by Republicans. This riled my father, who reported the matter the following week under a headline stating that "The Ass Brays Now Over in Currituck." He wrote:

"The Commissioners of Currituck County were treated to a strenuous and entirely uncalled for spectacle at their session last Monday when Walter Cohoon went before that body and proceeded to lambast *The Independent*, calling Mr. Saunders a mugwump, a Republican in disguise and a jail bird.

"Cohoon said he spoke as representing the Democracy of Eastern North Carolina and that, seeing *The Independent* making headway in Currituck, he thought it a duty he

owed to his party to thus speak before the Currituck Commissioners, that they might not be misled. . . .

"Mr. Saunders was present and maintained his composure
under the scathing abuse . . . and then he replied to Cohoon,
saying in part:

" 'I defy (Cohoon) to prove his assertions that Republi-
cans or Republican influence dominate the columns of *The
Independent* . . . Men of sense who read *The Independent*
know that the paper has no strings of any kind tied to it.
The Independent stands first for honesty in politics. Its
Democracy follows. If Walter Cohoon represents the
Democracy of North Carolina, I will have none of your
Democracy. I have known Cohoon for several years . . . I
have fought his Ring in Pasquotank, and for the first time
in twelve years it was defeated, polling only 149 votes in
the whole county with its best man.' . . ."

The other newspaper, *The Star* (formerly *The Tar Heel*
and dubbed by Saunders as the *Star Heel*), published
Cohoon's blast but didn't quote Saunders' remarks at all.
Then came this block-busting counterattack in *The Independent* dated Sept. 17, 1908:

WHO'S WHO?
In This Newspaper Quarrel
An Attempt to End This Thing For Once and For All Time

And so this is an attempt to end the controversy into
which myself and *The Independent* have been drawn by
The Star Heel in its desperate efforts to court publicity
by battling with a contemporary that has got the ear and
the respect of the intelligent masses of the Albemarle section—two things *The Star Heel* never had.

It is another case of the old hatred of Saul against David.

I realize that this controversy is growing tiresome to the

reading public. And yet I feel that I have another word coming and that any thing more to be said must be more interesting than what has gone before or it had best be not said at all. So here goes my dingdest.

But I wish to say right here that this blaze and thunder would not have taken place if "THE BRAYING ASS FROM CURRITUCK" had kept his pork chops off my meat block. I would have it understood once and for all that I was seeking legitimate business in a legitimate way when the whipper-snapper butted in with his fiddle-faddle. The public will understand from this that the controversy is forced and not sour grapes. The only thing that seems to stick out of the craw of *The Star Heel* is that *The Independent* has Radical propensities and that unless they can discover who owns *The Independent* they will bust a blood vessel or spring a leak, their back teeth being already under water.

The Independent doesn't claim to be a hidebound Democrat, as its name would readily indicate. Other things being equal, *The Independent* is Democratic. Still, when *The Independent* made its debut in this vicinity it found, to quote the words of a has-been friend, 'that the local Democratic party was a veritable omnium-gathrum of political odds and ends huddled together under the party blanket like household gods and barnyard refuse after a hurricane; a party controlled by grafters and mongrels, nincompoops and duds. As soon as I can get a new mainspring in my vocabulary, I shall pay my respects to the Radicals. That's me . . . Now for the facts . . .

WHO IS THE ASS?

"Who is the Braying Ass from Currituck? Walter Ludford Cohoon . . . Way back yonder the name was simply

4

Coon; then it was Cahoon until Walter came along, and the next generation probably will be Calhoun . . .

"Who has forgotten or can forget that terrific philippic characterizing the Braying Ass from Currituck, published in the columns of *The Economist* over the signature of Judge Geo. W. Ward, who was at that time Solicitor of the First Judicial District of North Carolina, and to which writeup the Braying Ass from Currituck had not the manly courage to reply? See the columns of that paper.

"Who was characterized in the columns of 'The Four Printers' in boyish but graphic language as 'at Wake Forest, taking another try at becoming a lawyer.'? The Braying Ass from Currituck.

"Who was it, in the face of all these antecedents, that was put up by the Democratic party as Bryan elector in this district? The Braying Ass from Currituck. Ye gods, what a sight! And this in the face of an editorial in *The Star Heel* advising Democratic voters to look closely into the political and personal records of every candidate before putting them on the ticket . . . Hear the Turgid Eddie in the Congressional convention characterizing the Braying Ass from Currituck as 'the splendid exponent of young democracy of North Carolina.' Surely, in that convention the Braying Ass from Currituck brought a price more nearly commensurate with what he thought he was worth instead of the real value of the product . . .

"And now I wish parenthetically to remark that the Braying Ass from Currituck is the cause of all this row. If he had kept his duck's bill out of my porridge over in Currituck, there would have been none of this. . . ."

Within a fortnight, some interesting notices were served upon The Independent Man, one of which went as follows:

"To W. O. Saunders, Editor and Publisher of *The Independent*:—

"You are hereby notified that the undersigned hereby alleges to be false and defamatory the following articles and statements therein hereinafter specified, made of and concerning the undersigned, to wit:

"That certain article published on September 17, 1908, in Vol. 1, No. 15 of *The Independent* on pages 1 and 3 of said issue, entitled 'Who's Who? in This Newspaper Quarrel.'

"First: 'And I wish to say right here that this last blaze and thunder would not have taken place if THE BRAYING ASS FROM CURRITUCK had kept his pork chops off my meat-block.'

"Second: *'The Star Heel* is represented by . . . and THE BRAYING ASS FROM CURRITUCK.'

"Third: 'WHO IS THE ASS? Who is the Braying Ass from Currituck: Walter Ludford Cohoon.'

"Fourth: 'And each and every word, sentence and statement in that part of the said article under the sub-title "WHO IS THE ASS?' and particularly the repeated reference to the undersigned as 'The Braying Ass from Currituck.'

"You are further notified that you are hereby required to make a full and fair correction, apology, etc."

This was signed by Walter L. Cohoon, of course. And, of course, no correction, retraction or apology was forthcoming.

Learning that he was to be indicted in the Superior Court on a charge of libeling Cohoon, Dad wrote on October 18, 1908, as follows:

"It seems to me that the only bone of contention is that Cohoon calls upon me to prove that he is a long-eared burro or a lineal descendant of one. I never made the charge that he was either, my reference being only in a figurative sense, as any man of ordinary intellect would readily understand.

However, if Mr. Cohoon has any evidence tending to show that he is not an Ass I should be glad to publish it for him. Everybody knows that he can bray. I take it that it will be difficult to justify on this proposition, after which the burden shifts and it will be up to him to prove he ain't what he says I say he is. It strikes me that this case will be very like the query in the country debating society: 'Did Bill Joneses House Burn Down or Up?' After a lengthy debate on both sides, the judges decided, 'It did.'

"One citizen has been fertile enough in his imagination to suggest that Mr. Cohoon, in denying that he is an ass, ought to leave that proposition to a vote of the people of this county and let them speak. I should have no objection whatever to this procedure, provided Mr. Cohoon would agree to abide by majority rule and not canter off to a county where he is not known. I made the reference simply as a matter of a joke, without any idea that Walter or his friends would treat the same seriously. I must confess considerable surprise that they . . . offered as their *causus belli* a proposition which defies proof only on the grounds of animalistic differentiation. I have never yet had occasion to pick a quarrel with Darwin for saying that man evoluted from a monkey, but my bellicose streak is at white heat because Darwin didn't take the proposition that man evoluted from an ass. . . . At the time that I wrote about the Braying Ass from Currituck, I didn't conceive how an exception to it could be taken by Walter, the ass being a designated emblem of the party for which he aspires to spout.

"But is not Walter making a mistake in thus taking judicial cognizance of this *nom de plume?* If I am convicted over yonder in Washington County, that bill of indictment will stand as long as the republic lasts, as a monument to Walter Ludford Cohoon. And when he is dead some tempted hand will not resist the opportunity to write on the cold stone at the foot of his grave, 'Here Lies the Braying Ass from Currituck.'

"I may be sent to jail but I shall have one satisfaction, that when I enter the door that act will forever seal upon him the *nom de plume* which I wrote merely in a spirit of newspaper banter."

The indictment came, not in Washington County but in Camden County, and the case went to trial in March 1909. Meanwhile, though, Dad had filed a countersuit against the Cohoons, charging that their newspaper had libeled him. The verdict of the Court was that both parties had published libels and that each newspaper should publish a retraction and its editor or editors be put under a peace bond.

Editor Saunders' retraction was a lulu. A bold black headline all the way across the top of the front page proclaimed:

WALTER COHOON IS NOT A BRAYING ASS

The Editor of The Independent Is Not a Buzzard

LIBEL SUITS ARE ENDED

"After many moons of quibbling and quarreling upon the part of many lawyers in many courts, the controversy between *The Independent* and *The Tar Heel* seems to have been terminated for once and for all by Judge Robert B. Peebles and a jury of twelve thoroly good men at the Spring term of Superior Court in Camden County this week.

"The Court holds that Walter L. Cohoon is not a Jack Ass.

"The Court holds that W. O. Saunders, editor of *The Independent*, is not a buzzard.

"And that's about all it amounts to except the bonds given by Mr. Saunders of *The Independent* and F. F. Cohoon and E. A. Womble of *The Tar Heel*. For two years to come these gentlemen must appear at each term of the Superior Court in Camden County to answer for their good behavior. We mustn't call each other Jack Ass and buzzard any more. The bonds are in the sum of $500 each.

"Taken all in all, it is another victory for *The Independent* and its policy of free speech. Last fall the status of the case was two warrants for criminal libel against Mr. Saunders, instituted by Solicitor Ward of the First Judicial District in behalf of Walter L. Cohoon and T. B. Wilson.

"It looked gloomy in those days for *The Independent* and its policy of free speech. The Democratic party and the bar of Eastern Carolina were working hand in hand to destroy this newspaper and imprison its owner. They came nearer succeeding than they knew. But that was last fall.

"At Camden Court this week *The Independent* was not so badly fixed. To conteract the suit of W. L. Cohoon, the Court found *The Independent* suing Cohoon's father for criminal libel and asking $10,000 damages of Cohoon. It was this countermove that blocked the little game of the enemies. When the jury found both sides guilty, the attorneys for the Cohoons very readily agreed to a compromise. They wouldn't ask for imprisonment of *The Independent's* editor if he would agree to withdraw the $10,000 suit.

"The enemy went further; it threw in the suit of T. B. Wilson to boot, sacrificing his vengeance as well to spare the elder Cohoon. And so *The Independent* will continue to be published by an editor at large.

"The suit of Walter L. Cohoon against the editor of *The Independent* was the first case called. It was shown that *The Independent* had referred to the Cohoon person as the 'Braying Ass from Currituck.' Counsel for Cohoon argued that to call a man an ass was a libel per se.

"Judge Peebles, presiding, said he didn't consider it a libel per se to call a man a Jack Ass, 'for,' said His Honor, 'calling a man a Jack Ass doesn't make him one nor does it create any impression that he is one.' The case went to the jury in an hour. The jury returned a verdict of guilty.

"The case of T. B. Wilson against *The Independent* was disposed of in equally short order, the jury returning a verdict of guilty."

That didn't close the matter, naturally. Less than six months later Editor Saunders was writing on the front page of *The Independent:*

"From inside rumors it is learned that the most powerful legal talent in Eastern Carolina will be on hand to assail *The Independent* before Judge George W. Ward, who will preside at the fall term of the Superior Court of Camden County on Monday, Sept. 13.

"On that date, the editor of *The Independent* will have to appear before Judge Ward to show that he has kept the peace for the past six months, and show that he has not libeled any good citizen, or forfeit a bond of $500.

"The publishers of *The Star Heel* newspaper are under the same sort of bond and will have to make the same sort of appearance, but the fight is on *The Independent.*

"Every effort is being made to stir up bad blood, encourage street brawls, noisy demonstrations and even bloodshed in advance of the convening of court at Camden.

"If the editor of this newspaper can be provoked to violate his bond, the grafters, poker players, blind tigers and corruptionists will have scored. The game is not so much to forfeit the bond of $500. The crooks want another sort of bond; they want the court to entangle the editor of this newspaper in a more embarrassing skein.

"A hotter head than the editor of *The Independent* would have fallen into the trap. Only a cool head could have passed through the blows and threats of the past two weeks without resenting them with a shotgun. But that is what Aydlett and his minions are wishing for, and *The Independent* has ever been slow to grant them their wishes.

"The editor of *The Independent* will appear before Judge Ward with a clean sheet on Monday, Sept. 13.

"Let the rascals howl!"

The desperation of The Independent Man's enemies was clearly revealed when E. F. Aydlett made the statement in a courtroom that W. O. Saunders might meet with foul play and his slayer could not and would not be convicted. This statement prompted Dad to pen this blast:

". . . The suggestion of E. F. Aydlett that if someone should kill me there could not be found a jury in this county to convict my slayer deserves some analysis. If anybody ought to kill me, Aydlett's the man. If what I have published about him is false, I deserve to be killed—not by another but by him. Why, then, does he not kill me? He seems to think it would be all right for somebody to do it. Is he, like the medical fraternity, afraid to take his own advice, or is the wish father to the thought? Aydlett knows better. He knows better. He knows that were foul play used in the taking of my life a thousand enraged men in this county would join a necktie party and string up my slayer before high Heaven. He knows that, just as I know it.

"Aydlett gave that hint either in the heat of passion, having entirely lost his head, or he did it in the hope that some minion would take the cue and do the deed. It may be it was because he was mad, for mad he was . . .

"Just why Aydlett's cup of wrath boils over at me is hard to understand. I have only published in the last twelve months what reputable citizens of this community have openly talked for the past twenty years—talked some things, too, that I have not published yet.

"I am here and here to stay. I am not afraid of a manly attack from any source. I have two good, healthy hands and in a fair fight can thrash any one of the mangy gang that stands ready to yelp when Aydlett blows the horn. There is not enough manhood in the whole band of dogs, including his burro, to face a sixteen-year-old boy. In fact, a sixteen-year-old boy armed with a rotten cornstalk could clean out the whole gang in the twinkling of an eye . . ."

This was strong stuff, no question about it, and it was soon to have its repercussions, but not before *The Independent* was to publish another challenging article under the headline:

THEY WOULD PUT THIS NEWSPAPER OUT OF BUSINESS
Petitions and Lawyers Employed Since Thug Violence Failed to End the Life of The Independent Man

The article went thus:

"Heaven and earth are being moved this week because a few men have been stripped of their masks and shown up in their hideous nakedness in this newspaper. It is a foregone conclusion that if *The Independent* continues to live in this community, there are some two or three gentlemen who will have to seek another climate. There is but one avenue of relief open to these gentlemen, and that is the suppression of this newspaper. They tried to do it twelve months ago and failed. Six months ago at Camden Court they tried the same trick and thought they had succeeded; but, lo and behold, *The Independent* has flourished since Camden Court last spring. And now for another try at it.

"Not sure that they will succeed with the courts by any meritorious plea; fearful even of the laws of their own making; distrustful even of their own imposing legal resources, the gentlemen who are afraid of *The Independent* have within this week circulated a petition requesting the suppression of *The Independent*. And somebody got up this petition asking the Judge to suppress *The Independent* in the name of order, in the name of law, and in the name of God knows what . . .

"It will be contended at Camden next week that *The Independent* has libeled E. F. Aydlett. And *The Independent* is prepared to show that it can prove every charge it ever made against E. F. Aydlett. Wonder if the petition scheme is his idea? . . .

"And the State will try to urge that if *The Independent* isn't suppressed, somebody will get shot. And as The Independent Man is the only man whose life has been threatened by the hit ones, it seems inconsistent that the enemies of this newspaper should be so anxious about the preservation of the life of the editor.

"And it will be argued that *The Independent* has kicked up a continual row in the community for fifteen months. And that is true, and a thousand petitioners will arise in a night within the bounds of this city to say that *The Independent's* brand of a row has done more for the taxpayers of this section than all the officeholders from Hugh Cale to Mac Sawyer.

"And it will be urged that *The Independent* has stirred up street brawls. And everybody knows that the street brawlers, the cowards who have waylaid in the dark and behind doors, are not of *The Independent* but of that toady class who hate *The Independent* for the good that it has done.

"There will be a lot of excitement at Camden Court next week; lots of fuss, fume, fury, fluster and superheated ozone. And in spite of much that has gone before, *The Independent's* faith in justice is so strong that it has no fears and *The Independent* will continue to be published in the future.

"There are compensations in life. If they get me in jail, *The Independent* will be published just the same—minus office rent. And before it's done let me say that the day I am jailed, that same day will I lift the lid and let out the malodor that is seeking the empty, vast and wondering air. I know who is the leading spirit in this thing, and when my liberty is taken I shall tell all I know, including that which I have promised God and my wife not to publish. That's what I said!"

Within two weeks, Walter Cohoon had again claimed he had been libeled, with the braying ass giving way in this instance to a burro. The notice he served on Dad went as follows:

"You are hereby notified that the undersigned specifies the following articles and statements therein as, and alleges that the same are, false and defamatory.

"That certain article published of and concerning the undersigned in *The Independent* in its issue of September 2nd, titled 'Mr. Aydlett Will Prosecute His Slayer' on page 1, column 2, as follows:

" 'I am here and here to stay. I am not afraid of a manly attack from any source, I have two good healthy hands and in a fair fight can thrash any one of the mangy gang that stands ready to yell when Aydlett blows the horn. There is not enough real manhood in the whole band of dogs, including his burro, to face a sixteen-year-old boy.

In fact, a sixteen-year-old boy armed with a rotten corn-stalk could clean out the whole gang in the twinkling of an eye.'

"You are further notified that you are required to make a full and fair correction, apology and retraction of each and every portion of the said article and statements therein as required by law."

To which Editor Saunders replied:

"In reference to the above notice served upon me by W. L. Cohoon, I wish to state that Mr. Cohoon's name is not mentioned in the publication and I am at a loss to see what expression therein Mr. Cohoon thinks refers to him., I did not have W. L. Cohoon in mind when I wrote it nor when it was printed. In view of this statement, I will state that if Mr. Cohoon sees fit to apply any of the names used to himself it is without any suggestion on my part and for which I am not blamable, and it is a matter entirely beyond my control."

In the next issue of *The Independent* there appeared this headline:

AYDLETT CUNNING FAILED TO LAND EDITOR IN JAIL

Prosecutors and Persecutors Lose Their Heads and Are Making Other Wild Endeavors to Put The Independent Man in Limbo, But They Must Fight It Out in His Home County

The story then went on to relate how certain unidentified enemies of Editor Saunders had altered court records in an effort to have a suspended jail sentence imposed. The Court ruled that no punishmment would be imposed on Saunders for the old conviction, and he further stated that any future

fights against *The Independent* and its editor would have
to be made in Pasquotank County instead of in other
counties.

(On the front page of that issue, "W. O." ran his own
picture and stated in the caption: "W. O. Saunders denies
all reports that he will engage in newspaper work else-
where and says he is here to fight it out and die with his
boots on if necessary.")

Dad wrote finis to this particular series of legal actions
and maneuvers with an article headed "And Still the Moths
Fly at the Flame—Aydlett's Gang Hot After The Independent Man All This Week—Malicious Persecutions Fail
As Usual." The story said, briefly:

"The fourth, fifth or fifteenth attempt to jail the editor
of *The Independent* and suppress this newspaper fell,
flunked, fizzled, blew up, busted and went the ultimate way
of all persecutions that are inspired by private malice.
Maybe some day, in some century yet to come, the spleen-
surfeited plotters of the plunderbund will learn the great
lesson of all history; that when the public good demands
the suppression of *The Independent* in this community,
then will *The Independent* cease to be. Until then, no private persecutions, maliciously manufactured, will fool the
courts, and this newspaper will run merrily on its way, its
machinery lubricated by the dollars brought forth by the
publicity it gets through its cases in the courts. . . . Judge
Sawyer found the defendant guilty and fined him $50 on
one count and one cent on a second. An appeal was entered."

Dad and his newspaper went through countless other
libel suits over a period of about fifteen years, and the fact
that he seldom had to resort to an apology and retraction
in order to escape conviction was due in part to his daring
philosophy of: "Be sure you've got your facts right, then

let them have it with both barrels, trusting to public opinion, a fair-minded judiciary and North Carolina's liberal
libel law to keep you from going to jail."

There was one case, however, in which Editor Saunders
stubbornly refused to retract an alleged libel and came close
to "doing time," as the expression goes. Ironically, this
was at the hands of the same Roscoe Turner who had collected the $300 fund used to start *The Independent* in 1908
and had been forced to repudiate the bill of sale he held
against the newspaper and its publisher.

Turner had in time realized his ambition to become county
judge, and when he got what he looked upon as a chance
to throw the book at Dad he didn't hesitate to do so. The
sentence he imposed was six months at hard labor, which
meant on a chain gang. Dad figured he could beat this rap
by fighting the conviction through to a higher court or
courts, if necessary, so his attorney noted a routine appeal.

Then came another display of the wit and audacity for
which The Independent Man was coming to be famous.
He had a friend draw a cartoon showing an obese W. O.
Saunders attired in convict's stripes, with a ball and chain
attached to his ankles and an upraised pickax in his hands.
Despite his potentially grave situation, Dad was pictured
as laughing. The caption merely said: "I should work hard
and grow thin." This struck the townspeople as being
funny as hell, and the result was that Dad's case was
laughed out of court.

Then, just when *The Independent* seemed well on the way
to establishing itself, along came the biggest libel suit of
all. The Grand Wizard had aspired to the office of United
States District Attorney, and Dad had published a series
of articles detailing six reasons why Aydlett should not
occupy such an office. Aydlett charged that the articles
libeled him.

The trial of this libel suit took up a ten-day session of the Superior Court. By this time numerous secret enemies of the Grand Wizard who had been nursing grievances of long standing came into the open and aligned themselves with Editor Saunders in a fight which might mean the extinction of the common enemy if *The Independent* could sustain its charges. The life of the newspaper and the freedom of its editor and publisher hung on a court decision— and Dad won. The Grand Wizard had begun to lose his grip and also was beginning to lose his taste for court defeats. Meanwhile, other forms of pressure and harassment were being brought into play.

Few mercantile houses in Elizabeth City dared advertise in *The Independent* in those early years. If they were not financed by capital advanced by E. F. Aydlett or Mac Sawyer, their owners were in some manner beholden unto those two individuals and dared not risk offending them by advertising in Saunders' newspaper. An effort was made, too, to array the town's churches against the young editor, it having become apparent that he was independent in his religious thought. They called Dad an atheist and an infidel, and one I. N. Loftin, pastor of Aydlett's and Sawyer's Blackwell Memorial Baptist Church, preached inflammatory sermons against him. How these sermons came close to resulting in the fatal shooting of my father is related in another chapter.

Then Loftin brought an old friend named Herbert Peele to Elizabeth City to take over Cohoon's languishing newspaper property and combat *The Independent*. After hammering away at his task for months with discouraging results, Peele gave it up and settled down to the business of running a strictly commercial newspaper and fattening on the business of the craven, the spineless and the subservient businessmen who shunned *The Independent* like a plague for obvious economic reasons. Of course, there was normally just so much advertising revenue available in a town the size of Elizabeth City, and Dad's little newspaper suffered in competition with a daily which strove mightily to butter up all the economic powers-that-be and offend no one. Meanwhile, Dad's operating and living expenses went on and the lawsuits went on.

Although the countless libel suits inspired or provoked by *The Independent's* dauntless reporting and bold crusading were taking a lot of my father's time and energy, they were not costing him much money. In the first place, he didn't have any money to speak of. Then, too, it developed that there were lawyers around who felt that they had been thwarted or otherwise wronged by E. F. Aydlett and were only too pleased to take up the cudgels on behalf of a courageous young newspaperman who dared to expose and stand up to the Grand Wizard.

One such unexpected ally was a bold and able Republican, Isaac M. Meekins, who later was to serve with distinction for two decades as a judge of the United States District Court for the Eastern North Carolina Circuit. *The Independent* had somehow offended Ike Meekins, but if he had little use for W. O. Saunders he had much less for E. F. Aydlett. In fact, it would not be wrong to state that Ike Meekins hated the Grand Wizard's guts.

As Aydlett continued to press his fight against my father, the realization came to Meekins that his days in the town would be numbered if Aydlett were to succeed in putting *The Independent* out of business. The upshot of this was that I. M. Meekins volunteered to defend Dad in many of the lawsuits brought or inspired by Aydlett, and the fact that Dad did not land behind the bars was due in some measure to Meekins' legal sagacity and his tenacious courage.

Another of Dad's courtroom allies was a young lawyer in Washington, N. C., the county seat of Beaufort County. Up to the time when he undertook to defend my father in a libel suit, young Lindsay Warren had done nothing to commend himself to E. F. Aydlett's attention, and the Grand Wizard looked with contempt upon this "young upstart" who dared to oppose him. But this case resulted in another acquittal for Dad and marked the beginning of a worthwhile and lasting friendship.

About eleven years later, in 1924, E. F. Aydlett announced his candidacy for nomination as U. S. Representative from the First Congressional District, and he thought things had been arranged so that no candidate of any stature would announce in opposition to him. But young Lindsay Warren threw his hat into the ring and, with the enthusiastic as well as effective support of *The Independent*, gave Aydlett one of the worst shellackings of his political career.

Lindsay Carter Warren went on from there to become an outstanding Member of Congress, and established such a record for soundness and integrity that Franklin D. Roosevelt in 1939 appointed him Comptroller General of the United States, or "watchdog of the Treasury." He served with distinction in the Comptroller's post until 1950, when he retired and went back to North Carolina to enjoy the life of a senior citizen and elder statesman.

Lindsay Warren was a lifelong friend of my father, and during the years when he was an influential figure in Congress he gave unstinting support to many of Dad's pet projects for regional betterment, such as erection of the handsome granite memorial to the Wright Brothers at Kill Devil Hills near Kitty Hawk, the development of the Cape Hatteras Seashore National Park, and the Lake Mattamuskeet Wildfowl Refuge.

5

Thus it was that the numerous libel suits that were brought against The Independent Man developed into assets rather than liabilities, enabling him to vanquish dangerous enemies and win valued friends at one and the same time.

SCHOOL OF
5.   HARD KNOCKS

My father had little talent for pugilism or the manly art of self defense, but he had one helluva proclivity for inviting mayhem. He disliked fighting but couldn't refrain from the use of fighting words. He rarely lost a fight of the journalistic or intellectual variety, and he almost never won one involving the use of fists or weapons.

One of the tenets of Dad's highly personal style of journalism was: "Be sure your man is of some importance before you attack him in print or publish anything scandalous about him." In other words, the pecadilloes of a shoe salesman or the pilferings of a hard-hit grocery clerk were more to be pitied than censured, in Dad's view, but the philandering of a deacon in the First Baptist Church or the misappropriation of public funds by a county judge were *The Independent's* meat.

There were quite enough highly placed individuals straying from the straight and narrow to keep Dad well supplied with targets who qualified under the above-mentioned tenet, but he would occasionally lapse into lowering his sights and leveling his fire at smaller fry. I have a vivid recollection of one such instance.

There was a political campaign on in Elizabeth City, and a faction headed by P. G. Sawyer, a son of the Boss Mac who figured prominently in an earlier chapter, was seeking to elect a majority of the members of the City Council who would be amenable to their views. About two weeks before election day, there suddenly appeared in mail boxes all around town a scurrilous piece of campaign literature aimed at the town's honorable and respected mayor.

Dad made the rounds of the other print shops in town until he found out where the offending card had been printed and somehow learned who had ordered the job done. He then published a reproduction of the card in *The Independent*, describing it as typifying the desperate, underhanded tactics of despicable peanut politicians and moronic ward-heelers of the anti-administration machine.

Considering the temperament of the individual thus castigated, this was an invitation to physical attack. Dad must have known this, but he was never one to run away from a fight, despite the fact that he abhorred physical or fistic combat.

On the morning when the paper appeared on the streets, Dad left the office and started walking toward the business section. Three blocks from his office and a block from police headquarters, two ruffians accosted him, muttering obscene curses. One of them struck Dad a glancing blow that knocked his eyeglasses to the sidewalk and then proceeded to blacken one of his eyes in a most effective manner. By that time others had reached the scene and peace had been restored.

Dad's assailant was charged with assault and battery and was arraigned before a Justice of the Peace. A $10 fine and costs of the court were levied against the defendant, who appeared to think the results were well worth the price, especially since it wasn't coming out of his pocket, anyway.

In the next issue of *The Independent*, Dad reported the entire incident without rancor under the headline "Editor's

Black Eye Delights Second Ward's Wild Babies." The story ran like this:

"A Chevrolet coupe rolled to a stop at the corner of Colonial Ave. and McPherson Street. A short-chunky, stern-visaged man jumped out of the car and advanced toward W. O. Saunders, editor of this newspaper, who was crossing the street at the moment. 'I want to speak to you,' said the man. And the man spoke by hitting the editor squarely in the right eye.

"The editor clinched with his assailant, received several minor blows in the mixup before the two were separated. 'And I'm going to beat you every time you put my name in your paper,' shouted the man as police took him in hand.

"The man was Elias Pritchard, proprietor of a Parsonage Street barber shop and until quite recently superintendent of the Sunday School of the First Christian Church.

" 'And I'm not a Sunday School superintendent any more,' he explained, 'and I can fight when I please.'

"Accompanying Pritchard was a young man named Wiley Long, who took no part in the fracas until Keith Saunders came on the scene and grabbed Pritchard. That was before the police came. Long then grabbed the younger Saunders and the two were stuck in a clinch until the police separated them.

"And this was an aftermath of the municipal election in Elizabeth City last week. This happened early Thursday morning. But early Wednesday night, after last week's issue of *The Independent* had gone on the streets, Second Ward gangsters were looking for W. O. Saunders. Eight or ten of them posted themselves near the shop of *The Independent* shortly after 8 o'clock that night. But W. O. Saunders had left the shop before they came and when he returned to his shop after 9 o'clock the police were already aware of the situation and the gang had dispersed. Pritchard says he was not a member of the Wednesday night gang.

"Pritchard insisted that his grievance was entirely personal, and he cited an article in last week's issue of *The Independent* condemning certain religious activities in the recent election. Pritchard said he took the article as a reflection on his party loyalty and it made him mad. Not having a newspaper at his disposal to strike back with, he used his fists.

"And Elias Pritchard knows how to use his fists; he is perhaps the best scrapper in the Second Ward and used to consider it a dull day when someone didn't give him an opportunity to display his fistic prowess. In recent years Pritchard had tamed down, joined a church, become a leader in the Sunday School and delighted in setting an example of good citizenship for his neighborhood.

"But shrewd politicians in Elizabeth City knew young Pritchard's weakness and, although he may have been unconscious of their designs, they have lost no opportunity to rig him for an attack on W. O. Saunders. When Pritchard rolled out of that automobile and attacked the senior Saunders, he probably was unaware that he was doing exactly what the scoundrel at the head of the Second Ward politics had planned that he should do.

"Pritchard was tried Friday morning on a warrant sworn out before Justice of the Peace H. Perry Davis. That was hard on Judge Davis, because Davis and Pritchard are bosom friends and as close as two peas in a pod. They have a brotherly regard for one another. It was Judge Davis' biggest court day; his court room was packed and the crowd overflowed on two sides of his place on Martin Street.

"Judge Davis was pale. The crowd knew his friendship

for the defendant. But Perry Davis is no fool. He was willing to give the defendant every benefit of the plea of provocation, although admitting that the defendant's plea of provocation was unreasonable. He offered to dismiss the action if the defendant would apologize and withdraw his threats. The defendant said his threats were conditioned and that he wouldn't apologize. The court imposed a fine of $10 and taxed the defendant with the costs.

"Before imposing the fine, the Court asked W. O. Saunders if he had any suggestion to make as to what penalty the Court should impose.

"Only this," said Mr. Saunders. "I trust that the Court will take cognizance of the threats made by the defendant. I have no desire to see this man punished. I hold no ill will against him, have no hard feelings against him. I know that this man has no real grievance against me; he is merely the victim of false friends who have taken advantage of his excitable nature to egg him into violence against my person. When he has had time to reflect upon what he has done, I believe he will think differently and feel differently."

"All seems to be quiet on the Pasquotank this week. The disturbing element in the Second Ward has quieted down after having become infuriated over one of the worst drubbings ever given a political organization in this town. . . .

"But the wild babies over in the Second Ward have some satisfaction in the black eye worn by *The Independent's* editor this week. They would have preferred seeing both eyes blacked, but half a loaf is better than no loaf at all."

Even when he had an opportunity to defend himself, Dad usually came out second best in the assaults his writing provoked. But in some cases he had no chance at all, as when Attorney Walter L. Cohoon ambushed him at night and beat him severely with a gold-headed cane. This was one of several attacks Cohoon made on The Independent Man, the most dastardly of these being one that occurred in 1909. Several months previous, Dad had suffered one of his rare losses in a libel suit and had been given a jail sentence which was suspended on condition that he keep the peace and commit no further libels for a period of six months. During this probationary period Cohoon fell upon Dad in a dark hallway and beat him brutally with a stick of hardwood, knowing full well that his victim could not defend himself except at risk of going to jail.

It can be judged from the above that Walter Cohoon was a vicious individual, hence it took a rare courage for *The Independent* to publish the following story on November 9, 1928 under the headline "Cohoon Threatens Life of Editor Saunders."

"W. L. Cohoon, Junior Orderite, saloonite, Ku Klux Klan supporter and stump speaker for the North Carolina anti-Smiths in the campaign just closed, declares that he will kill W. O. Saunders, editor of *The Independent*, if his name appears in the columns of this newspaper this week. Cohoon's threat was made openly and in loud tones in front of the Federal Building in Elizabeth City at 8:15 o'clock Wednesday morning. The editor was leaving the post office and passed Cohoon, who was in conversation with the Rev. E. F. Sawyer, Frank M. Newby and W. H. Anderson.

"I hope you are feeling good this morning, Saunders," said Cohoon as Saunders passed by.

"Feeling pretty good, thank you," Saunders replied without stopping for an argument. The editor had proceeded a distance of barely fifty feet when Cohoon said in a loud voice, "If you put my name in your paper again, I'll kill you, God damn you."

His threat was accompanied by a foul oath such as used by sailors and livery stable loungers.

"I'm glad you make the threat openly," said the editor, and continued about his business, followed by a tirade of abuse from Cohoon.

"Not satisfied with having made a threat in the presence of W. O. Saunders, Cohoon continued his harangue to the group gathered about him in front of the post office, and when David Cox, Civil Engineer of Elizabeth City, passed by, Cohoon called to Mr. Cox and volunteered the information to him that he would kill W. O. Saunders if his name appeared in *The Independent* this week.

"The editor of this newspaper will lose no sleep over Cohoon's threat. But it is hard on one's family to live in a town with an enemy of Cohoon's character . . . Living in the same town with a vicious and threatening personality like Cohoon is not conducive to the most comfortable feeling in the world but, knowing the nature of this person, the editor of this newspaper fears no immediate open encounter."

Cohoon did not carry out his murderous threat, but Dad did not know that such would be the case. However, this was not the first time that he had survived a threat of this nature, as the following editorial published in *The Independent* in 1909 reveals:

WANTS TO SHOOT

"Informing the rabble on every corner that he was going to kill the editor of *The Independent*, D. T. Gallop went forth on a tear last Thursday with something that looked like a gun in his pocket.

"He encountered the editor of *The Independent* on Main Street but didn't kill him. He compromised by declaring that the killing would come off the next time his name was mentioned in the columns of this newspaper.

"As Mr. Gallop's name is herein mentioned, those of my

friends who have tears to shed may prepare to shed them now."

In fact, threats against his life were common occurrences to The Independent Man during most of his journalistic career. As early as 1909, he was receiving so-called Black Hand letters threatening his early demise. The threats were signed by "The 4 Day Club," this purporting to be the name of the secret order that was to bring about the assassination of Editor Saunders. The first letter stated that it would employ one of two means in accomplishing its dastardly deed—poison to be placed in food by a Negro cook, or a pistol shot to be fired by an ex-convict who had been hired for that purpose.

Letter No. 1 was followed shortly by a second communication setting forth that "The 4 Day Club" meant business and that Mr. Saunders had been shadowed about town the night before. Dad did not go to the police with the threatening letters, but quietly pigeon-holed them while awaiting further developments. As he suspected, nothing came of these threats.

There came a time when the wrath of the wrongdoers of Elizabeth City and environs was diverted temporarily from the senior Saunders and his son was shot from ambush in January 1931. This inspired a first-person reaction story by my father that is worth reprinting in full because of its brilliant expression of an anti-fear philosophy. It follows:

"Do not ask me to describe the sensation of one when he is awakened from heavy sleep to hear the frantic bark of an automatic shotgun below his bedroom window, the pounding and shouting of someone at his front door, shouts from the other side of the street, the rush of footsteps in the street, and the screams of the women in his household.

"Do not ask me to describe the sensation: I didn't have

time to make notes when just this thing happened to my own household Thursday night, January 8. Jumping out of bed, groggy from sleep and a bad cold, I grabbed my shotgun, rushed downstairs to my front door, met my son Keith staggering into the door shouting, 'He shot me; I'm shot; get a doctor!'

"In front of me only black night and an innocent board fence, its white painting making it visible, staring at me from across the street. No one in sight. Back into the house I rushed to my boy, who was moaning with pain and begging for medical attention. I asked him where he is shot.

" 'My legs,' he replied. I note hastily that he is on his feet, that he is actually taking steps to and fro. Surely he cannot be fatally injured. I rushed back upstairs to comfort a hysterical mother. There is the detail of a doctor to be summoned, police to be called in, a wounded and frightened boy to be looked after, a frantic wife and mother to be calmed. And all the time I must keep my own head. I don't know how I commanded the thought and time to telephone the local fire department and ask those fine boys to get their men out to join with the police in searching the neighborhood for the dastardly coward who had fired from ambush and run under the cover of night.

"I get the boy upstairs, call for a basin of hot water and antiseptics. I remove his blood-soaked shoes and hose, remove his trousers, bathe his bleeding limbs, note with joy that no shot has entered above the knees, that no arteries have been punctured. I rush to the wife and tell her the boy's wounds are not serious, explained the nature of them, let her come and see for herself. No bleeding now; number five shot from a long range shell, fired at fifty feet, penetrate neatly; they do not tear. The clean, washed limbs showed only something like a score of small, red punctures where the shot had entered. No shot above the knees. The doctors come and their calm word of assurance that the wounds were not serious.

"That would-be assassin may have been lying in wait for me, but I had slept badly the night before and was sick with a cold, had come home early and gone to bed early that night. My son, Keith, came in at a much later hour. It was about 10:30 o'clock when he drove his car into the garage back of the house, came around to the front of the house and up the steps to the porch and the front door. He had barely reached the door when he heard the bark of a gun, turned and saw the spurt of flame, and heard the bark of a second and third gunfire. The first shot did not touch him; then two other loads of shot in quick succession. He was fumbling for his night latch key, pained by the wounds in his lower limbs, conscious of the fact that an automatic shotgun carries five cartridges, knowing not whether the next two loads would be aimed at his abdomen or his face and head. And there he stood under a porch light, a fair target for the dastard behind the board fence directly across the street from him.

"A windowpane crashed on the other side of the street. Someone shouted. 'Stop, help, police.' No fourth and fifth shots were fired. The shouts from across the street came from Leslie (Red) Armstrong, who lives on the corner of Cypress and First streets, diagonally across the street from my home. Young Mr. Armstrong is a special policeman who is employed from time to time for special police work or as a substitute police officer. He carries a gun. He had his gun on his person when he entered his home that night, some minutes before the shooting.

"Red Armstrong has an artificial limb in place of a foot and an ankle he lost in falling under a fire truck a few years ago. He had removed both his gun and his artificial limb and was sitting in the dark by a window when Keith Saunders' car entered the driveway beside my home. He saw Keith come around the corner of the house, mount the steps, go to the front door. At the same instant he saw a sinister figure emerge from behind a clump of shrubbery in his own yard and enter the yard of D. T. Singleton, next door, and directly in front of my house. The sinister figure, a white man about five feet, five inches tall, wearing a dark overcoat and a soft hat, carried a shotgun.

"Armstrong sensed danger, but his own gun was on a bed across the room and he had only one leg to get about with. Before he could act he heard the bark of the gun from Singleton's yard, saw the flame of it. Breaking out a windowpane, he began to shout. His cries probably alarmed the cur with the shotgun and saved Keith Saunders two more loads of shot.

"It is a frightful state to live in a town with degenerate and murderous cowards who have, previously, under the cover of darkness smashed the windows of your home on two occasions, burglarized your office on another occasion, and, finally resort to shooting from ambush. But take it from me, folks, we will have this state of things in our town just so long as administration of justice in this City and County is in the hands of Trial Judge Phil Sawyer, in whom certain criminal types are persuaded they have a friend and protector.

"It is notorious that this newspaper's attack upon (P. G.) Sawyer and certain of his underworld friends have been followed by reprisals. Whether my son and myself are victims of hired thugs, or whether thugs merely feeling that they have the sympathy of the local court are emboldened to prey upon me and my household, are matters for conjecture.

"Two poor timid Negroes, at whose home bloodhounds

faltered after following a tortuous trail, were held and closely questioned. No Negro fired those shots on my home. They were the work of a skunk of a white man, and many people other than myself think they know the skunk.

"Am I afraid for my own life? Yes and no. There are men higher up in this town who would gladly see me murdered and who would offer a reward and protection to any low creature who could be persuaded to do me harm. But I am not going to lose any sleep over that.

"This newspaper for nearly a quarter of a century has fearlessly exposed and lambasted not only the low crooks of the underworld, but has dealt even more harshly with the scoundrels higher up who wear the clothing of stewards and elders and prey upon the public under the cover of false sanctification. And, God helping me, I shall not let up on them at this late date. And that boy of mine is made of sterner stuff than his dad; those shots will not weaken him; they have only hardened him.

"My philosophy of life has little place for fear. If one stops to reflect upon life's hazards and vicissitudes, one may work himself up into a state of terror. The common hazards of life afford every basis for human fear. No man who leaves his home every morning is absolutely sure that he will return to his home alive that day. When you close your eyes in sleep at night, you have no absolute assurance that you will awaken to see another morn. But only here and there do we find humans who let the common hazards of life prey upon their minds, and there is no reason why one should have his peace of mind destroyed by some particular hazard.

"There isn't much to this life, anyway, and the greatest life's satisfaction is in seeing life through honorably and fearlessly. Let dishonor and fear be the afflictions of cowards who shoot from ambush, and of their protectors who skulk behind them. Ultimately these scoundrels will inherit the earth—six feet of it."

On another occasion, an irate citizen called The Independent Man an unprintable name and threatened him with a knife. Under the headline "Mr. Gordon Resorts to Low Language," this incident was recounted as follows:

"It seemed like old times Tuesday morning when your *Independent* editor was assaulted on Main Street in front of the Apothecary Shop by L. S. (Starky) Gordon, irate stockholder of the Carolina Banking & Trust Co. Funny how they always pick the Apothecary Shop corner.

"Armed with an umbrella and a pocket knife, Mr. Gordon accosted the editor and said: 'Can't you get anything right in that damned paper of yours?'

" 'I guess it would be impossible to print anything to suit you,' 'W.O.' replied.

"Backing off with his umbrella clutched in one hand and an old fashioned pocket knife in the other, gritting his teeth and hissing like a turtle, Starky ripped out an oath: 'You damn lying, thieving son-of-a B . . . .' frothed the blistered stockholder.

" 'Language of that sort means nothing to me,' said 'W.O.'

"Retreating, the angry citizen said: 'You'll apologize to me in your paper next week or I'll come to look for you. You are bigger than I am, but I know how to whittle you down to my size.'

"Turning to bystanders, 'W.O.' said: 'Small men have called me every kind of a son-of-a-B listed in the animal book, but that's the first time I was ever called a thieving one'."

It took a long time and a lot of lumps and scars to bring Dad around to the realization that there's a lot of truth in the childhood chant that "sticks and stones may break my bones, but words can never harm me." He described his ultimate awakening in these words:

"For years and years and years I suffered myself to smart and burn under the names that people called me, until at last it dawned upon me that so long as I chose to express opinions contrary to the established notions, bias and prejudices of my neighbors, just so long might I expect to have my neighbors rise up on their hind legs and call me names. And then it occurred to me that, after all, they were but exercising in a crude way the right which I reserved for myself and which I insisted upon exercising when and as I felt like it.

"In the light of the simple, obvious fact of the limitations of the human mind and the bewilderment of all human knowledge, isn't it silly for anyone to get mad with a fellow human who doesn't think on a given subject as oneself happens to think? But sillier still is the man who resents the inability of the other fellow to agree with him and who is provoked to near violence when the other fellow, whose viewpoint has been outraged, retaliates by calling names.

"I was born and reared in a narrow, bigoted and intolerant environment. I broke away from it, and for years I felt it my obligation to the cause of liberalism to impose what I was pleased to call my advanced views upon any assembly or audience. And in the name of liberalism I became as intolerant as those whom I opposed.

"I have had countless disagreements with my neighbors. I have been boycotted and ostracized by this and that group in my day, and there have been times when half the folks in my town wouldn't speak to me. Today, now that I have learned the value of tolerance, most of those people who formerly resented my views and sought to suppress me are my best friends, or, at least, are cordial enough.

"Most of the progress of humanity has been physical

or material progress. We have been so busy building our house and putting it in order that we have had too little time to think and talk about things relevant to our intellectual and spiritual improvement.

"We are going to have more time to think and talk about life's finer values, but the language involved will be so new and strange to many ears that all of us must learn to exercise a lot of patience, a lot of tolerance, and much good-natured indifference toward those who may, in our opinion, be unsocial or disagreeable."

With that sort of hard-won philosophy and tolerance, it is understandable that The Independent Man had a soft and reasoning answer for the hot-headed jerk who called him a "goddam lying son-of-a-bitch" on Elizabeth City's Main Street in broad daylight.

ASSASSINATION
6.   THWARTED

Dad published his swashbuckling, name-calling newspaper for more than a quarter of a century, during which period he must have made dozens if not scores of individuals angry enough to wish to murder him. It is one of life's little ironies that he never was shot (although he was shot at), whereas I managed to get myself peppered with shotgun pellets after working on *The Independent* only a couple of years.

But there was one occasion when only steel nerves and an acute sense of psychology—and some luck—prevented Dad from being shot, perhaps fatally.

Frank Grice was accounted one of the most substantial citizens in Elizabeth City and an upright man. He was the junior partner in one of the oldest and most successful department stores in the town and had built himself an imposing and comfortable home on Main Street, close by the business district, where the town's other rich men had built their homes. He was a sober-quiet-spoken, conservative citizen.

Grice had come from humble beginnings. Back in his young manhood he had earned a meager livelihood as a drayman, but he realized the limitations of his own earning power as a menial worker and he resolved early in life to acquire money. He salted away a goodly part of his limited funds, and as his pile grew he discovered small ways of making it work for him.

He loaned small sums to his less thrifty neighbors, charging usurious interest. He saw nothing wrong in that. Wasn't that the way all rich men got to be rich? He financed small tradesmen, staking his capital against their industry and sharing in their profits. Frank Grice was an uneducated man, with little practical business experience, but he was level headed, he was thrifty and he multiplied his dollars.

When Joe McCabe, one of the best retail salesmen in Elizabeth City, aspired to launch out in business for himself, he needed much more capital than he could supply, so he took Mr. Grice into partnership with him. Mr. McCabe stayed on the floor, regaled his public with yarns and moved the merchandise, while Grice bent over the books in the office, checking income and outgo. They made a successful team, and the firm of McCabe & Grice prospered and expanded with the passing years.

Most people had forgotten, and a new generation was unaware, that the well groomed, quiet mannered, distinguished looking Mr. Grice had been a drayman in overalls on the streets of the town.

He had passed the half-century mark and was living on Easy Street when he yielded to the importunities of friends and neighbors and let his name be used on the ticket for City Councilman. He was elected by a handsome majority, which pleased him perhaps more than he ever indicated by any outward show.

After two years as City Councilman, Frank Grice aspired to the mayoralty. Dad could not enthuse over his candidacy. He knew nothing about Grice's past history; he only knew that here was a highly esteemed citizen who was esteemed merely for his thrift and conservatism. He was neither modern nor progressive. And in commenting upon his candidacy, Dad said as much—and more. In an editorial in *The Independent*, he asked:

"What is the background or peculiar ability of Mr. Grice upon which he presumes to aspire to the mayoralty of an up and coming town?"

That question stung Frank Grice to the quick and wounded his pride to an extent that was unbelievable.

Dad happened to be out of town when the editorial was published. Mr. Grice read that editorial in his place of business, folded the paper, put it in an inside pocket and went to his home and to his bedroom. When his wife called him for supper that evening, he pleaded a headache and would not see members of his family. That night he paced the floor of his room, and his family became greatly alarmed.

The next morning, he refused to eat breakfast, despite his wife's pleading that he take nourishment and compose himself. Then he sent for his brother, Charlie, and the two were in solemn conference behind locked doors for some hours. Charlie Grice at last emerged from the room, put on his hat, went up the street and returned with Judge Ward, the family attorney. The lunch hour passed and Frank Grice never left his room, still refusing to take food.

Judge Ward left that room with tense, white features, returning later in the afternoon with a briefcase in one hand. There followed another long conference of Frank Grice with his brother and their attorney. Night drew on. Again came supper time, and still Frank Grice would take no food. All that night he again walked to and fro in his room. For two nights he had not slept.

On the morning of the third day, Dad returned to Elizabeth City, took the hotel bus at the Norfolk & Southern depot and alighted at the hotel on Main Street. Judge

Ward must have posted himself as to Dad's whereabouts and expected arrival time and was waiting for him when he stepped out of the hotel bus. Grasping Dad's arm with a tight grip, he hustled him into the lobby of the hotel, through the lobby into the washroom, and whispered hoarsely: "Go home, young fellow; for God's sake, go out the rear entrance of this hotel and lose no time in getting home. And stay there."

The judge was trembling with fear and excitement, and Dad sensed that there was something unusual and frightening in the wind. He demanded to know by what right the judge was ordering him to sneak out the back door of the hotel and go home? He then started toward the door leading into the lobby. Dad recounted the incident later as follows:

"Judge Ward almost screamed at me. 'Stop! For God's sake, don't do that. Frank Grice may be in the lobby now, and when he sees you he will kill you!'

"For the life of me, I couldn't grasp the reason for Judge Ward's emotion and fright, not having been filled in on the events of the past few days. I recalled the editorial about Mr. Grice, but I could not recall that there was any fighting language in it, let alone any cause for homicide. But I could see that Judge Ward was in dead earnest, I respected his judgment, appreciated his friendship, and said to him: "Very well, Judge, I'll do as you say, but I won't promise how long I will stay home."

"I went out a rear door of the hotel onto a back street and went quickly across town to my home. After greeting my wife and puttering around the house for a few minutes, I slipped a revolver in my pocket, kissed my wife goodbye and went back to the business district.

"Judge Ward had told me enough to assure me that Frank Grice was in the throes of an emotional insanity that might take days to run its course. And I had done some tall thinking about the situation.

"I had learned somewhere out of my own experience that a murderous resolve weakens once it is thwarted. It was months before I was to learn that Frank Grice had taken no food and slept not a wink for more than two days, and that in the interim he had made his will, armed himself with a Colt's automatic, and resolved to avenge a fancied wrong to his honor by killing me on sight. I went to look for Frank Grice.

"I first saw him in company with his brother, on Main Street in the middle of a business block. Without giving them a suspicion that I had seen them, I sauntered nonchalantly and unhurriedly into a drug store on the corner of the block. Quickening my steps once inside the drug store, I went out a side door and around the block, coming up on Main Street at the other end of the block. Sure enough, Frank and Charlie Grice had moved up the block and planted themselves, one on either side of the entrance to the drug store. I loitered on the corner at the other end of the block until I was sure that they had spotted me again. Then, looking at my watch, I appeared to be in a hurry to keep some engagement, cut across the street and did another disappearing act, only to reappear two blocks further down the same street a few minutes later. I observed that Frank Grice had again trailed me to the corner from which I had disappeared but a few minutes before.

"I walked back up Main Street in the direction of the man who was bent on gunning me, keeping my eyes on him all the while but striving to give no indication that I was aware of his presence anywhere on the street. When I was once more within a block of him, I did another disappearing act and went this time directly to my place of business on a side street. I fell into a chair, weak from the excitement of the chase.

"Regaining my composure, I called my printer, an unusually bright chap, into my office and told him just what had been going on.

" 'But how do you know Mr. Grice won't get you yet?' he demanded.

"I believe he is licked," I replied. "When a man gets murder in his mind and heart, he isn't thinking straight. Frank Grice is ordinarily a docile, peaceable, law-abiding citizen. Something that I have written about him—and I can't quite figure out what it was—has made him temporarily insane. For the past forty-eight hours he has been obsessed with one idea and has been utterly incapable of thinking straight. Now, when a man sets his head on doing a rash thing, nothing confuses and disconcerts him so much as being confronted with an opportunity to do that thing and then missing his opportunity.

"Frank Grice thinks he has missed three fine opportunities to plug me with the automatic in his pocket. Each time he missed what he thought was an opportunity, he lost a lot of his nerve. I suspect that by now he has become very shaky and that his mind is functioning something like normally again. I believe that at this moment he is a badly whipped man and thoroughly ashamed of himself. Anyway, I'll gamble my life that I'm right. Follow me and see."

" 'Hold on,' cried my printer, 'I think a lot of you, boss, but I think a helluva lot of my life, too. Damned if I want to get mixed up in any shooting scrape!'

"I don't ask you to expose yourself to any danger," I told him. "I merely want you to follow me at a safe distance and, if the unexpected happens, be prepared as a witness that Frank Grice killed me deliberately and with malice.

And now I am going to look for Frank Grice again."

"I left my print shop and passed over toward Main Street, my printer following me at a safe distance. But even before I got to Main Street I suddenly and unexpectedly came upon Frank and Charlie Grice. I must confess that my blood ran a little cold and that my heart was not functioning normally, but with a show of indifference and nonchalance I sauntered past the pair, speaking respectfully as I passed, just as if nothing in the world had happened. Nothing happened. Nothing.

"A moment later my printer joined me on Main Street, wiping the perspiration from his brow.

" 'My God!' he exclaimed. 'Did you get a good look at Frank Grice's face? He has aged ten or twenty years since I last saw him.'

"I had not seen Mr. Grice's face. I suspect that I was seeing a funeral procession, an open grave and a lot of flowers when I passed him."

In retrospect, I am inclined to think that Dad was a bit foolhardy in this instance and placed too great a reliance on a psychological assumption, but the important thing is that he escaped with a whole skin and *The Independent* thereby survived for nearly thirty years instead of a mere decade.

A DARINGLY
7. DIFFERENT NEWSPAPER

Most readers either admired *The Independent* a great deal
or they hated its guts. Not many people who read it could
be neutral about W. O. Saunders' newspaper.

Back in the 1920s, the *State Port Pilot*, a weekly newspaper published in Brunswick County, carried a box at the
top of its front page proclaiming: "Most Cussed Newspaper
in North Carolina, Outside of Elizabeth City." And there
was no gainsaying the fact that *The Independent* was
cussed and discussed a-plenty. It was admired and respected, too.

H. L. Mencken, the skeptic and caustic Sage of Baltimore, once wrote that "If the South had forty editors like
W. O. Saunders it could be rid of most of its problems in
five years."

In the mid-1920s, John H. Casey, Professor of Journalism at the University of Missouri, surveyed the field of
12,000 editors of country weeklies in the United States and
named an All-American "team" composed of the eleven
whom he regarded as outstanding. The editor of *The Independent* was designated as left halfback and co-captain,
which was no small honor.

As one of the country's most vigorous and most colorful
practitioners of a crusading personal journalism, my Dad

was cautioned by a friend on one occasion about the dangers of printing certain information about an important citizen of the community. He unhesitatingly replied: "What a a private individual does may be his own private affair, but what a public man does is the public's business. An editor, if he stands at all, stands between the public and those who would milk or betray the public."

It was such statements as this, backed up by deeds, which prompted the late Dr. Parkes Cadman, eminent theologian and lecturer, to say that W. O. Saunders was a great force for righteousness, and as such a real asset to his community.

What did *The Independent* stand for? It stood for a lot of things; more importantly, perhaps, it stood *against* a lot of things. Early in the paper's career Dad wrote an editorial statement of his credo. This remarkable statement follows:

"The people of Eastern North Carolina have witnessed in 15 months the remarkable growth of *The Independent* from a four-page, semi-boilerplate, issued from a 10 x 12 attic room, to a quite respectable looking illustrated weekly with a circulation that long ago outstripped its one lingering competitor after witnessing the funeral of another.

"*The Independent* was launched on a borrowed capital of $300. It was worse handicapped by the business incapacity of its founder who, even now, couldn't be induced to open a set of books.

"Spite of its lack of financial backing, spite of slack methods of business, spite of the devil himself, *The Independent* has grown and the town is as wild over it today as it was on June 9, 1908 when we caught our first grafter and held him up to public contempt, dangling by the heels, as it were.

"*The Independent* today has a circulation of 2,200 copies every Thursday, is read by 15,000 persons and is known in every honest household in five or six counties. Tho boycotted by the moneyed interests of the town, *The Independent* carries more advertising than any newspaper in the city. There's a reason. And the reason is plain. *The Independent* has stood for something, and that something is clean government.

"And we haven't stopped at nailing that fundamental to the masthead and leaving it there to flap itself to tatters in the wind; we have rallied every grain of energy, ability and moral courage to the standard and fought night and day against the enemy in the open and the enemy in the dark.

"We have exposed corruption wherever we could prove it. Often finding corruption, but without the proof, we published the hint so broad that the rascals were frightened from their spoils and the public saved that much. The very presence of *The Independent* in the community has saved untold thousands to the people, for grafters must be wary, wary, where beats the footsteps of this tireless sentinel.

"*The Independent* believes in clean politics and believes that there is no way to clean up politics till the party machine and the pie counter are eliminated.

"We believe in putting in office men who will as jealously guard the interests of the public as they would their own, and any man who is not capable of taking care of his own business has no place in the business management of a city, county or state.

"*The Independent* believes in religious liberty and stands with head uncovered in the presence of every true religious devotee, black or white, high or low. *The Independent* has no patience with religious hypocrisy, with religion for policy, and hates the ground that's trod by a two-faced scoundrel who is arm in arm with the devil all week and first in church on Sunday. This town's full of that brand of skunks. They have been the damnation of the country. They give a thousand to foreign missions on Sunday and on a Monday go out and rob a credulous stranger of a like amount to make up the deficit. To hell with all such.

"*The Independent* stands for the square deal business man. Business is the backbone of the nation. Business is the great civilizer. Business creates all property. Without property there is no law, no order. *The Independent* has a helping hand for every worthy business enterprise in this country. On the other hand, we detest unfair methods of business. We oppose business men who by the strength of their capital and numbers would crush competition and deal unfairly with their weaker brethren. There are business men of that kind in this town. To hell with them.

"*The Independent* stands for the women of this town, this county and this country. Our main fight is for them. They have no vote; they are as disfranchised as the lowest black— but infants before the law. *The Independent* works for them. It shows them how politics affects their everyday life and how those politics are corrupted by men. We put the woman in a position to talk intelligently to her male dependents and persuade them in the way they should conduct all public affairs.

"We stand for everything that is worthwhile to the women, the mothers of men. We fight for better schools; saner investment of our school moneys; more competent teachers. We fight for clean streets, a clean fire department, a clean city. The women are interested. Their children are robbed every time the city's boss takes the city's money for his own neighborhood and leaves their streets in filth.

"*The Independent* stands for little children. We have a mailed fist ever ready for the lowdown corruptor of childhood. For the defiler of an innocent little girl we make such protests as gives the courts a pause, and no more can a brutal seducer of young girlhood walk out of a Pasquotank court room under a paltry $200 bond.

"Last but not least, *The Independent* stands for the masses of this town, this county and this district. We stand for the underdog, for the poor man; for the remote farmer; for the fellow who works all day in the shop, on shipboard or in the field, too busy making an honest living to pay much attention to the idle classes who make laws for him, tax him to death and manipulate political parties to control his vote and lead him blindly to perpetuate their rascality.

"We say we stand for the masses, not in a socialistic or anarchistic sense; but for a square deal in all matters of public concern. We strive faithfully to look out for the man who can't look out for himself. If he is then inclined to vote for crookedness because the Boss Crook has a mortgage on his little house, that's not our funeral.

"And believing these things and fighting for these things, *The Independent* has an eye to its own household. We print no whiskey and patent medicine advertising to tie our hands against these frauds. We truckle to no advertiser, and when given our choice of losing paying business or keeping silent towards corruption we have lost the money."

With such a credo as that, it is no wonder that *The Independent* never made much money.

It's hard to conceive of a country weekly newspaper without correspondents who send in social and personal items from every crossroads community in its circulation territory, but such a newspaper was *The Independent*. Explaining this departure from the norm, Dad once wrote as follows:

"For more than 20 years this newspaper has been conducted without country correspondence. Occasionally, I print a letter from some rural neighborhood, not because we consider it always worth the space but out of courtesy to friends and correspondents. I have never believed columns of personals and social items are worth the room they take up. And if *The Independent* is today one of the outstanding home weeklies in a land of more than 12,000 weekly newspapers, it is because I have paid my rural readers the compliment of believing them to be interested in more important things than the comings and goings of Sue, Jane and Carrie, Tom, Dick and Harry.

"And if Sue, Jane and Carrie, Tom, Dick and Harry secretly resent the fact that their names do not appear in the columns of *The Independent* every time they go a-visiting, they read *The Independent* more eagerly because it gives them many columns of lively, entertaining and informative matter. And if Sue, Jane and Carrie, Tom, Dick and Harry ever do anything important or of more than family interest, this newspaper will very likely carry a picture of them if it can procure a good picture.

"I believe that you can lay it down as a general proposition that the family that takes a paper simply because it carries the visiting news from its neighborhood, reads nothing more than the personal items from their own village or rural route and throws the paper aside because there is little in it worth saving. But the rural home that receives *The Independent* reads this paper from front to back, missing nothing in between, and then saves it for the neighbor next door who is a regular borrower.

"I could far more easily edit *The Independent* and have a lot of desirable leisure for myself by letting country correspondents fill my columns with their trivialities. I have to work hard and fast to fill these columns with matter that is largely of local interest and yet so well written that it interests readers even in other states.

"And now let me throw a bomb into the big myth about

the value of country correspondence to a weekly newspaper. The average country correspondent is interested only in his or her own little coterie of friends and neighbors, and his or her personal items carry the same names from the same restricted circle every week, ignoring the vast majority of people who live in the same region. And so, the country newspaper that makes a circle of lukewarm readers by printing their names every week or so loses the interest and provokes the contempt of the greater numbers of those who are not favored by the correspondents.

"What is more exasperating about the country correspondent is the fact that he usually misses the big news in his community. If there is a suicide, a murder, a raid on a moonshine still, a fire or a calamity of any sort, they either presume that everybody already knows about that, or they consider the subject too big for them to handle properly and they don't write about it at all. The village of Hatteras had the highest tide in its history recently; the village was flooded. But it received no more attention from the Hatteras correspondent than an item about Willie Dough visiting his aunt at Rodanthe. The flooding of Hatteras was easily worth half a column of newspaper space. I bet I could have written two columns about it that would have been read with as much interest in New York as at Manteo.

"I am intensely interested in the important news events of every neighborhood in the Elizabeth City trade territory. But the country correspondent is a disappointing source of real news; your country correspondent is most often a chronicler of trivial travels, catering to the petty vanity of his or her own little social set."

Like every other newspaper editor, my father received letters from his readers. Most of these communications were signed but some were not, and the writers of the latter type inspired some of Dad's choicest invective. One editorial paragraph on this subject ran as follows:

"Hardly a week goes by that the editor of this newspaper doesn't get an anonymous letter from some person, telling him to write up this person or that. Tips on all sorts of scandals come to this newspaper from anonymous letter writers. These unsigned communications make no impression on the editor and publisher of this newspaper. People who resort to that sort of letter writing are dirty little curs, dastardly and vicious cowards, venomous little vipers, bootleggers of social poison, moral prostitutes and mental masturbationists. Next!"

A couple of years later, more such letters resulted in the writing of another editorial titled "Pardon the Digression." It went thus:

"The ugly compound 'son-of-a-b....' is popularly considered the vilest epithet that can be applied to a human being. I have searched my vocabulary for a viler epithet to apply to that low-down order of humanity with which an editor is afflicted. I refer to those dirty, yellow, lousy-minded, unspeakably villainous wretches who write abusive, slanderous and defamatory letters to editors and sign no names to them. These bubonic plague carriers are forever attempting to assassinate the character of someone they dislike and, having not the faintest spark of manhood or womanhood, they write anonymous letters to editors. They are far lower down in the scale of human degeneracy than any Son-of-a-B could be. If there were such a thing as a human Son-of-a-B, I should say that the anonymous letter writer is an intestinal worm out of such an animal. And now I've gotten this off my chest."

There are some four-letter Anglo-Saxon words that never appeared in *The Independent*, but damn was not one of them. The following brief editorial titled "Wrong Dam

Spelling" tells how Dad felt about this particular word:
"Readers of this newspaper are due an apology. A headline on the front page of this newspaper last week carried
the words: 'CAME DAM NEAR KILLING TWO,' referring to Frank Scott's automobile accident. A large number
of copies of the paper went out before the error was noted
and corrected. What I wrote was: 'Came Darn Near Killing
Two.' I never use the word 'DAM' as an expletive in my
headlines or anywhere else. When I say 'damn' I mean
damn and spell it with four letters: D-A-M-N, just like
that."

Understanding friends of The Independent Man sometimes told him that one of his newspaper's troubles was that
it was ahead of its time. Dad finally was moved to write
on this subject in these words:

"The trouble with *The Independent* is, it has always been
15 to 20 years ahead of its time. *The Independent* is forever advancing ideas and espousing causes before the rest
of the country has caught up with its thinking. Take the
matter of Russian recognition, for instance. *The Independent* was advocating recognition of Soviet Russia back in
1917. *The Independent* said then that the Sovietization of
Russia was one of the boldest and most promising political
experiments in human history.

"A lot of people resented *The Independent's* editorials
on behalf of Russian recognition back in those days. I was
called a bolshevik, and some went so far as to drop their
subscriptions to this newspaper. Washington's recognition
of Russia last week is but the late fulfillment of a prophecy
which this newspaper dared to make a good many years
ago.

"This newspaper fearlessly opposed America's entry into
the World War and dared to dispute the claims of the
illustrious Woodrow Wilson that i° was a 'war to end war

7

and make the world safe for democracy.' For all of which my patriotism was called into question and Department of Justice spies put on my trail.

"When advocacy of birth control was a new and frightful thing in this country, I not only advocated it but brought Mrs. Margaret Sanger, founder of the birth control movement, to Elizabeth City to defend the cause.

"And so may I suggest that all who quarrel with the editorial ideas of this newspaper give them the test of time. Verily, what is heresy today may be quite orthodox ten or 15 years hence."

8. LUCK

Dad had a great bent as a reporter, and when he interviewed men and women in all walks of life in gathering material for a newspaper story or a magazine article, he not only got his story but he nearly always learned something useful besides. For example:

One morning in the early summer of 1925, Dad sat with Julius Rosenwald in his presidential suite in the administration building of Sears, Roebuck & Co. in Chicago. He had been sent to interview the head of that great mail order house by the editors of *The American Magazine*. He thought he had never met a more meek or modest man.

When he had concluded the interview, he paused to ask Rosenwald a question not at all relevant to his editorial assignment. And the question was this: "Mr. Rosenwald, to what specific thing, if any, do you attribute your unique success?"

"Luck," Rosenwald replied.

At that moment a gong sounded in the outer hall. Moments later the tramp of hundreds of feet, of men going from their desks to a basement cafeteria, smote their ears. Mr. Rosenwald rose from his desk and led Dad into the outer office and to the door opening upon the hall. He opened this door and held it ajar, asking Dad to observe the men who were passing.

In just a short while the hallway was empty again, the last of the men having disappeared around a corner and down a stairway leading to the basement. And then Mr. Rosenwald spoke again.

"I said that I attribute any success I have made to luck. You have seen in these brief moments perhaps as many as a hundred men pass this door who could have made a greater success of Sears, Roebuck & Co. than I have made of it. But those men just haven't had my luck. Imagination, ability, industry and the qualities of leadership are not exclusive with executives; they are inherent in great numbers of men who may never have an opportunity to demonstrate them. That I am head of one of the greatest mail order houses in the world was not due to my own contriving or initiative. It was my luck."

Dad thought a great deal upon that interview with Julius Rosenwald and became convinced, through years of observation and experience, that the Chicagoan was fundamentally right. Dad recognized that it was through sheer luck that he had escaped from a butcher shop in a country village to the field of journalism. And in later years he insisted that it was luck that lifted him from the obscure position of a country editor to the ranks of nationally known journalists and contributors to national periodicals. Here is how that particular bit of luck came about.

In the summer and autumn of 1921, Dad learned of a certain wealthy sportsman who had acquired an island of some 5,000 acres in Currituck Sound and was spending money lavishly in improving the place. Mackay Island, the retreat in question, was hardly more than 25 miles from Elizabeth City, and Dad wandered over there one day looking for a story. The owner was in New York and no one on the place seemed to know anything about him. They knew him only as "Mister Knapp" and had a vague idea that he was in the calendar business. They called him "Knapp, the calendar man."

Dad roamed about the island, noted the modest but beautiful and comfortable home, boats and shooting equipment, and observed among other things that some 50 acres had been cleared and put in condition for farming. The dairy barn, poultry house, piggery, etc. were models of their kind. But there were no cows, no pigs and no poultry to speak of.

One of the overseers who was guiding Dad about the place explained that Mr. Knapp was going to buy a couple of thoroughbred cows up north some place and send them down later.

"We've got a lot of cattle on the island now," he said, "but they're all scrubs and mostly bulls. I believe we've got forty-two head in all and there ain't but two cows in the lot."

"For gosh sake!" Dad exclaimed. "What is this man doing with a herd of forty bulls and only two cows?"

"Well, he doesn't know they're mostly all bulls," said the overseer. "You see, it was this way. There's a lot of underbrush on this here island, and Mr. Knapp had an idea that a lot of scrub cattle turned loose on the place would clear up the underbrush. He told us to go over to the mainland and buy some scrub cattle and turn 'em loose over here. It seems that the folks on the mainland who had scrubs to sell didn't want to sell anything but bulls. We see now that we made a mistake. Those forty bulls spend all their time fighting over those two cows; the bulls are fighting all day and all night back in them woods."

This information amused Dad but he attached little importance to it until he got back to his office and reached for *Who's Who in America* to get a line on this man Knapp.

He found that Joseph Palmer Knapp was a son of the late Joseph Fairchild Knapp, founder and former president of the Metropolitan Life Insurance Co., and that Joseph P. Knapp was chairman of the board of the Metropolitan, which placed him at the head of what then was probably the greatest financial institution on earth. He found that Mr. Knapp was only incidentally in the calender business, being head of the American Lithographing Co. He was also principal owner of the Crowell Publishing Co. and P. F. Collier & Son Co., publishers of *The American Magazine, Woman's Home Companion, The Mentor, Farm & Fireside* and *Collier's Weekly.*

Mr. Knapp didn't mean any more to my father than any other rich man who happened upon some out-of-the-way place where the shooting was good and spent barrels of money trying to make it liveable. But the fact that Mr. Knapp was incidentally identified with *Farm & Fireside,* one of the oldest farm journals in America, gave Dad a lead for the story about Knapp's Mackay Island place for his newspaper. The story he wrote was this:

"Joseph P. Knapp, chairman of the board of the Metropolitan Life Insurance Co. and active head of the American Lithographing Co., is incidentally principal owner of *Farm & Fireside,* one of the oldest and most widely read farm papers in America. Mr. Knapp contemplates an experiment on Mackay Island that will enable him to put into practice some of the fine theories that his *Farm & Fireside* editors have been trying to drum into the heads of American yokelry for many years. Mr. Knapp is planning a model farm on Mackay Island, in the heart of Currituck

Sound. He will engage in mixed farming, producing both field crops and livestock.

"But his initial herd, consisting of forty bulls and two cows, is causing his retainers on the island much loss of sleep. The ratio of cows to bulls being only one to twenty, twenty bulls are fighting day and night for the possession of each cow. The pawings, snortings and bellowings of two-score bulls on that otherwise peaceful island makes the nights hideous. And the small human population that Mr. Knapp has domiciled on the island is fearful that the sex-crazy bulls, tired of fighting among themselves, will turn upon them and rend them with horns and hooves. But the principal owner of *Farm & Fireside*, the great American farm monthly, is proceeding blithely with his plans to become a gentleman farmer."

There followed nearly a column more of similar foolishness, lampooning the adventurings in agriculture and animal husbandry of an excellent gentleman who was only casually interested in a farm publication. After reading the proofs of the story Dad had a mild hunch that if the great Mr. Knapp ever saw it he would be highly offended and would never be counted among the subscribers to his paper. But he didn't know Mr. Joseph Palmer Knapp. It turned out that he was a true sportsman, with a fine sense of humor, who thoroughly enjoyed Dad's impish satirization of him and contrived to get marked copies of my paper into the hands of his friends back in New York so that they could enjoy a laugh at his expense.

Mr. Knapp thereafter became a regular reader of *The Independent*. And being himself a publisher of national publications designed for mass consumption and sensitive to all the ignorance, pettiness, bigotry, prejudices and intolerance inherent in the human herd, Mr. Knapp undoubtedly got a kick out of the unconventional journalism of a country newspaper that called a spade a spade and a backhouse a backhouse.

In a later account of the Knapp influence on his life, Dad wrote:

"It takes a lot of morons and small minds to run the circulation of a national periodical up into millions. To be a successful publisher, one must cater to a low level of intellect. It must irk publishers of the Knapp type to contemplate the limitations placed upon their editorial policies through the economic necessity of playing forever to the galleries of small minds. I can understand why he got a kick out of *The Independent*.

"Mr. Knapp not only read *The Independent*, but clipped and filed a number of unusual editorials that he found in it. One day in New York, utterly unknown to me, he passed a sheaf of these editorials over to the late John M. Siddall, at that time and until his death a few years later, editor of *The American Magazine*. John M. Siddall read the editorials placed in his hands by Mr. Knapp and wrote for more. I wrote Mr. Siddall that I would be in New York the following week.

"It was my first lucky break, and I was determined to make the most of it. Luck is one thing, but Luck is a coy lady who but winks her eye and invites pursuit. She is no lady of easy virtue to yield her favors to a lazybones.

"I sat at luncheon with John Siddall in the Vanderbilt Hotel in New York City a few days later. He asked me a lot of questions about my experiences as a free-lance editor in a conservative little town down South.

" 'I feel there is good copy in you for *The American Magazine*,' Mr. Siddall said, 'but I don't know just where to peg you.' He puzzled for a moment and said: 'If you will attempt a piece of about 5000 words for me and call it The

Autobiography of a Crank, I'll pay you four hundred dollars for it if I can print it'."

Four hundred dollars in one lump sum looked like a fortune to Dad back in 1922, when the income tax was negligible, and he was quick to act upon Mr. Siddall's suggestion. "The Autobiography of a Crank" was published in the June 1922 issue of *The American Magazine*. Dad followed it with a score or more of contributions in subsequent issues, found a market for other articles in *Collier's* and did special editorial work for *Collier's* in 1925. Subsequently, he contributed numerous articles to *The Country Home*, *Nation's Business* and other national publications. He had come a long way. But Dad readily conceded that it was all a matter of luck for him.

"I would perhaps have been an obscure country editor still, unknown to millions of magazine readers throughout the length and breadth of these United States, but for my stumbling upon the fact of Mr. Joe Knapp's herd of forty bulls and two cows on Mackay Island in the summer of 1921," he confided, adding:

"But don't misunderstand me. It is the fast worker who captures Lady Luck when she gives him the flirtatious eye. If I hadn't followed up John M. Siddall's invitation to call on him in New York with some alacrity and with a plan and a determination to make the most of the opportunity, nothing would have come of it." When one considers the many tough breaks and innumerable formidable adversaries with whom he had to contend over the years, one can only conclude that The Independent Man certainly had need of a little luck.

9. LESSONS IN POLITICS

Not all of The Independent Man's scorn, contempt and invective was reserved for medicine fakirs, crooked lawyers and shekel-gathering preachers; some of it he lavished upon politicians, of whom he once wrote:

"A politician is a person who knows how little the public knows, and who keeps his public in his confidence by never taking it fully into his confidence. Your successful statesman or politician is a successful statesman or politician because he accepts the human factors of ignorance, inertia, selfishness and prejudice as his stock in trade."

"I could never be either a successful statesman or a successful politician," he added, "because I have too many lapses in which I credit my public with more knowledge and reason than it possesses and lay my cards on the table at the wrong time."

Nor was Dad's disrespect for politics and politicians diminished at all by reason of his service for one term as Representative from Pasquotank County in the North Carolina General Assembly.

He decided to run for the seat and won the nomination because the politicians in the town and county, hardly one of whom was not against Dad to some degree, inexplicably failed to enter anyone against him in the primary. Maybe they just thought they could get him off their backs for a spell by sending him to Raleigh. Nomination on the Democratic ticket in North Carolina was then, as it is now, tantamount to victory in the general election in November, so off to Raleigh he went, filled with zeal and ideas.

There were three things which Dad much desired to accomplish in one brief session of a General Assembly which functioned under a machinery with which he was woefully unfamiliar.

He was determined to raise the age limit of children in industry in North Carolina from twelve to fourteen years.

He wanted to abolish the electric chair and capital punishment in North Carolina.

And he desired to place on the statute books of North Carolina an honest package law which would prohibit the use of any but standard packages for farm produce and prescribed honest grades for such produce.

This was in 1919, and in those days the common practice with growers and shippers of farm and orchard produce was to undersize packages when they thought they could get by with it, fill a barrel nearly full of little apples or potatoes and top it off with enough big apples or potatoes to make it pass for fancy grade. Of course, the poor farmer who did this sort of thing generally fooled nobody but himself. Shrewd buyers turned his barrels upside down, opened them from the bottom and paid for them on the basis of the lower grade.

It is exceedingly doubtful that Representative Saunders could have selected three measures better designed to dispel any illusions he may have entertained as to the patriotism, wisdom and integrity of state lawmaking bodies. He just didn't see how anyone could seriously oppose a bill to abolish capital punishment. But when he dropped his bill in the hopper it met with instant and violent opposition all over the House. Leaders of the General Assembly went to him and asked him: "What would you do with a nigger who had raped a white woman?" Why, North Carolina had to have a gallows or a death chair if only for niggers who committed rape, they argued with considerable vehemence!

And when Dad replied that he would castrate the colored man and confine him to hard labor for the rest of his life, they looked upon him as a demented individual and shook their heads. Dad tried to reason with his fellow legislators: "Would a farmer kill a vicious and unruly stallion that attacked his womenfolk, as vicious and spirited stallions will do on occasion?" he asked, going on to say: "Of course not.

"He would call in a veterinarian and take the fire out of the brute by a simple surgical operation and convert him into a perfectly docile and reliable work animal. And that's exactly what we ought to do with unruly human males, both black and white, who can't control their sex urge. Nothing is accomplished by strapping the brute in an oaken chair and shooting several thousand volts of electricity through him until he is dead, dead, dead. Electrocution doesn't deter the next criminal; it never has done so and never will."

All Dad's pleadings and writings were to no avail, and the bill to abolish capital punishment was defeated early in the session. Capital punishment remains the law of the state to this day, the only difference being that the supposedly more humane gas chamber has been substituted for the electric chair. However, I witnessed several gas chamber executions while working as a reporter with the *Raleigh Times* and I can only say damn the difference.

The next of Dad's bills to come up for consideration was the one proposing to raise the age limit of children in industry. Thousands of children in North Carolina were working long hours in textile mills. Some of these children were actually under twelve years of age; ghostly little caricatures of children crawling out of bed before dawn and going into the mills to work until after sundown. Certainly, Dad told himself, no one would object to giving these pitiable human beings a chance to have some semblance of normal childhood. But objections there were, and plenty of them. Opposition to the bill came not only from the mill owners of the state but from the parents of the children themselves. Even the agricultural forces opposed the legislation, because farmers were told that the bill was but a step in legislation that ultimately would prevent a farmer from working his own children in his fields at harvest time.

One farmer member of the legislature rose to his feet when the bill was under discussion and said:

"Mr. Speaker, I want to ask a question of the gentleman from Pasquotank. I want to know if he would deprive the poor little children of North Carolina of the right to earn enough bread and meat to keep their poor little bodies and souls together?"

Hell flew into Dad as the gentleman ended his question, and he promptly shot back: "If it has come to this in North Carolina, that thousands of innocent little children would starve to death if taken out of our slave-driving industries, then God damn North Carolina!"

Bang! went the Speaker's gavel, and Dad was sharply reprimanded for the use of unseemly and intemperate language on the floor of the House.

However, with the more influential newspapers of the state and many of the best citizens behind it, the bill was finally amended by the manufacturers to fix the age limit at 13 years instead of 12, and the emasculated bill was enacted into law. But before it was passed Dad had made so many enemies in the House that any legislation sponsored by him had two strikes against it. When his honest farm packaging bill came up for consideration there was a chorus of objections and the measure was ordered to be tabled. A lot of strategy was required to bring that bill back to the floor of the House and get it passed.

Needless to say, Dad's respect for government and its lawmakers was not heightened by his legislative experience.

"Legislation is largely a matter of compromises effected by much trading among utterly selfish groups," he wrote in *The Independent*. "It goes much like this: If you will vote for my bill to permit commercial fishing of big-mouth bass in Shallowbag Bay, I'll vote for your bill to permit construction of a private toll bridge over Mill-Tail Creek.

"The average member of a state lawmaking body seems to have little mind or opinion of his own, taking his cues from this or that faction leader or pressure group. Often as not, he votes his Ayes and Noes without really knowing what he is voting on. He sits dumbly through a session of the legislature and then hurries to his hotel room to read a newspaper and find out what the session was all about.

"That state that has a strong political boss with a state-wide organization has the most efficient legislature. It may be a bad legislature, but it does things because it has a mind and direction behind it. The Boss is for a thing or he is against it, and that settles the matter. To go against the Boss is to commit political suicide. Without a Boss, your legislature is without a mind and it is dangerous to call it together, for without a mind, good or bad, it will become a headless body of dissenting and quarrelsome groups that will wrangle for months and eventually adjourn without getting a substantial part of its job accomplished."

"Of his fellow Assemblymen, Dad gave vent to this distinctly unflattering opinion:

"Your legislator is a man of two minds. On matters on which his constituents or his boss have no settled conviction or self-interest, he may vote his own mind. On other matters he votes the will of his constituents or boss. . . . Your Legislator is called a Representative. And that is what he is; he is fairly representative of the political or social body that elects him. He is no better and no worse than his constituents. If he is anti-social, selfish and crooked, you can be reasonably sure that he has a lot of anti-social, selfish and crooked people in his constituency back home."

Looking back on the matter, I find myself a little amazed that Dad ever got elected to one term in the Legislature.

There were enough political shenanigans on the local scene to keep The Independent Man busy, but he nevertheless found time to comment on state and national affairs on occasion.

In 1924, shortly after the famed Scopes trial in Tennessee, so graphically depicted in the movie "Inherit the Wind," North Carolina's Governor Cameron Morrison decreed that the theory of evolution must not be explained in North Carolina's public schools. *The Independent's* headline said: "Refuses to Stand up Alongside Monkey— Governor Morrison Isn't Going to Invite Chance of Someone Seeing a Resemblance." The story went thus:

"The Theory of evolution must not be explained to the children in the public schools of North Carolina for the next five years. Such is the edict of the Governor of North Carolina. Cameron Morrison says he doesn't want to see a picture of himself and a monkey on the same page. The pleasure of the monkey has not been consulted.

"Seven hundred textbooks to be used in the North Carolina public schools for the next five years have just been approved. Governor Morrison has ordered that two textbooks on biology be excluded from the list. The one to which the Governor particularly objected was Traskins' 'Biology of Home and Community.' There is a chapter in that book that made the Governor so hopping mad that the wonder is that he didn't swallow a pint (more or less) of the tobacco juice he carries in his face." (The rest of the article is a quote from the Traskins biology text)!

In a subsequent editorial on the same subject, Dad made the following radical suggestion.

"Herbert Spencer, the most popular if not the greatest of all English philosophers, stated the theory of evolution in a single sentence more than 50 years ago.

" 'Evolution,' said Spencer, 'is an integration of matter and a concomitant dissipation of motion; during which the matter passes from an indefinite, incoherent homogeneity to a definite, coherent heterogeneity; and during which the retained motion undergoes a parallel transformation.'

"Our late lamented Col. William J. Bryan used to quote that sentence with great glee to uneducated audiences and convince them out of their own illiteracy that evolution was a senseless and preposterous theory, the insanity of which its supporters had endeavored to conceal in a confounding concatenation of unintelligible words.

"Wouldn't it be a good test of the eligibility of a member of any legislature to pass upon the question of evolution that he be able to read and explain the Spencerian definition of the term? We demand of illiterate voters (if they are dark of skin) that they read and explain the Constitution of the United States of America. Would it be more unreasonable to demand that a member of the legislature, who presumes to contend that the theory of evolution should not be taught in our public schools, should be required to demonstrate his ability to read and explain fairly and intelligently just what the theory of evolution is?"

Needless to say, this suggestion was never acted upon in North Carolina or any other state.

The political bug bit The Independent Man again in

1926, when he ran for the Legislature on an anti-Ku Klux
Klan and anti-Fundamentalist platform. The *Independent*
subsequently chronicled its editor's defeat in a news story
headed "Isaac, Jacob and Abraham Got the Vote—Fundamentalist Pasquotank Gives 'W.O.' a Spanking at the Polls
for his Liberalism."

It said:

"It couldn't be done, folks! And nobody knew better
than W. O. Saunders that it couldn't be done; but it was
just like Saunders to throw his hat into a ring with no
likelihood of ever recovering his hat, Saunders would call
it his devotion to the cause of religious liberty, freedom of
speech and scientific progress. More practical-minded folk
call it 'butting his head against a brick wall.'

"W. O. Saunders, running on an anti-Ku Klux and anti-
Fundamentalist platform for Representative of Pasquotank
County, was overwhelmingly defeated in the Democratic
primary last Saturday. His opponent, J. Kenyon Wilson,
a corporation lawyer and the choice of the professional politicians of the county, beat him nearly two to one.

"It was a rainy day, the sort of day when most of the
folks who vote have to be dragged out of their homes and
hauled to the voting places. . . . Saunders had no organization, his enemies did. They got out their Bibles, got out
their corn liquor, hired automobiles, sent their workers forth
with specially marked tickets, and when the polls closed at
7:26 o'clock Saturday evening the poll holders had to go
to the bottom of the ballot boxes to find votes for Saunders."

In the national political campaign of 1928, *The Independent* took the unpopular (in Dry and Protestant North
Carolina) stand of supporting Wet and Catholic Al Smith.

"W.O." felt that his fellow Tar Heels should not drink
wet and vote dry, and that the mere fact of a man's Catholicism should not keep him out of the White House. He wanted

8

to report firsthand on the doings at the Democratic National Convention in Houston and somehow got himself named as a delegate.

In his convention story in *The Independent* of August 3, 1928, he told of the perfidy of the North Carolina delegation and then told how his own efforts to put North Carolina on record as standing for religious tolerance got him into a fracas. Here's how that part of the story went:

"An exciting moment in the convention came Wednesday when Senator Robinson of Arkansas, favorite vice presidential possibility, spoke as chairman of the convention, stressing the principles of Jeffersonian Democracy. Robinson declared that the Constitution of the United States required no religious test of any candidate for public office. This was a signal for a great demonstration. Friends of religious liberty began a march around the great auditorium, carrying the standards of their states. W. O. Saunders, who was occupying a front seat with the North Carolina delegation, grasped the North Carolina standard and attempted to join the parade. B. O. Everett, Durham politician and (Cordell) Hull supporter, attempted to take the standard from Saunders. W. O. Newland, chairman of the North Carolina delegation, and others joined Everett, and a tussle ensued in which the standard was wrecked before the police arrived.

"Saunders is not easily licked. In the rear of the auditorium there was another North Carolina standard marking the alternate section. To the back of the hall rushed Saunders, seizing the standard from the alternate section and joining the parade. Saunders carried the North Carolina standard to the very stage of the auditorium and held it aloft while thousands cheered. This only riled Carolina Hullians more, and when Saunders came down from the stage he was rushed upon by the Hullians, led by J. A.

Brown of Chadbourne, and the standard was broken to pieces in his hands by the enraged Hull supporters. There are many North Carolinians under the hateful (F.M.) Simmons who have no use for religious liberty and would repeal that amendment to the Constitution if they had their way. . . ."

Later, Dad found an opportunity to express his feelings about North Carolina's anti-Smith Democrats by printing in his editorial column the following story:

"The most talked about speech made in the recent session of the North Carolina General Assembly never got into print. And I guess I'll have to print it, being as how I'm supposed to print everything worth printing.

"There was a dog tax measure before the Senate and one of its sponsors was contending that a $1.00 tax on male dogs and a $2.00 tax on females was an equitable tax.

" 'I agree with the gentleman,' said the rotund Senator Persons of Franklin County, 'but I would make the tax go a little further. I would put a tax of $1.00 on male dogs, $2.00 on bitches, and $3.00 on sons of the latter. Over in . . . . County, where 7,000 Democrats voted anti-Smith in the last election, the $3.00 tax would yield a revenue of $21,000 for that county."

On another occasion, editorializing on a gubernatorial candidate who was distasteful to him, Dad wrote:

". . . Here is a fat-headed, mealy-mouthed, pussy-footing intellectual nonentity without a single characteristic to commend him to the serious consideration of any thoughtful North Carolinian, and yet he is one of the greatest vote getters North Carolina has produced . . . This fat-head, this mealy-mouth, this pussy-footer, this intellectual nonentity, is a disturbing possibility; he is going to make trouble. . . ."

People called The Independent Man a lot of names over

the years, but not even his worst enemy would have ever thought of calling W. O. Saunders "a mealy-mouthed, pussy-footing, intellectual nonentity."

TWO TALKATIVE
10. CHARACTERS

The Independent was a widely read, widely quoted and widely respected country newspaper, largely because it mirrored the personality of an editor with profound convictions; a rare facility for self-expression; a penchant and a zest for crusading; an above average knowledge of religion, philosophy and psychology; a Rabelaisian sense of humor; and a distinct affinity for the common man.

One of the newspaper's most popular features in the 1920s and 1930s was a front-page column called "The Bank Clerk and the Soda Jerker," in which two readily recognizable small-town types discussed current topics in language that was easily understood.

In a preface to a collection of these columns published in 1934, Editor Saunders told how this column came into being.

"Just how did this column of yours get started in *The Independent?*" asked the Bank Clerk of the Soda Jerker.

"It started before your day and mine," said the Soda Jerker. "It was about like this. Way back ten or twelve years ago, W. O. Saunders was sitting at that table over there when Guirkin Cook, who was a teller at the First & Citizens National Bank, came in and got in an argument with Vincent Hughes, who was squirting soda here at that time. The argument was about bird dogs or something, and 'W.O.' thought it was funny. When he got back to his office he wrote out their conversation about as he remembered it and published it under the heading of 'The Bank Clerk and Soda Jerker' without calling any names.

"The piece was the talk of the town and everybody was asking 'Who is the Bank Clerk?' and 'Who is the Soda Jerker?' The next week *The Independent* ran another dialogue between the Bank Clerk and the Soda Jerker which probably was the invention of 'W.O.' himself. The second piece made a hit and *The Independent* has been featuring the column ever since.

"It has been a great stunt. People generally like to hear two sides of an argument, and the Bank Clerk and the Soda Jerker give two sides. And when the editor has some viewpoint he hesitates to voice in his editorial column, he lets the Bank Clerk and Soda Jerker say it and get away with it."

"And he's worked off a lot of stuff on us that he's been ashamed to put under his own name," said the Bank Clerk.

"Well, you see, it's like this," said the Soda Jerker. "The Bank Clerk and the Soda Jerker is realistic and it's human; it's written like everyday men think and talk. When two men get together and enter into a talkfest, their talk is often pointed up with a funny story that may be just a little off color. Sometimes such stories get into this column, but never if they don't make a wholesome point or afford a little harmless humor that affects no one's morals.

"Still I don't just see how 'W.O.' gets away with some of the things he prints," said the Bank Clerk.

"I'll tell you how he gets away with it," said the Soda Jerker. "For years and years he was prosecuted and persecuted by lawyers and politicians who tried to make him out a liar and a slanderer; he always came out with flying colors and persuaded his public of his honesty, truthfulness and intellectual integrity. Whenever he made a mistake, he was man enough to apologize for it. With his reputation established, he can get away with a lot of things."

On one occasion, the Bank Clerk and the Soda Jerker were discussing an article in a medical journal advocating the teaching of anatomy and physiology in the public schools.

"I agree with the doctor," said the Bank Clerk. "School children should be taught everything there is to know about their bodies, the various organs, what they're for and what to expect if they abuse them."

"Very true, very true," said the Bank Clerk, "but school boards and parent-teacher associations are still made up mostly of old-fashioned folks who would be horror-stricken at the idea of teaching anatomy. There might be something in the anatomy books about sex, and grown folks mustn't admit to young folks that there is such a thing as sex. It is part of orthodox religion to try to conceal from young folk the biological difference between the male and the female."

"As if you could conceal anything from youngsters in this day and time," said the Soda Jerker. "The average twelve-year-old boy and girl of today knows more about sex than some of the oldsters, although much of what they know is wrong. Did I ever tell you the stork story?"

"I don't think so," said the Bank Clerk.

"Well," said the Soda Jerker, "little Johnny asked his Daddy to tell him how he got here. The old man told him the stork brought him. 'And how did you get here?' asked Johnny. 'The stork brought me,' said the old man. 'Well, how about Grandpa? How did he get here?' asked Johnny. And the old man told him the stork brought Grandpa, too. Little Johnny gave his old man a curious look and ran to find his sister. 'Anybody who believed that line of baloney he handed me about how we all got here would have to believe there ain't been no fun in this family for three generations,' he told her.

"No sir, old folks who try to keep scientific facts from youngsters in this age are just kidding themselves. You ask little Johnny."

In another discussion on much the same topic in another year, the Soda Jerker told this story to point up the precocity of youngsters with regard to matters anatomical:

"A little girl whose head just came to the top of the counter came in the other day and wanted a chocolate boy baby. I gave her a chocolate baby from the candy display case and she pushed it back over the counter, saying, 'I don't wanna girl baby, I wanna boy baby.'

"I told her there wasn't any difference between the chocolate boy babies and the chocolate girl babies.

" 'Es it is a difference,' she said. 'Boy babies got a iddle bit more chocolate on 'em than girl babies'."

Back in the early days of Franklin D. Roosevelt's New Deal, Dad's Main Street pals fell into a discussion one day about "Our Most Serious Crop Surplus," saying:

"I've about made up my mind to quit this job of slinging soda and rent a farm," said the Soda Jerker to his friend the Bank Clerk.

"And what are you going to raise on your farm?" asked the Bank Clerk.

"I ain't planning to raise things," said the Soda Jerker. "I got a great hunch this morning when a farmer friend of mine showed me a government check for $50 for not raising 25 hogs this year. That's the greatest gravy I've ever seen or heard tell of. It made my head dizzy thinking about it. Now just suppose that farmer had been real smart and not raised 500 hogs; he might have gotten a government check for $1,000. And if he hadn't raised 1,000 or 2,000 hogs he could have been rich.

"Of course, I gotta find out what's the best kind of farm not to raise hogs on, the best strain of hogs not to raise, and just how to keep an inventory of hogs I'm not raising. The only thing that worries me is how the government is going to find enough money to keep on paying for all the hogs that ain't raised. Mind you, I ain't going to buy a farm; I just plan to rent one, because the government may go broke before long and not be able to pay for the hogs I don't raise."

"Oh, I'd buy a farm and be done with it," said the Bank Clerk. "You can buy a farm now at any old price. Both the commercial banks and land banks are loaded up with them and eager to unload at almost any price you want to pay. And once you get a title to a farm you are in line for all kinds of government dole, subsidies and favors. You stand to turn right around and borrow from the government twice as much as you paid for the farm, and if you don't choose to repay the loan you just let the government step in and take the farm and you pocket a cool 100 per cent profit, the difference between what you paid for the farm and what the government loaned you on it."

Ever ready to discuss almost any topic, the B.C. & S.J. got into a discussion of bigotry one morning in a column titled "Kikes, Niggers and Jackasses."

"I see by the papers that Mr. Gardiner, manager of the Chamberlain Hotel at Old Point Comfort, has apologized to the Jews for having advertised that he didn't want their business," said the Soda Jerker.

"And if I were a self-respecting Jew I'd never set foot inside the Chamberlain, since the State of Virginia and the United States Government had to force the apology," said the Bank Clerk.

"I don't reckon Mr. Gardiner ever intended any reflection on self-respecting Jews in the first place," opined the Soda Jerker. "I reckon self-respecting Jews were always welcome at the Chamberlain and that Mr. Gardiner valued their good will and their business. But it was the other kind of Jews he was trying to keep out of the hotel. There are Jews and there are Jews. Or to put it another way, there are Jews and kikes; just as there are Negroes and niggers, Southern gentlemen and crackers.

"Some of the finest folks I know are Jews. Two of the finest characters on the U.S. Supreme Court bench are Jews. President Roosevelt values the ability and integrity of a number of Jews who have been given key positions in his administration. One of the best friends the South ever had was a Jew. But American capitalism has produced a peculiarly offensive and obnoxious type of Jewish upstart. Without breeding or education and possessing only a kind of Oriental cunning which he mistakes for brains, he gets into business and by hook or crook makes a wad of money. Money is his god and he thinks he has a passport to society and an open sesame to all the good things of life. He likes to splurge in fashionable hotels and restaurants, follow the native rich and make himself conspicuous by his clothes, his jewelry, his vulgar spending and his bluster and bumptiousness. This type of Jew has ruined many a good hotel. He is as offensive as a bumptious nigger and holds his race back just as the bumptious, half-baked nigger holds back the decent, self-respecting element of the Negro race."

"In which particular the Jew and the Negro are not at all unlike our own people," said the Bank Clerk. "We have our own ignorant, vulgar, loud-mouthed, swaggering, chiseling white Christian Nordics, the same as the Jew has his kikes and the Negro has his niggers."

"Yes," replied the Soda Jerker, "but with this difference.

The Jew and the Negro are minorities and we are in the majority. Our own breed of jackasses so far outnumber us that we long ago gave up the idea of handling them, so we take it out on the Jew and the Negro with their less formidable numbers."

It was inevitable that those two characters, the Bank Clerk and Soda Jerker, should discuss religion now and then, which they did in this discourse titled "And Still We Are Pagans."

"Did you hear Bishop Mouzon at the First Methodist Church last Sunday?" inquired the Soda Jerker of the Bank Clerk.

"I did," replied the Bank Clerk

"And what did you think of him?"

"I think he's a great preacher, and I enjoyed his sermon. He is an able exponent of Christianity, but as a booster for organized religion the Bishop is a flop. In his sermon Sunday morning he said that the world had gone back to paganism, and that America is ruled by the same forces today that ruled Pagan Rome and brought that mighty empire to a fall.

"Now if I were the bishop of a Christian church, I wouldn't make a statement of that kind, because it's a mighty poor advertisement for the church. This is supposed to be a Christian land. We have more than a billion dollars invested in church property, we employ more than 100,000 salaried preachers, and our church organizations are composed of more than a million Sunday School teachers and officials. Now, for a bishop to say that after eighteen hundred years of Christianity and such an investment in its enterprises, the world has turned back to paganism sounds like a flat admission that organized religion is a failure. The Bishop renders a very poor account of Christian stewardship, to say the least."

"To what do you attribute the failure?" asked the Soda Jerker.

"I attribute it largely to the fact that organized religion has not kept in step with human progress," said the Bank Clerk. "If the world is pagan today, is it not reasonable to look for the cause of its paganism in a paganistic theology? Everything changes except theology. Ecclesiasticism in the Twentieth Century offers the enlightened mind of modern man the same crude spiritual fare that satisfied a lot of semi-barbarians in the first century of our era.

"Our preachers still pose as magicians or miracle workers who can change black goats into white sheep and allocate celestial mansions to human misfits who are incapable of appreciating a decent shelter in the here and now. They have trafficked in mysticism and played upon human emotions to the neglect of ethical culture and the principles of right living. And what is worse, they have made religion such an expensive luxury that the average church worker may be pardoned for thinking he has fulfilled all his obligations to God and man when he has responded to the multitudinous demands made upon him by his pastor and the various church boards.

"And now they tell us that, after all the billions they have collected and expended in the business of making the world better, we are still a lot of pagans. I consider it a rather damaging indictment of ecclesiasticism, coming from the mouth of an eminent ecclesiastic."

"Well," said the Soda Jerker, "do you think you would like to live in a world that is not Christian?"

"That's the only kind of world I have ever lived in," responded the Bank Clerk.

The Bank Clerk, who is generally broad-minded about new mores, found nothing but revulsion in a dance that was the rage briefly during the Roaring Twenties. Here's how the dialogue went:

"What do you think of this new dance craze, the Black Bottom?" asked the Soda Jerker of the Bank Clerk.

"What I think of it would furnish the lexicographers with ample material for an unabridged dictionary of profanity in all languages," replied the Bank Clerk.

"The Black Bottom is a low, dirty, vulgar, nasty, loathesome, disgusting, coarse, ribald, ignoble, hideous, revolting, repugnant, nauseating, abhorrent, lewd and obscene distortion of everything terpsichorean. It is the antithesis of all elegance and refinement, offensive in every sentiment of decency, decorum and modesty, and is merely a low-born, vile, degraded dance atrocity borrowed from the jungles of darkest Africa and introduced to American society via the waterfront dives of the Mississippi delta and black-belt towns and the black and tan dance halls of New Orleans and Chicago.

"Black Bottom is an appropriate name for it. The name probably is derived from the black bottoms or black alluvial lands of the Mississippi delta, where a very low type of black, blue-gum, burr-headed Negro is found and where one would expect to find a semi-barbaric race of jungle folk affecting just such a manner of dancing. But, if you will pardon the vulgarity, Black Bottom is, correctly speaking, just what its name implies—a dance for black bottoms— and every white girl or woman who has so little regard for the primary elements of chastity and good manners as to publicly perform such a dance should be taken out in a back alley and her bottom blacked with an application of coal tar or chimney soot.

"The ancient world had an army of gods and goddesses, most of whom have retired to their respective heavens or

Olympian heights to appear no more in the drama of human life. But one of those goddesses still lives; that goddess is Nemesis, the goddess of retributive justice.

"For all the injustices, brutalities and ignominy heaped upon black folks by their Nordic ancestors, we, their descendants, are paying a fearful price in the degradation of our own folk.

"The Africans were not of one type, but of many types. Anthropologists have found something like 125 different types of Negroes, ranging from pigmy cannibals, but little superior to the apes, up to stalwart, high-browed, docile, highly spiritual types from whose ranks came the mighty Pharaohs of Egypt.

"We gathered our black slaves indiscriminately without regard to their type or ancestry. We brought to America black men with the souls of artists and souls of gods, and black men with the low minds of ape-like barbarians and no souls at all. Both were musical. From the two variant and remote types we may choose the most moving spiritual and the lowest jazz in the realms of music. It seems to me that we have chosen jazz.

"Nemesis has struck her blow. Blinded by racial prejudice to all the beauty and nobility of the higher type of Negro life and character, we have seized upon and adopted for our divertissement and amusement the worst that the Negro could give us. The white man once upon a time conquered and enslaved the black man by force of arms; the lowly blacks today are seducing, degrading and enslaving the white man with their lewdest and most immoral jungle music and dances."

One wonders what the Bank Clerk, were he alive today, would think of the twist.

The Soda Jerker kept well abreast of all the scandal in

town without even half listening to the unceasing chatter of the females to whom he served cokes and other concoctions all day long. But it finally got him down, as the following column attests:

"These gossips make my crupper tired," said the Soda Jerker to the Bank Clerk the other morning.

"What's ailing you now?" asked the Bank Clerk.

"I met old Mrs. Thingsmadoodle on the street this morning and she gave me a gimlet-eyed look, shook her finger at me and said: 'I've been hearing things about you.'

"And I said, 'Yes'm, I expect you have, because there are a lot of nasty old busybodies in this town.' And then I says to her: 'I've been hearing tales about you, too, but if you don't pay more attention to what the tattle-tales say about me than I pay to what they say about you, we'll both be happy'."

"And what did she say to that?" asked the Bank Clerk.

"She didn't say," replied the Soda Jerker. "She stuck her nose in the air and beat it up the street. I reckon she's forgot about the time when folks talked about her. That was when she had the looks that she ain't got now and was full of pep instead of vinegar."

"What satisfaction do you suppose small town gossips get out of their snooping and tale-bearing?" interrogated the Bank Clerk.

"They don't get satisfaction," said the Soda Jerker. "There ain't any satisfaction in life for them any more; that's what ails them. Show me any tattle-tale woman who is forever back-biting other women and tearing other people's reputation to tatters and I'll show you a discontented woman who is simply dying to do all the things she condemns in others. You can mark it down as one of the truest things in the world; a woman who is always raising hell about somebody else's morals has simply got a grouch on the world because she hasn't the opportunity or the nerve to have a fling of her own.

"These female gossips are almost invariably a lot of sexual perverts who break the seventh commandment in their hearts every time they read a marriage announcement or see the lights dimmed in a neighbor's bedroom.

"The worst gossip in our town is a woman who ran her husband away from home and has been regretting it ever since because she has discovered that she has no sex appeal for any other self-respecting man in town."

"You haven't much use for gossips, I see," observed the Bank Clerk.

"I can't say that I have, but I am not repudiating them utterly; when I cease to be attractive to the young and giddy ones I'm going to begin to make up to some of these gossipy, middle-aged ones, for I've got their number and I know they are only cackling and secretly yearning for a chance to talk baby-talk to a real he-man."

Never lacking for versatility, the Bank Clerk and Soda Jerker could and would discuss almost any topic under the sun. For instance, in the foregoing conversation they forecast more than thirty years ago the current trend toward fuschia slacks, lime shirts, orange slippers and other many-hued items of raiment with which the male animal today adorns himself when away from the office:

"Folks say this is a great life if you don't weaken, but I have an idea that the fellow who does weaken can get a helluva kick out of it for a season, at least," said the Bank Clerk.

"What's on your mind now?" asked the Soda Jerker.

"I have just come out of the raw cold, a muffler around my neck, Arctics on my feet, wool mittens on my hands, and all buttoned up in a heavy overcoat. The thermometer is down to 10 above zero. And I walk into this female social club and see these women folk sitting around in thin silks just as if they were taking tea under the palms at Palm Beach. I'll bet you that little evolutionary flapper who just went out of here didn't have a darn thing on under her coat except a pair of chiffon hose, thin rayon bloomers, a brassiere and a one-piece georgette silk frock that wouldn't weigh three ounces."

"What kind of a flapper did you call her?" asked the Soda Jerker.

"An evolutionary flapper," said the Bank Clerk.

"What is an evolutionary flapper?" asked the Soda Jerker.

"One who has been monkeyed with," replied the Bank Clerk.

There was a pause in the conversation and then the Soda Jerker said:

"You seem to be always worrying about the way women dress."

"Not at all," said the Bank Clerk. "I have figured that the trend of feminine styles these past few years is a fair indication that the he-male is coming back into his own.

"In the great economy of Nature, the male was originally intended to be more beautiful than the female. It is so throughout all animal creation; the male of every bird and beast is gaudier than the female, and the male makes it his business to vamp the female.

"Several thousand years ago a lot of bewhiskered old men on the plains of Palestine got afraid of God and began to dress in severely plain and uncomfortable clothing. Men ceased to care for their personal appearance. They became decreasingly active in hunting mates. The women were not to be slighted in any such way and they took up the burden of chasing their mates, which men in their weakness had relinquished. And so it has been for centuries.

"But scientists and students of human nature are noting an interesting change. Women are wearing fewer and fewer clothes and men are wearing more. Women have bobbed their hair and are trying to look more and more like men. Man is wearing fancier hose, fancier shirts, fancier neckties and gayer clothes generally. He displays a fancy colored silk handkerchief in his outside breast pocket, wears a gay silk muffler around his neck, and wears pajamas of brilliant oriental colors. Men's clothing today is a riot of colors. Man is coming back into his own.

"Man may yet be the gorgeously arrayed and strutting rooster that he used to be and women the plain, unadorned, drab little hens that God intended them to be when he took a short rib from the side of Adam and gave it a hank of hair for Adam to play with. Everything moves in cycles. In a thousand years or so life, with all of its changes is, after all, but one damn thing over and over again. Women have have their day for a thousand years. Maybe we are on the threshold of a millenium for men. Who knows?"

I could quote many more hilarious columns, as well as some serious ones. Hundreds of them were published over the years and they afforded the readers of *The Independent* a lot of belly-laughs as well as a lot of horse sense and homespun philosophy. I am glad that I had the privilege of knowing the Bank Clerk and the Soda Jerker.

WHEN THE LAW
11. IS "A ASS"

Prime targets for The Independent Man's editorial barbs included, but not necessarily in that order, preachers (The Lord's Annointed), itinerant evangelists (Shekel-Gathering Pulpiteers), the makers and purveyors of patent medicines, crooked politicians and lawyers.

It was the latter group that was most responsible for the harassment and persecution that hounded Dad when he was struggling to get his little newspaper on its feet. And from this same group came most of the men whom he regarded to be the biggest scoundrels in Elizabeth City and Pasquotank County.

"Where Is the Majesty of the Law?" asked a 1932 *Independent* editorial which went as follows:

"The indignation of the citizens of Elizabeth City at the appearance of their County Court officers at the recent term of Federal Court in this city in defense of violators of the national prohibition law is general and emphatic.

"There can be no such thing as majesty of the law in a community where officers sworn to enforce laws in one court go into a higher court to impede the enforcement of the very laws they are sworn to uphold in their lesser court.

"All law and the legal profession is made cheap, venal and vulgar in the eyes of a public that already has too little respect for law and courts of the law. And therein lies the true gravity of the offense of Pasquotank County's court officers who hired themselves out to the bootleggers at last week's term of the United States District Court in this city.

"And then lawyers wonder why the public should regard their profession with undisguised contempt! Here and there we hear some men higher up in the legal profession say that the profession as a whole should not be condemned for the conduct of a few members of the profession. I have no patience with that sort of argument in view of the fact that not once in the history of the profession in this city and section, that I know anything about, have the lawyers themselves made a protest against the rascality of one of their own profession. On the other hand, when the perfidy and general cussedness of one of their profession has been exposed time after time, the lawyers themselves are first to endorse that perfidious member for public office when he gets a bee in his bonnet. And I defy any honest man to employ a lawyer of note in Elizabeth City to prosecute a claim against another lawyer.

"If the lawyers themselves will not clean up their house, they have no right to expect the public to withhold a finger from its nose when it passes their threshold."

Again indulging in lawyer-baiting, Dad wrote an article titled "Philadelphia Lawyers Ain't Got Nothing on Members of our Local Bar" saying:

"Elizabeth City has some smart lawyers. Three Elizabeth City lawyers got a total of $6,337.33 out of one estate with total assets of $5,000, it was revealed this week.

"The estate of the late Joseph Ellis, a World War veteran who died in May 1930, consisted of $5,000 in U.S. Government Bonds representing his war risk insurance. Lawyer W. L. Cohoon, who qualified as Administrator of the estate, got $4,662.16, or what remained of the estate after Ellis' funeral expenses had been paid and the Administrator's fees deducted.

"All efforts to make Cohoon disgorge the money due the Ellis heirs failed. Within the past few days the American Security Co. of New York, who bonded Cohoon in the sum of $10,000, paid off the estate. The security company's check was for $5,025.51, part of it representing interest due on the deferred settlement.

"And then two other smart lawyers, J. H. LeRoy, Jr. and M. B. Simpson, stepped in and claimed one-third of the settlement, their third amounting to $1,675.17.

"Figure it out for yourself: $4,662.16 Cohoon got; $1,-675.17 Messrs. LeRoy and Simpson got—a total of $6,-337.33 out of an original estate of $5,000.

"Elizabeth City has some smart lawyers."

Next to E. F. Aydlett, the Cohoon referred to in the above-mentioned legal triumvirate was the worst and most persistent enemy of The Independent Man over the years. He assaulted Saunders several times and sued him for libel on numerous occasions. That he was not altogether lacking in provocation may be adduced from the reading of the following editorial from the files of *The Independent*.

TIME FOR W. L. COHOON TO GET AFFLICTED AGAIN

"If many local guesses are justified, then the Honorable Walter L. Cohoon, local attorney, soon is expected to have a recurrence of the various and sundry ailments with which he became suddenly afflicted last June on the eve of his scheduled trial on a charge of embezzling $5,000 from the heirs of an ex-serviceman who left that amount in war risk insurance. . . .

"When the Cohoon case was called for trial in Superior Court here on June 7, Mr. Cohoon's physician, Dr. Howard

J. Combs, appeared in court with a certificate to the effect that his patient was physically unable to appear in court since he was afflicted with nephro something-or-other, cystitis and atrophy of the prostate gland.

"Local lay opinion boiled all this medical phraseology down to mean simply that Mr. Cohoon was suffering from cold feet.

"Mr. Cohoon had good reason for not wishing to appear in court at that time. Presiding at that session was Judge M. V. Barnhill, a fearless jurist who is noted for not temporizing with rich or influential lawbreakers. Judge Barnhill suspected a ruse, knowing something of Cohoon's reputation, so he sent another physician to examine Cohoon. That physician, Dr. W. H. C. White, also reported that Cohoon was a sick man and unable to attend court. So the case was postponed until the November term, at which Judge Walter L. Small was scheduled to preside.

"But now comes the rumor that Judge Small has requested that the Governor send a substitute here in his place, since it would prove embarrassing to him to have to sit in judgment upon a follow townsman and a fellow barrister in a case so serious as the Cohoon case. And it is further rumored that Judge Barnhill will be sent here to preside over the November criminal term of Pasquotank Superior Court.

"If this be true, Cohoon is no better off by reason of the postponement than he was before. So the guess is that he will suffer a relapse shortly of the numerous ailments which put him to bed the day before his scheduled trial in June, but from which he recovered a day or so after the court session was over and apparently has not experienced from that day to this. In the meantime, many citizens are wishing Mr. Cohoon the best of health."

But Cohoon finally had to stand trial, was convicted of

embezzlement, and was sentenced to from five to eight years in the State Prison. Editor Saunders heralded this development in a news article headed "A Lawyer Can Be Convicted in the Courts of North Carolina," in which he wrote, in summation:

"The Cohoon case was simply a case of a man reaching the end of his rope . . . a case wherein justice, represented by a jury of twelve good men and true and a fearless and uncompromising Superior Court judge, triumphed!"

(Then followed details of the trial and background of the case.)

A few months later *The Independent* ruefully reported the news that Cohoon would not have to go to prison after all, due to a bungling prosecution which left a legal loophole on which an appeal was successfully based.

This news in turn impelled Dad to write an editorial titled "When the Law is 'a Ass'," as follows:

"The recent opinion of the Supreme Court of North Carolina reversing the judgment of the Superior Court of Pasquotank County in the case of W. L. Cohoon need not have surprised anybody. The conviction of Cohoon would not have been possible upon the mere evidence put in the record by the State's Solicitor, Herbert Leary. Cohoon was convicted not upon the State's evidence but upon the evidence generally known to the Judge and the jury and upon Cohoon's general reputation for cussedness.

"The evidence upon which Leary undertook to convict Cohoon was an affidavit made by Cohoon himself on a sick bed with a view of having it accepted in lieu of his personal appearance. If that Affidavit had been introduced by Cohoon's attorneys, the State would have proceeded to tear it to shreds. But when the case came to trial, with Cohoon himself present to speak for himself, our numbskull of a Solicitor introduced Cohoon's affidavit instead of leaving

Cohoon himself to go on the stand and subject himself to cross-examination.

"The introduction of that affidavit by the State bound the State by Cohoon's own version of his alleged embezzlement. It is a fundamental of law that the State cannot rebut its own witness. Any law student just out of college should have known that. . . . It is a bad thing for the State when a man like Walter Cohoon can go scot free in the light of his known character. It gives the public a contempt for the law and for its courts. The poor and ignorant layman can well say with truth and emphasis that 'If it had been me instead of Cohoon, I would have gone to the penitentiary.' . . ."

Saunders then pointed out that the "seldom-brained Solicitor" was a candidate for renomination on the Democratic ticket and promised that if the Democrats didn't vote for Leary's capable and honest opponent *The Independent* would support the Republican nominee and work for his election.

But Cohoon had in him a streak of viciousness, and it was this latter attribute which eventually proved his undoing. He finally went too far and assaulted a young lawyer with a horsewhip and knife. This led to a 60-day jail sentence. Editor Saunders called this a light sentence and in the following editorial expressed the fervent hope that Cohoon would not be able to escape serving it:

"And so, according to P. G. Sawyer, member of the local bar . . . it's bad for the community to send a lawyer to jail. Sawyer said as much in his passionate appeal to Judge Henry A. Grady, in the Superior Court here last week, to revoke or suspend the sixty-day jail sentence imposed upon Walter L. Cohoon.

"Lawyer Sawyer's appeal for judicial clemency in behalf of Cohoon fell upon the ears of a courtroom audience that is right well convinced that the best thing that could happen in this community would be to send a lawyer to jail.

"On account of my personal dislike for Walter L. Cohoon, I have tried to refrain from commenting upon the sentence imposed upon him in the Superior Court here last week, but when men of the community standing of the Hon. P. W. McMullan and Judge J. B. Leigh back up a person like P. G. Sawyer in an effort to keep . . . Walter Cohoon out of jail, I can no longer restrain myself. Cohoon has been an unrestrained terror in this community for more than a quarter of a century . . . And the courts have always glossed over Cohoon's acts of terrorism. He had come to regard himself as a person above the law.

"But came a day within the past two years when Cohoon was brought to book, charged with the embezzlement of nearly $5,000 from the heirs of a deceased veteran of the World War. He professed to have loaned the money to his wife on a third mortgage on a water-logged farm up in the Dismal Swamp. But, despite the fact that through ignorance or connivance the State's Attorney waived the State's own witness aside and tried Cohoon upon his own written affidavit, a jury in Pasquotank convicted Cohoon of embezzlement and he was sentenced to serve a term of five to eight years in the penitentiary. When the Supreme Court reviewed the case on appeal some months later, it reversed the judgment of the lower court, finding that the defendant could not be convicted on his own testimony. All the time Cohoon was insisting that he would make restitution to the heirs if the courts would let him off. Months and months have elapsed since the Supreme Court relieved Cohoon of that penitentiary sentence, and yet he has done nothing in the way of paying back that money. He let the surety company with which he was bonded settle with the orphan heirs.

"J. Henry LeRoy, one of the younger members of the local bar, was retained by the surety company to represent its interests. No other lawyer in town would take a case against Cohoon. From that day Cohoon marked young LeRoy as a personal enemy and began to accuse him of persecution. One day in June of this year, when LeRoy inserted language in a court order that was offensive to Cohoon, Cohoon laid for LeRoy with a horsewhip and a knife . . . After lashing LeRoy mercilessly and cruelly with the horsewhip which he had bought for the purpose, and after threatening him with the knife, Cohoon shouted in a loud voice that the next time he would meet LeRoy with a Colt's automatic.

"Cohoon, a lawyer above the law, confidently expected to go into court, plead guilty to simple assault and be let off with a fine of five or ten dollars. Instead he was confronted with an indictment for 'secret assault with a deadly weapon with intent to kill,' and the case was sent up to the Superior Court. Judge Grady discreetly had the indictment changed to 'assault with a deadly weapon,' knowing that a conviction for the greater offense would hardly be confirmed by the higher court. Upon conviction, Cohoon was sentenced to 60 days in jail by Judge Grady. His Honor said subsequently, in reply to prayers to change his judgment, that if Cohoon had been an ordinary citizen the lawyers would have demanded a sentence of 12 to 18 months on the roads. And that's exactly what the lawyers would have done.

"Judge Grady's sentence meets with general approval in the city, county and district. His judgment was tempered with extreme mercy and a deep feeling for the defendant's age and physical infirmities. Failure of Cohoon to serve that sentence would enrage every sense of fairness and decency in this community and fill the hearts of the people with hatred and contempt for the courts of North Carolina."

Cohoon tried every legal trick and maneuver in the book but was unable to escape serving that jail term. Needless to say, The Independent Man felt that this was a triumph for justice as well as himself.

Grand Wizard E. F. Aydlett, Dad's other principal antagonist, was not the type to commit physical assault upon an enemy. He punished or sought to punish his enemies either through law suits or through political manipulations and machinations. One of Dad's editorial attacks on E. F. Aydlett started off in this vein:

"Some blind and benighted admirers of the Grand Wizard behold and hail him as a mighty Bull of Bashan—a behemoth of old who splashed the waters of a river and drank up the same—a man who perverts the prophets and falsifies the Psalms. But the scales are falling from the eyes, first this one and then t'other, and ere long he will stand stripped of his gilded coat of many colors, the naked Judas of twenty centuries. . . ."

On another occasion, Dad got off this nifty as a filler at the end of his editorial column:

"E. F. Aydlett was seen in the courthouse one day this week with his hands in his own pockets."

There is no disputing the fact that over the years lawyers gave Dad a bad time of it, but he managed to give it back to them in good measure. If the law is "a ass," as has been said, then that was one ass that The Independent Man beat time and again—and with obvious relish.

BIRTH CONTROL
12. CAMPAIGN

W. O. Saunders' eternal, untiring quest for worthy causes to champion, false idols to smash and hidebound traditions to jolt led him into strange avenues on occasion.

Large families were encouraged in the economic age and the rural locality in which Dad was born. Cheap farming required an abundance of cheap labor. The more brats an ignorant, hook-wormy yokel could beget, the more corn-hoers and cotton-pickers he could command. And when he finally moved to town, to fetch up in a mill district, the sum total of the wages of his large brood of brats in the mill would enable him to live in comparative comfort.

The problem of feeding, clothing, sheltering and educating a lot of children was no problem at all in those days. There were no compulsory school laws, and a shiftless or impecunious parent just didn't have to provide decent clothing and school books to enable his children to go to school. At home they lived on cheap rations of fat pork, corn meal, yams and molasses, and slept four or five in a bed.

This community environment left an indelible impression with my father, an impression which showed clearly some years later in a Bank Clerk and Soda Jerker column titled "Our Biggest Crop Surplus of All." It went as follows:

"I want to ask you what you think of this AAA idea of

hiring farmers not to raise hogs and not to grow cotton?" said the Soda Jerker to his friend the Bank Clerk.

"I don't think a durn thing of it," replied the Bank Clerk. "In the first place, the government has undertaken to curtail the wrong kind of production. What the world needs is not less meat and not less clothing, but fewer mouths to feed and fewer backs to clothe. Now if the government had gone to our tenant farmers and into the slums and mill districts of our towns and cities and contracted with all the jobless, weak-minded, sickly and poverty-stricken individuals to reduce the baby crop, the government would be getting somewhere, and many of our worst social and economic problems would be solved . . . While the government is about the business of regulating everything under the sun, it ought to do something about regulating the baby crop. With fewer babies to grow up into adult problems, there would be little need for so many CCC, CWA, FERA and SOB government activities that threaten to swamp us with debt."

The views that the Bank Clerk expressed in the above colloquy were views Dad had held for sometime, certainly as far back as 1916, when he brought Margaret Sanger to Elizabeth City for her first birth control lecture in the South.

When Mrs. Sanger got under way with her birth control movement, Dad resolved that here was one of those things of which the South stood in dire need. He preached birth control in the columns of *The Independent*, published everything he dared to publish on the subject, and finally invited Mrs. Sanger to come to Elizabeth City.

She arrived there in the summer of 1916, this being her first appearance south of the Mason-Dixon line and probably the first birth control lecture ever made in the South outside of the agricultural colleges, where control in the breeding of pigs, sheep, cattle and horses is given much emphasis, but from which emanated not a word on the limitation or scientific control of human offspring.

So little was known of the birth control movement in the South back in 1916 that the ministers of Elizabeth City were not alarmed about it, and when Dad asked them to announce from their pulpits that Mrs. Margaret Sanger would lecture on the birth control movement, several made the announcement to their congregations.

Dad had rented the local movie house for a Sunday afternoon, and the Standing Room only sign was out long before Mrs. Sanger mounted the rostrum. It was a mixed audience, and men and women alike hung eagerly on her words. She spoke for nearly two hours, but when Dad announced that she was through not a person stirred from his or her seat. These people had heard something about the birth control movement, its whys and wherefores, but not a word about the techniques of birth control. The immobility of the audience was embarrassing; the situation was growing tense. Sensing the heart hunger of hundreds of women in that audience, Dad went to the platform and asked the men to leave the house. He said:

"I know exactly what you good women in this audience want to hear. Fortunately, there is not a word in the statutory laws of North Carolina prohibiting the dissemination of birth control information by word of mouth. Our lawmakers have taken infinite pains to prescribe frightful penalties for printing such information, but there is not one word against oral instruction. So, if the men in this audience will depart quietly and then leave the house to the women, we shall have a birth control clinic here this afternoon, that women may learn truths that will indeed make them free."

The men departed reluctantly, and for nearly two hours

Mrs. Sanger talked frankly to her feminine audience and answered hundreds of intimate questions. It was a red letter day in Elizabeth City. That night, upon invitation from the pastor of one of the largest Negro churches in the town, Mrs. Sanger conducted a birth control clinic for Negro women in the church itself.

This was certainly one of the most popular things Dad ever did. The women of the town were frightfully ignorant not only of available methods for the limitation of offspring, but of the simplest facts of elemental hygiene. They learned much from Mrs. Sanger that they had long yearned to know and very much needed to know.

While Mrs. Sanger's preachments were welcomed and practiced avidly by many women in *The Independent's* territory, they made no impression whatever on certain husbands, as is clear from this news story published January 14, 1927:

"Who is northeastern North Carolina's nearest competition to Reuben Bland of Martin County, who, by being the father of 34 children claims to be the champion papa of the United States? Edward Markham of Weeksville is only in his early fifties, and he is the father of sixteen, which makes him the nearest competitor in Pasquotank that this newspaper has heard of.

"John Sanderlin in Currituck is reported to be the father of twenty children, and he is probably the nearest competitor in the entire district. *The Independent* never has encouraged large families, but folks are generally interested in a large family that has already happened, and this newspaper will be glad to hear from readers living anywhere in this section of the State, telling of the largest families they know of, whether by one wife or several wives, and giving all available details.

"Carl Goerch, editor of the *Washington Progress*, pulled

a great publicity stunt last week in taking Reuben Bland to Washington, where Congressman Warren presented the champion papa to President Coolidge and to Congress. But it looks like somebody ought to take more Blands to Washington. Of course, the present Mrs. Bland is the mother of only about nineteen of his children, but it looks like being a mother of nineteen is a greater accomplishment than being the father of 90 would be. If Reuben fed and clothed them all properly, he would certainly deserve some recognition for that.

"Louis Bell says that Reuben Bland took his family to the Martin County Fair at Williamston to see a champion bull. The man at the entrance saw Reuben trying to line up the crowd and herd them into the tent, whereupon he yelled out: 'Wait a minute, Mr. Bland, we want to bring the bull out to see you.'

"One would expect a woman to be the last person in the world to congratulate Reuben Bland, but here is the telegram reported to have been sent by one in Kansas City: "Reuben, Reuben, I've been thinking, you are quite a nifty man; to your health I now am drinking, you have done what few men can."

"Congressman Lindsay C. Warren in presenting Reuben to Congress said, in part: "Just prior to the holidays the gentlemen from Georgia, Mr. Upshaw, introduced to the House with great satisfaction a constituent who was the proud father of 28 children. Such a feat was not permitted to go unnoticed by this body and we paused in the consideration of an important bill to pronounce our acclaim. And so today, when the national defense of the country is being debated, it is fitting that we stop again and pay tribute to the man who has and is contributing more to the manpower of the Nation than any other citizen.

"Incensed and indignant that one would be so bold as to

attempt to usurp his well-earned laurels, Reuben C. Bland of Robbinsville, Martin County, N. C., my most famous constituent, has come here to Washington and sits yonder in the Speaker's gallery. He is the father of 34 children, and this wonderful accomplishment has been the subject of song and poetry for many, many years. He stands in a class alone. He is the champion papa of America. He is a walking advertisement of the great section of the country he hails from. He is supreme in his line, unequalled and unexcelled."

Dad couldn't let the matter rest there, and two weeks later the Bland case inspired an editorial titled "Thank God for Monogamy." It read as follows:

"Enough of Reuben Bland. A smelly and bewhiskered old peasant from Martin County, has, by the hideous night work of half a century or such a matter, begotten 34 children of record. And Carl Goerch, a Washington, N. C. newspaperman with a ghastly sense of humor and leisure for a lark, parades this procreant bull of the Martin County hinterlands around the country, introducing him to President Coolidge, and putting him on the picture pages of metropolitan newspapers.

"For what? It is certainly not for the glory of the country, the state, its manhood or its womanhood, that one old man has laid around home for half a century and made a stud record that would provoke only a mirthful hee-haw of contempt from a two-year-old jackass.

"Thank God for human monogamy! What a state we would be in if polygamy were tolerated in a land where Reuben Blands are exalted."

The Independent Man had many brushes with the law as a result of his writings, but the editorial which got him in the hottest water of all was one in which he advocated a foeticide in the case of a 13-year-old orphan girl who had

10

been debauched by a man who had adopted her and taken her into his home. In an editorial titled "Where Society Wrongs," Dad told the story of this outrage and then wrote:

"And now, laying aside all false modesty and all the hypocrisy of rote refinement, I want to demand of this county, this state and the society under which we live: By what process of reason do we compel this little girl to go through with this thing and ruin her life forevermore?

"It is true, the very act by which she became entangled in her pitiful physical predicament tainted her innocent life forever; but the world forgives a shame, the world never forgives the badge of that shame.

"I do not advocate foeticide unreasonably, but I do deplore the crime of forcing into being a ruined life that ruins another's life as well, when the prick of a needle or a prescription of ergot would give society one bastard less and give an innocent little girl another chance to make good the life which another had abused."

Dad's enemies read this, sensed that they had discovered a chink in his armor, and had him indicted by a Federal grand jury and prosecuted for obscenity and for advocating an abortion. He barely escaped a prison term in that case, but did have to pay a $50 fine.

Some years later Dad was to have this final utterance on the subject:

"My views on birth control have undergone no change with the passing of years; the more I see of the sorry spawn of the barnyard run of human, the more I am grieved.

"The limitation of offspring among the mentally, physically and economically weak should be compulsory. I resent the doctrine of the Roman Catholic Church that no resort shall be made to any unnatural practice looking to the restriction or limitation of offspring. But at the same time

I make a reverent bow to a church that maintains so many institutions in which the misadventures of its daughters are adroitly concealed and their progeny provided for in skillfully conducted foundling homes.

"If it preys upon ignorance and superstition and fear, the great Church Mother has a deep and sympathetic understanding of human error and does very well look after its own."

The Independent over the years carried many editorials advocating the sterilization of sex criminals. One, titled "What the World Needs," went as follows:

"What the world needs, among other things—and God knows it needs a lot of things right now—is fewer judges and more surgeons. For the second time within a few months the Elizabeth City police have arrested and arraigned a white woman for consorting with a black man. The white woman is sent to jail for 18 months, the black man for 12 months. For a period of 12 months in one case and 18 in the other, the taxpayers of this city and county would feed, clothe and shelter a pair of ignorant, immoral wretches at considerable expense, at the same time lowering the morals of other inmates of the county jail by subjecting them to the degrading influence of an unfortunate woman of the lowest order. The fact that the man and woman were later set free by a Superior Court judge does not affect the argument.

"The most ignorant farmer in dealing with unruly livestock in his barnyard or pasture could have dealt more sensibly with the problem created by the case cited. The farmer would have sent for a veterinarian or would have whetted his old barlow knife and performed an operation himself. And this is just one of millions of cases of human infamy and degradation that could be cured by surgery. We are spending millions in coddling and perpetuating the socially undesirable and unfit, forever sacrificing the biology of the race to the pathology of the unimportant individual.

"What the world needs, among other things, is more surgeons and fewer judges."

Rough language, that, but The Independent Man wrote strongly on subjects about which he felt strongly. That's the kind of man he was.

THE LORD'S
13. ANOINTED

My father had nothing but contempt for what he once called "the Lord's anointed." The biggest rascals in Elizabeth City paraded themselves as religious men and devout workers in the vineyards of the Lord.

"These people," Dad wrote, "are in no sense Christians, but they are devout believers in a God in whose words, as recorded in the Old Testament, they find divine authority for their rascality. For was not David, a robber chieftain who ravished the wife of a friend and then had that friend put to death, looked upon as a man after God's own heart?

"And is it not written in the 21st verse of the 14th chapter of the Book of Deuteronomy that, although the favored of God may not eat of the flesh of an animal that dies of disease or by accident, 'thou shalt give it unto the stranger that is within thy gates, that they may eat it; or thou mayest sell it unto an alien'."

"The Old Testament abounds with like examples of the low ethics of a primitive and barbaric people who regarded everyone not of their faith as enemies of God. Ergo, what the faithful contributed toward the undoing or despoilation of the other fellow is okay with God. Skin your competitor alive, sell tainted meat to your country, unload watered stocks and fraudulent bonds on widows and orphans, and praise God, Hallelujah! Amen!"

"I do not question the faith and devotion of the rascals at all," he continued, "because they can find authority for their every act of knavery and iniquity tucked away somewhere in the forty books of the Old Testament. And if they read the New Testament at all, they translate the Golden Rule to read: 'Do it unto the other fellow first, before he does it unto you.'

"With a very real feeling of great, great righteousness, they prey upon the ignorant and gullible and contribute liberally to priestcraft and the church. And the preacher fawns upon his rich and rascally pewholders because they are his financial mainstay. The poor are devout, prayerful and humble enough, but they have little cash."

I am constrained to believe that Dad was not lacking in justification for his strong and vituperative feelings with regard to "the Lord's anointed."

The political bosses in Elizabeth City half a century ago were devout church members, and both of them belonged to the same church—Blackwell Memorial Baptist. This church had the largest congregation in town because the flocks tend to follow the rich. The pastor, one I. N. Loftin, was a simple, sincere sort of fellow with a background of ignorance and poverty, and he was profoundly grateful for the liberal contributions of his rich pewholders and members of his church board of deacons. It followed that he was sorely grieved over my father's attacks on the money-bags.

It was profoundly shocking to him that this interloper, this stranger within the gates, who had the audacity to impugn the purity and integrity of pillars of the church, was an agnostic, a free-thinker, a member of no church— hence an infidel and an atheist.

The little pastor read Dad's attacks on his brethren and prayerfully decided that something should be done about this disgraceful situation. He began a series of sermons directed against infidelity and atheism. He called no names at first but denounced in scathing terms the town's "atheistic assassin of character and emissary of the devil."

His sermons became so vitriolic and sensational that mobs of curious non-churchgoers surged to Blackwell Memorial on Sunday mornings and nights to be entertained. On a Saturday before one of his diatribes was to be delivered, he would plaster the town with handbills announcing his subject. In one of his handbills he called the name of W. O. Saunders outright.

Dad attended his services, heard the sermon and heard himself denounced as a pest and a scourge. The pastor said, among other things, in referring to *The Independent:*

"Here is an institution that is a far worse evil in our fair community than a house of prostitution; for a house of prostitution only destroy's men's bodies; but in this newspaper and W. O. Saunders we have an institution that destroys men's souls. I call upon the Christian manhood and womanhood of this town to rise up in its might and put it down. Let us pray."

He lifted his hands and eyes to the heavens and prayed fervently in a shrill staccato voice for God to manifest Himself as of yore and send down a scourge upon this infidel in their midst. After which the congregation lustily sang "Onward, Christian Soldiers."

There was an ominous fervency in the singing of that hymn, and when Dad left the church that night he was not surprised that a large number of the males of the congregation followed at his heels. We lived only about two blocks from the church and he lost no time in getting home; stepping quickly inside the front gate and closing the gate

behind him. The mob that had by this time gathered
banked itself in front of our home and pressed against the
picket fence.

A voice out of the crowd spoke up: "In the name of God,
we order you to leave this town in twenty-four hours or we
will get you."

"Let's get him now," shouted another voice.

Dad's only firearm was a cheap little nickel-plated 32-
calibre revolver, the kind the mail order houses used to sell
for about $3.95. If you shot at the flagman on the caboose
of a freight train you might hit the engineer in the cab of
the locomotive.

"The first man who enters my yard will have to be toted
out," Dad shouted back.

There was a frightening silence except for the heavy
breathing of the mob massed in front of the house.

"Get away from here," Dad shouted, "or I'll shoot into
the crowd, and I mean business."

"He hasn't got a gun," someone taunted. Whereupon
Dad quickly fired three shots into the air. He reasoned that
his adversaries, hot from the House of God, had not gone
to worship with firearms in their pockets (although he had
done just that) and had not had time enough to arm themselves since leaving the church. But he reasoned wrongly.
Some of them not only had gone to church armed that night,
but used their arms now, pouring a volley of steel in Dad's
direction. My mother, attracted by the disturbance, had
come out of the house and was standing beside Dad when
the shots were fired.

Bullets whistled by their heads, one bullet barely grazing
Mother's arms and another imbedding itself in a wooden
post only a few inches from Dad's head. At this point
Mother swooned and Dad dragged her into the house.

He then rushed to an upstairs window and again ordered

the mob to leave, threatening to shoot to kill if they didn't. And the mob left; in fact, it fell all over itself in its mad get-away. For only a few of the men in the crowd were of murderous bent; most were but curiosity seekers who augmented the mob's numbers in quest of excitement. It wasn't their row and they had already seen enough fireworks.

During the entire episode, Dad had not lost his head or become excited. He now hastened downstairs to look after Mother, whom he had left unconscious on the floor. Halfway down the stairs his knees buckled and he fell in a flop. His legs wouldn't function; he couldn't walk; he had to drag himself downstairs on his bottom. The reaction from so much excitement and terror had been too much for him.

Of course, Dad didn't leave town in the next twenty-four hours. He stuck and fought it out. The next day, and for days to come, many of the best people of the town and countryside rallied to his support, and subscriptions to his paper poured in. Dad had closed his shop the Saturday night before, wondering where he was to get enough money to buy a ream of paper for his next edition. Now the money was coming in. He bought two reams.

That week he published a horrific account of the Sunday night affair and assailed the rabble-rousing preacher with all the invective and vitriol at his command. A few weeks later he served notice on Loftin that two could play at being rough. An editorial titled "Loftin Still At It" went as follows:

"I am informed by a responsible witness that Preacher Loftin continues to harp on the subject of Saunders and *The Independent*. These two weeks I have tried to let Loftin alone. But if this inciter of rioting doesn't keep his mouth shut, I'm going after him again. And if he starts another gang of rioters after me I am going to kill the first dastard that crooks a finger.

"Furthermore, I want to say that if I am dragged out of my house by any of Loftin's banditti, the next mob-frolic will be at the corner of Pennsylvania Avenue and Cypress St., and Ike Loftin will be the beautiful spectacle to be arrayed in a genuine coating of tar and feathers.

"Not since that outrage of a month ago has Loftin expressed regret at the conduct of his members who stormed out of his church to threaten me and shoot up my home. If that mob hadn't done just what Loftin wanted it to do, he would have apologized for it from his pulpit ere now, and expressed his regret at such hot-headedness through the medium of the press. But Loftin hasn't done any such thing.

"On the other hand, I hear of him valuing the church property held by the various religious denominations in this town and declaring that if the united institutions, worth more than $100,000, were to rise up in their might they could 'drive the devil out of the community.' I am the devil he referred to.

"Not satisfied with the foolhardy efforts of his own crowd to mob me, Loftin would persist in his incendiarism and try to recruit from the other churches and other denominations in the town.

"And I want to say right here to Loftin that he had better steer clear of the other churches in Elizabeth City. If the other churches had had anything to do with Loftin, they would have given him his walking papers months ago.

"And now there's another thing I want to say to Loftin, and it is this: I will let you rest for a while now if you will keep your mouth closed and spare us the odor of your bad breath. But if you can't keep your infernal mouth shut, I will give you something else to howl over . . .

"Take the hint?"

Naturally, The Independent Man was not going to let Preacher Loftin and his flock rest from there on; he had to keep the pot boiling, which he did with an article provocatively titled "Bing!" It went as follows:

"In last week's *Star Heel*, my weekly contemporary, there appeared an article contributed by the Rev. I. N. Loftin entitled 'Moral Conservation.' In the body of this article there appears the following quotation: 'A man who goes to the bawdy house one night and the next night leads church work makes a terrible thrust at moral ideas.' Right. I would like to know the gentleman's name. Indeed I would. If Loftin will give me the name, and proof vouched for by someone other than himself, I will hold up the picture before the people of this community until the man becomes as loathesome as a leper. Lead in Christian work fresh from a bawdy house! . . . However, let me tell Loftin he had better apply the soft pedal or he will run amuck again. Some of his male members are quite unlike him . . . I know men in his church who, when they reach Norfolk, make a bee-line for Belle Brown's. Thence they zigzag from one hooker joint to another until the last poor girl is slobbered over, nature balked and knocked from a living perpendicular to a dead level.

"This conduct on the part of a church member is bad enough but is not comparable to the conduct of the Sunday School Superintendent who squeezes the lady pianist so hard that her brother threatens to shoot him. Because, in the first instance, the church member is seeking to gratify the lust of flesh among those who have already gone the gait; in the latter, the conduct of the superintendent is calculated to add another 'soiled dove' to the flock.

"Damn a church member who goes 'a-hoppin' and then leads the holy meeting with the smell of the harlot yet upon his garments; twice damned the church leader who scruples not to make love to his typist; thrice damned is the preacher who presumes to play fast and loose with the heart of a lady school teacher. 'Whosoever looketh on a woman to lust after her hath committed adultery with her already in his heart.' But this subject is getting too interesting. Bing!"

To which I would be inclined to add: Wow!

Well, the clashes from pulpit and press continued for a while longer, and again Loftin made the comment that Dad and *The Independent* were a worse evil than a house of prostitution. What did he know about houses of prostitution, Dad wondered? A little digging revealed the fact that there was only one brothel in Elizabeth City at that time, and, by God, Preacher Loftin was the landlord of the premises, whether he was aware of it or not.

The poor reverend was never the same again. His congregation raised his salary, built him a new church annex, praised him and promised him undying loyalty and devotion. But he was a sick man. He just wasted away after that and in a few years died without making another ripple in the town.

Dad seems to have had more trouble with Baptist ministers than those of any other denomination, but he had his set-tos with ministers of other faiths. Notable among them was a stalwart Episcopal reverend, a hot-headed impolitic cleric who indiscreetly shook his finger at my father one day and said: "We are going to get you!" Dad published a facetious piece in *The Independent* that week, reporting his threat and suggesting that the reverend gentlemen had better keep away from the First Ward, else old man Andrew Chesson might get him on account of the chickens he had bought from Old Man Chesson two years before and had never paid for. Or the officers of the law might get him some night when he was sneaking into town from Doc Lowry's vineyard with a jug of wine concealed under his buggy robe. Those were horse and buggy days; Main Street had not been paved; the automobile was yet to arrive in Elizabeth City.

That Episcopal preacher sought out Dad next day with blood in his eye. He shook his fist in Dad's face and invited him to fistic combat. Dad told him he didn't fight that way.

"Of course, you will not," the preacher thundered, "for I could put your back on the ground in three minutes."

In the next issue of his newspaper Dad reported the episode and asked, innocently, "Will the good reverend tell the town whose back he last had on the ground?" That jibe raised a question and started a flow of gossip that caused the poor parson to leave town under a cloud.

Another cleric whom Dad drove out of Elizabeth City was a young Catholic priest. The lid began to blow off this story in July 1934, when *The Independent* ran a front page story under this headline: "Fr. Howard Lane, Hot-Headed Catholic Priest, Raises Hell at Sunday Morning Services— Likens His Altar Boys to Jackasses, Tells Their Mother to Get Out of Church and Orders Call for Police." The story follows:

"Incensed at the ungentlemanly and tyrannical behavior of the Rev. Father Howard V. Lane, communicants of St. Elizabeth's Roman Catholic Church in Elizabeth City are considering taking steps to have Lane removed and another priest assigned to their parish.

"In the little more than two years that Priest Lane has been in Elizabeth City he has made many enemies by his amateurish egotism, his bumptiousness, his arrogance, his insolence, his intolerance and his tyranny over his congregation. He has even gone out of his way to bulldoze local tradesman not members of his church and has threatened the extinction of *The Independent*. Two years ago he gave this newspaper just one year to live, making the boast that he had rich and influential Catholic friends in the North who would smash this newspaper with their wealth and prestige. The destruction of *The Independent* hasn't materialized after two years, although the depression did its durndest to vindicate the priest's boast . . ."

Then followed an account of how Lane lost his temper because of the slowness of one of his altar boys and bawled out the boy from the pulpit. Then, when the boy's mother started to leave the church, Lane shouted after her to "Get out, get out of here."

The Independent's story went on to say that "Lane should have lived in Spain during the Inquisition, when he could have gouged eyes out with red hot irons, broken the bones of his victims on the wrack and burned their corpses at the stake. How the Catholics in Elizabeth City have contrived to tolerate his conceit and tyranny for more than two years is as hard to explain as most other religious phenomena. But his exhibition of rage and insolence last Sunday was too much for most of his flock, and they will hardly tolerate him much longer."

Father Lane's reaction was prompt and violent, as reported in the next issue of *The Independent*. The self explanatory headline went as follows: "Roman Catholic Priest in Drive to Get Advertisers to Boycott This Newspaper—Spiritual Descendent of the Hellish Torquemada Vows that this Newspaper shall be Crushed and Boasts of Support of Outside Agencies Aiding Him with Their Cash and Magic."

In the same issue, Editor Saunders put the matter up to the diocesan bishop with the following brief editorial:

"Does the Rev. Howard V. Lane, the ferocious and ungodly priest who rules over the Roman Catholic parish in Elizabeth City, represent the spirit and policy of the Roman

Catholic Church? The Rt. Rev. William J. Hafey, bishop of the North Carolina Diocese of the Roman Catholic Church, can answer that question. The proper answer from the Bishop would be the immediate demotion or unfrocking of Lane. Lane is not only a menace to society but a menace to the progress of Roman Catholicism in North Carolina. But if Lane represents the spirit and principle of Roman Catholicism in America, then by all means he should be encouraged and exalted by his Bishop. We shall see."

One week later *The Independent* was able to headline: "Exit the Rev. Fr. Howard V. Lane, the Catholic Priest Who Was Too Big For His Cassock." The gist of the story was in these words:

"By order of the Rt. Rev. William J. Hafey, bishop of the North Carolina Diocese of the Roman Catholic Church, the Rev. Fr. Howard V. Lane has been removed from St. Elizabeth's Parish, Elizabeth City. Lane departed last Sunday for parts generally unknown. . . . Lane was vigorous, aggressive, bumptious, egotistical, carnal—a tyrant, a braggart and a bully."

On another occasion, when a Baptist preacher in Camden County attacked Editor Saunders in a sermon, Dad tore into him and his church in an editorial titled "He Can't Help It," in which he wrote:

"It comes to my ears that I was the subject of an attack by the Rev. Jesse McCarter, pastor of Sawyer's Creek Baptist Church, in his sermon last Sunday. I haven't bothered to try to find out what he said about me. It really doesn't matter.

"This cadaverous, ascetic, hard-headed parson McCarter is a good man according to his lights. But his lights are terribly dim. Life to him is distorted, as if illumined by the dancing flames of the Inquisition. Mr. McCarter does not belong in this world at all, but to heaven. I feel no un-kindness toward Mr. McCarter; he is the helpless product of a very bad theological system.

"There are 25,000,000 Protestants in America and they have produced, according to the latest statistics, 180,815 preachers, or one preacher for every 141 church members. A system in which preachers are so plentiful and so cheap is bound to produce a lot of ignorant, hateful meddlesome, tactless preachers. It would perhaps be possible to perfect a clerical army of 10,000 intelligent, refined, tolerant, re-spectful and respectable clergymen in America, but not 180,815. . . ."

Then there was the time when a Charlotte (N.C.) minis-ter accused The Independent Man of denying "the infallible Word of God," and Editor Saunders challenged the preacher to subject the Bible's alleged infallibility to a fair trial in a court of law and before an ordinary jury.

In the next issue of *The Independent*, Dad told how the Charlotte minister had crawled in his hole. The story follows:

"The Rev. S. D. McLean, pastor of Wilmoore Presby-terian Church of Charlotte declines to bring his Bible into court and present the preachers' evidence of the infallibility of the book to a common jury of North Carolina.

"Having challenged W. O. Saunders to come over into the church because the church is the 'concomitant' of a book that is 'the infallible word of God,' the Rev. McLean now feels affronted because the editor of this newspaper chal-lenged him in turn to show proof of the Bible's infallibility according to the rules of law and evidence prevalent in ordinary courts of law.

"By such a test, hearsay testimony, theological deductions and mere opinions would be ruled out. It would be necessary for the preacher and his attorneys to explain to a jury how the books of the Bible came to be written, when they were written, and how they had been rewritten, subject to numerous translations, revisions and interpolations until today it is admitted that no translation is satisfactory.

"Even the Roman Catholic Church, safe custodian of the Bible for nearly 1500 years, during which time there were no Protestant churches and no English editions of the Bible, is right now completing a new translation of the Bible to take the place of the Bible the Methodist Church has proclaimed infallible for nearly nineteen centuries. In recent years, the Protestants have rewritten the Bible several times, and their much-heralded Moffat translation no more reads like the King James version than G. Bernard Shaw reads like Shakespeare.

"W. O. Saunders knew that the Rev. Mr. McLean would refuse to come into court because no one knows better than a preacher that the book which they hold up as THE IN-FALLIBLE WORD OF GOD is no more infallible than this newspaper or a copy of the *Congressional Record*. And the preacher who proclaims the Bible the infallible word of God is either ignorant or insincere.

"Holy Man McLean in evading challenge of the editor writes a very long letter in getting away from the point. His letter will satisfy millions who are content to 'believe,' but it leaves the earnest truth-seeker just where he was before. Those whom God has endowed with reason are out of luck; they can get no help from the clergy who damn them."

On another occasion, when a Norfolk (Va.) preacher objected to some language used in a Saunders speech and referred to the editor as "a half-boiled potato" in a Sunday radio sermon, Dad termed the preacher's attack uncalled for, explained what he had said and in what context, and concluded with these words:

11

"But it is a fine thing to get off with being called 'a half-boiled potato.' Just a few centuries ago (Preacher) Holland and his kind would have had me tried for heresy and burned at the stake. We have made some progress. There are millions today who will agree with me that even a half-boiled potato sets better in the stomach than a half-baked Baptist preacher."

If The Independent Man proved anything in his many fights with the clergy, it was this: a frock coat is not always long enough to cover up clay heels.

HEYDAY OF
14. HOOCH

The Independent made its debut some years before enactment of the Volstead Act, which brought back national prohibition of distilled spirits. It lived through an era in which moonshinning, bootlegging and hijacking were rampant, and it faithfully reported on all aspects of Prohibition, from the amusing to the tragic.

Dad reported the apprehension, arraignment, trial and punishment of liquor-law violators, but he held no rancor for them. If given the opportunity, he would gladly excoriate the wholesale grocer who piously passed the collection plate in the Methodist Church on Sunday and sold barrels of sugar to known moonshiners the other six days of the week. He would go after the judge who accepted a bribe for letting a bootlegger off with a light fine instead of a jail sentence. But he looked upon the typical moonshiner and 'legger as the weak and hapless victims of a bad law.

On one occasion, he reviewed the prohibition movement and wrote, in part:

"And so prohibition, a dishonest law contrived to regulate the appetites and conduct of others, added women and young people to the nation's quota of liquor addicts and resulted in a deplorable state of scofflawism and an alarming breakdown of morals.

"Out of it all grew a new, bumptious, arrogant, law-defiant undercover industry in our rural regions. Industry had invaded our agricultural districts and was making life for the farmer and his sons less and less secure. Moonshining and bootlegging offered the prospect of a more lucrative and more adventurous vocation than farming. The rural church had driven the grog shop from the crossroads, and now the outlawed distiller of hooch brazenly set up his still in the wooded acres back of the country church.

"We thought it would be a fine thing to raise our children in a saloon-less country where they would never know the smell or taste of booze. As things turned out, they had forced upon them, and had cultivated a taste for, more abominable distillations than their forefathers ever knew."

The Independent was not against liquor *per se;* it was only against the abuse of liquor and the social evils connected with its manufacture, sale and consumption. It stood for temperance, as the following editorial, titled "Let's Talk Turkey," reveals:

"What the country needs, it seems to me, is more Temperance talk and less Prohibition talk. In all of the windjamming pro and con over the merits and demerits of National Prohibition, we have been permitted to lose sight of the evil of drink itself. Alcohol, a poison, the poisonous nature of which was in utter disrepute a decade or so ago, has become respectable under Prohibition. And I think this is true because we have lost sight of the true chemistry and harmfulness of alcohol in a fog of discussion about Prohibition. We may never settle the question of whether Prohibition is good or bad, but there is no question about the evils of intemperance.

"While their elders are making much noise over the effectiveness or lack of effectiveness of laws, millions of young people today are soaking their entrails with alcoholic stimulants that will in many instances destroy their will power and impair their health in adult life. . . .

"I, for one, would like to hear more honest-to-God discussion about the evils of alcohol and less about Prohibition."

"Boy Bootleggers in Town Are Mopping Up," proclaimed a headline appearing in *The Independent* above the following news story:

"Youngsters operating about the corners of Main and Road and other streets would give Horario Alger another type of prosperous youth to write about. Some of these boys are making upward of $100 a week, selling liquor at $1.50 and $2 a pint.

"They find ready customers in traveling men who visit the city. It's easy to spot a stranger now, for he drives a car with an out-of-town license. One boy barely 17 years old hopped into a traveling man's car the other day and casually mentioned that he was disposing of some 200 pints of liquor a week. The traveling man got his pint for $2.

"The boy bootlegging racket began some time back when a youngster in need of cash, and with no other way in sight to get some, slipped a few pints from his father's five-gallon carboy. The profits were good and the sale so easy that the lads soon got to buying their own at $3 to $5 a gallon. They keep their liquor stored in toilets in poolrooms and other convenient places about the city, and fill orders as needed.

"Little else could be expected of boys in a town that makes no effort to provide wholesome recreation and industry for the younger generation."

Sometime later, Editor Saunders scolded the bootlegger behind the operations of these boys, terming him "a modern-day Fagin."

Another news item of the prohibition era heralded the information that the "First Methodist Church Has Its Own Blind Pig." It went thus:

"That a bootlegger occupying an imposing residence on Church Street, Elizabeth City, numbers among his customers prominent and influential members of the First Methodist Church of this city was the startling information imparted to the congregation of that church by the pastor, the Rev. F. S. Love, in his sermon last Sunday.

" 'And that is what makes prohibition so hard of enforcement,' declared the pastor—the fact that the bootlegger is aided and abetted by prominent citizens. 'How are you going to put an end to the bootlegger when he is encouraged and supported in his business by church members who ought to be earnest crusaders against the rum traffic and making war on bootleggery instead of patronizing it?' he asked.

"Mr. Love did not call the name of the bootlegger or name the members of his congregation who are among the bootlegger's customers. The public is making two guesses as to the name of the bootlegger and not guessing so much as to who the brethren are who are drinking bootleg liquor.

"The bootleggers are not pleased with Mr. Love's attacks. A friend of this newspaper reports a conversation in which he heard a bootlegger complain that the churches won't let a bootlegger rest until they get him in the church, and that after he joins the church the church members won't let him rest until he supplies them with more liquor. The bootlegger seems to be thoroughly in accord with the pastor that the church member who buys and drinks hooch is the more culpable party."

Again on the light side, *The Independent* reported the following social note:

"If a hoax perpetrated at the Elizabeth City Country

Club Monday night, February 18, was intended as a sly poll of prohibition sentiment, the results were not satisfactory to Volsteadians. Punch was served from a barrel, drawn from two spigots, one on either side of the barrel.

"One spigot was labeled SPIKED. There were 200 or more guests present and only five of the entire number drew their punch from the spigot labeled UNSPIKED, and four of them were women. The only male to tap the UNSPIKED spigot was N. Howard Smith, and Carl Blades insists that Howard was drawing it only for a chaser.

"It should be stated that both spigots tapped the same contents of the punch barrel, and the punch was not spiked at all. Spiking punch is considered an unnecessary procedure, now that so many carry their own 'spike' on their hips."

Actually, The Independent Man was less harsh on those who broke the prohibition law than he was on those who abetted in the lawbreaking and those who subverted the law. He frequently chided the sheriff or the prohibition agents for not raiding certain stills, and on one occasion he all but drew a map in an article headed "And Why Don't the Dry Officers Get This Outfit?" It read:

"*The Independent* is not trying to break up the liquor industry in this section; it is today one of our most important industries and puts a lot of money in circulation in the city and section. But this newspaper will lose no opportunity to expose the stupidity, inefficiency or venality of Federal prohibition agents.

"Within the past few weeks *The Independent* stirred up a hornet's nest by asking certain officers point-blank why a certain still in this county was not raided, since the owner of that still has boasted that he was protected. The agents got busy and together with the sheriff of the county made a belated raid on the still in question. *The Independent* will now ask them another:

"One of the biggest and boldest bootleg organizations in this section is domiciled on the main highway between Great Bridge and Northwest, Va., just a few miles over the North Carolina line. The place is conspicuous by the large number of automobiles and trucks that are parked about the place all hours of the day and night. The place is known to everybody along the road, and truckloads of whisky are moved to the place over the main highway in broad daylight, the contents of the trucks poorly disguised.

"This newspaper is informed that the liquor for this Virginia distributing organization comes from East Lake, is brought to Elizabeth City on boats and here loaded on trucks and transported to the Virginia destination.

"It is common talk around Moyock, Northwest and Great Bridge that the senior member of the Virginia outfit boasts that he pays certain officers for protection and carries a gun for others who might interfere with him.

"Surely the prohibition enforcement officers know all about this outfit. If they don't know about it, this fact alone condemns them as a lot of boobs. And if they know about it and do nothing about it month after month, then isn't the public justified in assuming that somebody is being paid for protection? This newspaper is seeking information."

When North Carolina voted to retain prohibition at a time when most states were voting it out, the lead on *The Independent's* news story went as follows:

"In one of the most spectacular political landslides in its history, North Carolina that gave wringing wet, gin-guzzling Bob Reynolds a majority of more than 250,000 votes over Dry Cam. Morrison in 1932, went to the polls

Tuesday on an out-and-out Repeal issue and voted better than two for one against a repeal convention and for the retention of the Eighteenth Amendment. The cantankerousness of North Carolinians defies explanation."

Later, North Carolina voted for local option, and Pasquotank County was one of 25 or so counties in the state to go wet. *The Independent* reported on the ending of "the long drought" in a news story headed "Corn-Swilling Huskies Use New 3.2 Beer for a Chaser Merely—Which Isn't Going to Help Cause of Temperance." It went thus:

"Legalized 3.2 per cent beer made its debut in Elizabeth City this week in a mild orgy of intoxication, just as the W.C.T.U. and other dry organizations had direfully predicted, but the intoxication was not the result of drinking 3.2 beer but rather was caused by the amount of liquor consumed by those who were disappointed in the 'green' taste and near-beer impotency of the long anticipated 'real' beer.

"People who have become accustomed over a long period of years to the taste and 'kick' of raw corn liquor and powerful home brew failed to find any exuberance in drinking the new 3.2 beer. So, after sampling a bottle or two of the new brew, they resumed the drinking of home brew and corn whisky. One man told the story briefly when he said: 'This 3.2 beer's all right, and don't let anybody tell you different. Take three drinks of liquor and two bottles of beer and you'll sure have that floating power and free wheeling.'

"Another remarked that 'This stuff ought to be called three pint-two instead of three-point-two—three pints of liquor and two bottles of beer as chasers will make a whole party high.' . . ."

By the time the Eighteenth Amendment was repealed, this country was in the throes of a depression, and *The*

Independent again was struggling to make ends meet. Pasquotank had an A.B.C. liquor store and *The Independent* could have had a most helpful boost to its revenues by accepting liquor advertising, but this it refused to do. The following editorial "Restatement of Policy" was published in 1935:

"Funny how the 'dry' newspapers in North Carolina that have been yelping against the legalization of liquor emitted nary a yelp when a bill was passed by the General Assembly last week to permit the advertising of whisky in North Carolina newspapers. One may confidently expect most of the 'dry' newspapers in North Carolina to immediately begin an eager solicitation of whisky, gin, brandy, and rum ads, accepting this business with the same alacrity that they accept the paid advertising of common patent medicine frauds.

"The liquor business is going to be fat pickings for the newspapers in North Carolina and the spending of vast sums of money by the distillers in North Carolina in newspapers probably will make them as respectful toward the liquor interests as they are towards the cigarette industry. We shall see.

"Fortunately or unfortunately (according to the point of view), *The Independent* shall hesitate to participate in the profits that will accrue to the press of the state through liquor advertising. When *The Independent* was established in 1908, it excluded both whisky and patent medicine advertising from its columns. It is not convinced that it should alter its policy in this, the 27th year of its career.

"For years this newspaper has held to the firm conviction that the way to temperance is to encourage the use of beer and wine in moderation and discourage the use of hard liquors. The human system has a peculiar affinity for alcohol, and those who do not drink alcohol manufacture it within their own systems through the consumption of excess carbohydrates. Since this natural human craving for an alcoholic stimulant seems to exist, the polite use of milder alcoholic beverages is vastly preferable to the consumption of the harsher liquors that have a demoralizing, brutalizing and ugly effect upon millions who play with them.

"Adhering to this conviction after many years of experience and observation, this newspaper is not enthusiastic over the new law and is disinclined to accept any advertising extolling the merits of any brand of whisky, rum, or gin, or encouraging the use of these intoxicants. This business it prefers to hand over to its contemporaries.

"*The Independent* will continue to accept advertisements of beer and wines of recognized purity."

Again, as he had done so many times in the past, The Independent Man chose to put principle above profit. It just wasn't in him to do otherwise.

WHEN AN
15. ASS AIN'T

If he hadn't found a niche in the world of journalism, I feel that my father would have enjoyed more than a modicum of success in some field of endeavor having to do with instruction of his fellow man.

He had a gift with words, an ability to express himself in such a manner that there could be no mistaking as to his meaning. But it was not logic and rhetoric alone that made Dad a forceful and understandable writer and speaker; it was a certain common touch he had which enabled him to communicate effectively with rural and small-town America—the real America.

A distinctive element of this "common touch" was his enjoyment of a bawdy or ribald story, and his use of such a story to get a point across to the readers of his newspaper. One never knew when overtones of Balzac or Rabelais might crop up in the columns of *The Independent.* For the most part, Dad employed salty humor to drive home a moral or illuminate an incident, but he sometimes used a shocking word or story just because it tickled his fancy to do so—just for the hell of it, in other words.

He once told a close friend: "An ass is a beast of burden; the posterior or rump of a human is an arse. But I lay you a wager that nine out of ten persons you meet on the street would spell the latter with a double ess." Then, chuckling, he recalled that the Norfolk (Va.) politician who threatened him with violence back in 1907 had not said he intended to kick Dad's arse in public; he was going to kick his ass.

Well, Dad could not for long ignore this fundamental shortcoming in his readers' knowledge of semantics. Imagine, then, the consternation of thousands of good rural folk in Northeastern North Carolina one day when they saw on the front page of *The Independent* a headline like this:

BRIDE OF THREE WEEKS
BEATS ASS OFF HUSBAND

That is what the bride literally did, but a prudish and ignorant public thought she had beaten the arse off him, which is what a lot of brides should do to their husbands, Dad suggested privately.

In neighboring Camden County, a young woman, attracted by the cries of her husband emanating from the back premises, rushed to the stable and found her husband cornered in a stall and being kicked savagely by an ass. Grabbing a stout cudgel, the bride of three weeks rushed into the stall and beat the ass off her husband, probably saving his life.

Now, the writing of newspaper headlines is something of an art. The headline writer has many sizes and styles of type to play with, but he can get only so many letters of a given style and size of type into a balanced line. The Camden bride story merited a two-line head, admitting of a maximum of about twenty-one letters to the line. The words "Bride of Three Weeks" made one good line of 20 letters. In the next line, the headline writer was forced to conserve his words. He couldn't have said "Beats Jackass off Husband" because that would have been too long to fit into the available space. So Dad used the word "ass" instead of "jackass," telling himself that, after all, an ass is an ass and an arse is an arse.

The publication of that properly balanced and correctly worded headline shocked so many prudish readers of *The Independent* and brought on so many cancellations of subscriptions that Dad felt impelled to try to enlighten his readers as to the distinction between an ass and an arse in a subsequent issue.

A feature of his newspaper for some years had been a weekly dialogue between two hypothetical characters found on every Main Street in America, the Bank Clerk and the Soda Jerker. These two individuals were permitted to exchange sophistries, banalities or philosophical banter on everything under the sun—from philandering to philanthropy, from nudism to Buddhism—as the mood suited them.

And so "The Bank Clerk and Soda Jerker" indulged in the following bit of dialogue in their column shortly after the bride of three weeks beat the ass off her husband.

"You look as if someone had stolen your marbles," said the Soda Jerker to his friend the Bank Clerk, as the latter worthy came in for his morning sugar toddy today with a frown on his face.

"I am getting tired of these durn candidates for county offices asking me for my support. I can't come on the street without running into some bozo who tells me he is running for this or that office and will appreciate anything I can do for him. I have just been button-holed by a bird running for constable who, honestly, hasn't got sense enough to get in out of the rain. He wouldn't know his ass from a hole in the ground."

"Ssh-h!" shushed the Soda Jerker. "Go slow on that rough stuff; there're females around."

"What do you mean, rough stuff?" exclaimed the Bank Clerk. "You give me a pain in the neck; like most low minds, you don't know the difference between an ass and an arse. I said that this bird I am talking about don't know his ass from a hole in the ground. Must I tell you how that saying originated?

"Well, it was like this: there was a certain old farmer who used to live up in the Scratch Hall township in Gates County whose only mount was a jackass. This old farmer rode his jackass to church regularly every Sunday morning. Obviously, he couldn't tie his donkey to the common hitching rack with the fine animals owned by his more affluent neighbors, so he found a hitching post close by one of the church windows and tied his donkey there.

"One winter day the church caught fire from a defective flue, right in the midst of the morning service. There was a mad rush for the doors and the old farmer feared the crush. Suddenly he bethought himself of his ass tied just outside the window, rushed over to the window, raised the sash and jumped for his donkey. But the old boy got the wrong window and landed in a well instead of on his donkey. The old fellow explained the accident next day by saying that he had become so old and near-sighted that he couldn't tell his ass from a hole in the ground."

"Well," said the Soda Jerker, "I should say that a man who doesn't know his ass from a hole in the ground shouldn't go to church."

"If you remove that class from our churches, the preachers would starve to death," said the Bank Clerk.

"It is folks who don't know their ass from a hole in the ground who provide communicants for every doxy in the land and follow every new cult that comes along. Our pulpits are filled largely by preachers who don't know their ass from a hole in the ground. The same can be said for our State and National legislative bodies. And not only in religion and politics and secret orderism, but also in the avenues of trade, the world is disordered by misfits who don't know their ass from a hole in the ground."

"I guess that's why I've got a job," said the Soda Jerker. "If folks knew what's what they wouldn't be filling their bellies with soda fountain slops from breakfast to bedtime and I would be out of a job."

"And so would the patent medicine manufacturers and most of the doctors," said the Bank Clerk.

This was a rather far-fetched way of educating his readers in the meaning of language, but it must have worked, because this piece of journalistic deviltry brought no cancellations of subscriptions, and readers of *The Independent* were able to chuckle at a later date when Editor Saunders ran this caption under a photo of the young man who married one of his daughters:

"Introducing the Editor's handsome, long-legged new son-in-law, Albert Sydney Smith, Jr., who hails from Edenton and works with the State Highway Department. Nobody calls him anything but Pete, but he ought to feel lucky to get off that lightly with the initials he has."

Getting back to the story about the Gates County farmer, Dad used that yarn in *The Independent* a long while ago, mind you—in the early 1920's—and I had almost completely forgotten it until I saw a modified version of it in a magazine in the late 1940's or early 1950's. Since then I have seen several variations of the same story in public print.

I would not profess to claim that Dad concocted this highly illustrative story. It may well be a bewhiskered folk tale of rural America which he had heard and used to point up a lesson in semantics. I only know I had never heard or seen the story until it appeared in *The Inde-*

pendent, and it was nearly a quarter of a century later before I saw it again.

Which proves, if nothing else, that Dad knew how to pick a durable yarn.

AN ADVENTURE IN
16.   DRESS REFORM

"Saunders? Oh, yes, he's the one who paraded down Fifth Avenue in his pajamas."

Such was the comment that followed on many occasions when, with what I thought was justifiable pride, I identified myself as the son of W. O. Saunders of Elizabeth City. Whereupon I would feel it necessary to rise to Dad's defense and try to explain that the pajama episode was not the act of a crackpot or exhibitionist but that of a well-intentioned crusader who sometimes used dramatic or shocking means of getting a point across.

Dad did walk down Fifth Avenue in pajamas in broad daylight and was probably the first person who had appeared on that thoroughfare in such attire unless driven into the street at night by a fire in a hotel or apartment building. I am sure he felt like a fool, albeit a noble one, when he took that much publicized stroll in New York, but he had his reasons.

The widely misinterpreted episode in my father's generally productive and constructive life had its genesis in Dad's strong personal feelings about sensible dress—for males and females alike.

Typical of his views were the following two editorials

from *The Independent*, both published in 1926.

LET 'EM STRIP

"Pick up the Monday morning issue of almost any daily newspaper anywhere in America and you will find a report of a Sunday sermon in which some minister is protesting against the way women dress. These ministers are forever expressing their conviction that the scanty attire of modern woman is leading men astray.

"I am wondering if these birds who are so upset about women's clothes are not, in many instances, belliaking because they haven't been led astray?

"Fresh in my mind are the days when women wore long skirts, high top shoes and cotton hose. They were leading men astray then, as now. The masculine mind is sorely prone to stray, and there never were female garments long enough, full enough and numerous enough to protect the feminine figure from the imagination of the lusty male.

"The new styles adopted by women within the past few years are here to stay because they are healthful and sensible. Women's legs don't excite anyone any more. And I have an idea that if the dear creatures stripped down to their hair nets and sandals, nothing in the female anatomy would excite anyone any more, for millions of women there are who could never excite one of the opposite sex in all their lives were it not for the clothes they wear to conceal their awkwardness and their imperfections."

The above commentary on women's clothing was followed the same summer by this editorial, titled "When Will Men Be Sensible?":

"We poke all sorts of fun at women about their clothes, when, indeed, we are not actually nasty about them. When I was a boy everybody deplored the fact that women wore high heel shoes, wasp-waist corsets, bustles, imitation busts, skirts that swept the floors and petticoats that carried enough yardage to sail a ship.

"The years roll away and women shed their bustles, their corsets and their pneumatic busts, shorten their skirts, discard the cumbersome and insanitary old petticoats and dress within two pounds of the way nature intended they should dress. And menfolk are still raising the devil about the way women dress. A poor old fellow who is a pillar in Berea church came to town the other day and said it was a shame the way the young girls of this day and time tempt old fellows like him. 'It's all an old fellow like me can manage to go straight,' he said. I had to laugh.

"Why don't we men be as bold as the women and adopt a more sensible dress? The women change their styles, adopt this new thing and that, discard the things they don't like and keep on experimenting until they find real comfort in their clothes. But we fool males go right on wearing collars and cuffs and woolen suits in summer when we could be a darn sight more comfortable in a suit of pajamas."

The latter editorial was a tip-off to what was to happen just one year later.

On a torrid day in the summer of 1927, Dad went home from his office at the close of the business day, wringing wet with perspiration. He discarded a wilted collar, unbuckled the leather belt about his waist, shed trousers and shirt, relieved his legs of binding garters, took off the rest of his sweaty garments and got under a shower.

Instead of returning to conventional clothes for the rest of the evening, he donned a suit of pajamas, slipped his feet into easy house slippers and went down to dinner. He commented, and the family agreed, that this was the sensible thing for a man to do on such a hot day. After all, he pointed out, he had been stewing around all day in about ten pounds of clothing, whereas the girls in the family were clad in featherweight raiment weighing less than fifteen ounces.

After dinner, he went out on the screened porch and settled himself in a glider to read the evening newspaper. If any neighbors or passersby took notice of his night clothes, they made no fuss about it. Later in the evening, when Mother suggested that they go for an automobile ride, Dad said:

"If it's all the same with you, I'll go along just as I am."

"Well, I don't see why not," answered Mother. "You certainly look comfortable and decent."

They rode about town and out to where a certain road paralleled the river, then came back to town and stopped at a drug store and had curb service from the soda fountain. No one noticed Dad's pajamas, which were not of the loud variety so often chosen by men for their nightwear but were a light tan lounge type, with collar and lapels, open at the throat.

Dad had spent a delightful evening and no one had noticed or made any protest regarding his unconventional attire. After that experience, he made it a practice to exchange his conventional clothing for pajamas at the end of a hot day. Some of the neighbors eventually took notice, and a few congratulated him for daring to be sensible. That was in 1927.

In the summer of 1929, at the height of a heat wave of unusual severity, Dad's friend Louis Graves, who published the *Chapel Hill Weekly* at the seat of the University of North Carolina, wrote an editorial in which he advanced the suggestion that men should rebel against their conventional sartorial stuffiness and go in for clothes adapted to hot weather comfort. He suggested pajamas.

Dad immediately challenged Graves to practice his

preachment and agreed to appear in pajamas on the streets of Elizabeth City if Graves would appear in pajamas on the streets of Chapel Hill. Graves then reneged, satisfied with having had his say editorially.

But the press of North Carolina made much of Dad's challenge to the Chapel Hill editor and didn't want to let the matter die. An alert newspaper correspondent in another town sent Dad a telegram, asking if he would make a public appearance on the streets of Elizabeth City in pajamas and stand to be photographed for the metropolitan press. Here was a real opportunity to make great publicity in behalf of hot weather dress reform for sweltering males, and Dad was too much of a crusader and had too much awareness of the power of the press to let this one go by the boards. He wired the correspondent to come on to Elizabeth City and then proceeded to plan a real show for him.

The plan was simplicity, itself. Dad was to walk down Main Street in pajamas and be arrested by Chief of Police Leon Holmes. Whereupon his friend Jerome Flora, mayor of the town, would step into the picture, order Dad's release, and issue a proclamation affirming "the right of every citizen to dress as he pleases and go and come as he pleases, so long as there is no indecent exposure of the person." All of this was prearranged, of course.

At the appointed hour Dad walked up Main Street and through the business section of the town. Chief Holmes laid hands on him and Mayor Flora ordered his release and issued the prearranged proclamation. The incident was emblazoned on the front pages of newspapers in this country and abroad.

The next day, the newsman for whom Dad had staged the performance sent over prints of the photographs which he proposed to sell to a Sunday supplement issued with metropolitan dailies and having a circulation of probably more than six million copies.

Dad looked at those photographs and knew what it was like to yearn for the earth to open up and swallow one. It had never occurred to him how sloppily tailored were sleeping pajamas then being made for men. They sagged in the seat of the pants, and they sagged in the belly. And they were creased on the sides, not fore and aft as trousers are. Dad felt that those pictures made him look like a lunatic escaped from his asylum in oversize nighties. He shut himself in his office, groaned inwardly, and then put his mind to work.

How could those absurd pictures be kept out of the Sunday papers?

The first move was to obtain from a local haberdasher the name and address of one of the country's largest manufacturers of pajamas. Dad then put in a long distance call for Harry Hardie, president of the Faultless Manufacturing Co. in Baltimore. Hardie came on the line and without any introduction or explanation at all Dad proceeded to ask him:

"Why the hell don't you pajama manufacturers put some semblance of tailoring into your product?"

"We do," Hardie shot back.

"You don't," Dad retorted.

And then he told Hardie of his predicament and tried to make him see that if those pictures of a pot-bellied, middle-aged male in those ill-fitting pajamas ever got into the public prints it would not only make a laughingstock of W. O. Saunders but would be a black eye to the nightwear industry as well.

The manufacturer saw the point. In a few minutes Dad had given him his exact measurements, described the type of garment he wanted, and told him they must have pockets in the trousers as well as in the coats. Hardie agreed to put his designer on the job immediately and to rush two suits of pajamas to Dad's specifications through the factory the following day, and to have those suits in the hands of his New York City sales manager the morning following their completion. He was as good as his word.

Two days later Dad arrived in New York, registered at the Roosevelt Hotel and found the Faultless man waiting for him with two beautifully tailored pajama suits, one of fine quality Rajah silk, the other a maize colored rayon.

The coats were provided with patch pockets, and breast pockets had not been overlooked. The trousers were cuffed and had side pockets, hip pockets and the usual watch pocket. The trousers were snug fitting and correctly pressed, and the designer had shown pleasing skill in the design of the collars and lapel. The coats were pleated in the back and belted.

Dad selected the Rajah silk suit, picked a tie of a pastel shade of green, put on a panama hat with turned-down brim, discarded his heavy shoes for a pair of Roman sandles with crepe soles, rolled his socks, and sported a malacca cane.

The Raleigh (N.C.) correspondent of the United Press had tipped off the New York newspapers, and a dozen reporters and half as many cameramen were on hand when Dad emerged from the Forty-sixth Street exit of the Roosevelt. The reporters and camermen attracted attention and a mob of spectators trailed them over to Fifth Avenue, down Fifth Avenue to Forty-second Street, thence west to Broadway, where Dad was compelled to take refuge in the Paramount Theater to get the crowd off his heels. A reporter for one of the New York papers asked him how a fellow felt walking down Fifth Avenue clad in pajamas.

"I can only speak for myself; I feel like a damphool," was Dad's candid reply.

In the artificially cooled interior of the Paramount, he found his attire not so comfortable, although he wore beneath the pajamas a silk undershirt and linen shorts. He lingered in the theater until the curious crowd on the sidewalk had dispersed, after which he emerged and walked nonchalantly out on Broadway again.

Without the cameramen shooting him fore and aft, his costume attracted little or no attention. He went into a Schrafft's soda dispensary packed with women, and no one seemed to notice anything unusual about his costume. Just another fellow from the South wearing a lightweight summer suit! He strolled over to Fifth Avenue again without causing any excitement, and in front of the New York Public Library met an old friend from Norfolk, Va., whom he had not seen in several years. They paused and exchanged a lot of conversation, shook hands and parted.

That night the telephone in Dad's room rang. His Norfolk friend was on the line. He had seen the afternoon newspapers.

"Jesus Christ!" he exclaimed. "Why in hell didn't you tell me you were pulling that pajama stunt? I'd have given something to have been on the sidelines."

Having talked to Dad face to face for a matter of several minutes in broad daylight, he had failed to notice anything unusual about the way he was dressed.

Dad felt that he had achieved the object of his New York trip. He had anticipated the appearance of those goshawful photos made on Elizabeth City's Main Street by getting a more respectable showing in all the daily metropolitan papers before the Sunday supplements could get in their dirty work. It was a case of the timeworn military stratagem that a swift offense sometimes is the best defense.

And something had been achieved in the interest of summer dress reform for men, which was Dad's sole objective. Pajama parades and pajama parties sprang into vogue that summer, and all over America sky-larking young bucks broke out on the streets in pajamas. A young Jewish boy in New York ventured out in yellow and red pajamas with pants that had no buttons down the front. An Irish cop gave him a ride to the hoosegow. The Rotary Club in a North Carolina town challenged the Kiwanis Club to play a game of baseball in pajamas. Society had turned out for the event, and the grandstand was packed with women when a Rotarian sliding for first base lost his pants. That broke up the game.

But when the sky-larking was over, America did not accept pajamas for daytime wear. Enterprising pajama manufacturers who tried to introduce P.J.'s for street wear found that they couldn't get their product displayed or sold in men's wear stores. The merchants figured they would sell fewer woolen suits if men took to wearing street pajamas, and there was more profit in woolens.

Dad insisted that they were being short-sighted, since a man who adopted pajamas for street wear would require a dozen suits of pajamas to one suit of woolens. The light and airy fabrics of which pajamas are made show dirt and cannot be worn more than one or two days before going to the laundry, whereas a man could go around in a woolen suit for weeks or months and collect an enormous amount of soot, dirt, grease and odors without his uncleanliness being detected, because pressing his woolen suit only packed the dirt into its fabric. Such was Dad's reasoning, but he couldn't sell it.

He later remarked, facetiously, that a great depression might have been averted or its distress mitigated if America had taken to pajamas in 1929. A new market for cotton would have been created and millions poured into the pockets of impoverished Southern cotton planters. The textile industry would have been given a needed boost and jobs created for thousands of workers in that industry. The laundry and dry cleaning business would have experienced a new and unprecedented era of prosperity.

"But you can't expect a nation in which seventy-five per cent of the population goes to bed in its underclothes to enthuse over pajamas," Dad remarked, noting that Department of Commerce figures showed that less than twenty-five per cent of the populace used nightwear of any sort.

So Dad's pajama "crusade" fizzled out, but if he didn't succeed in selling America on pajamas for hot weather street attire, he did very well succeed in throwing a mild panic into the retail clothing business, with the result that suits of linen crash and lightweight tropical worsteds were offered for the first time in smart men's shops in New York and other cities north of the Mason & Dixon line the following summer, soon to be followed by slack suits and other comfortable summer-time attire.

The above is a factual account of the famed pajama episode. It was a publicity stunt, true, but one carefully calculated to give the utmost mileage to Dad's campaign for summer dress reform that would benefit sweltering mankind. It didn't achieve its purpose—not quite—but no one can say that it didn't take more than a little intestinal fortitude for Dad to saunter onto Fifth Avenue wearing pajamas in the summer of 1929.

FOE OF FRAUD
17.   AND FILTH

My Dad once wrote, with pride and sincerity, I am sure:
"In the nearly 30 years of my publishing experience,
I never accepted for publication or printed the advertisement of a patent or proprietary internal medicine, and if
every newspaper in America were to follow suit, Americans
would recover from most of their female troubles, kidney
troubles, nerve disorders, halitosis, athlete's foot, etc. almost
overnight. Millions are made ill by the suggestions conveyed to them in the advertisements of nostrums that are
claimed to cure this or that ailment."

There developed in my father a belief that the same power
of suggestion that makes the sick well can make the well
sick. He came to believe that most of the so-called female
trouble with which American womanhood is afflicted is the
result of a form of hypnosis induced by the reading of
Lydia E. Pinkham and Wine of Cardui almanacs and advertisements. He felt sure that literature detailing the symp-
toms of this or that disease subtly poisons the mind of the
naive person who reads it and makes him or her a real or
an imagined sick man or woman. In either case, the manufacturer and vendor of the advertised nostrum snare a victim
and reap a profit. And when the sucker takes the prescribed
nostrum and imagines he is well again, he is easily induced

to write a testimonial letter to the quack, who then publishes it for the allurement of other suckers long after the writer of the testimonial is dead.

And so it was inevitable that Dad would someday write a blistering editorial in which he teed off on the fraternity of medicine fakirs in these words:

"The average man and woman of us are but children groping our way through the fogs and mists of a mundane morass between the cold and distant peaks of two inscrutable eternities. From the cradle comes no sign of that world whence we came; from the grave comes no word of the other world. Our journey from the cradle to the grave is beset by countless doubts and fears and disappointments. We are easily confused, wounded or thwarted. Such is our plight that the doctor and the priest, professional conveyors of sympathy and consolation, seem absolutely essential to the peace and happiness of our rank and file.

"But when the purveyor of patent nostrums by malicious suggestion preys upon the fears and credulity of men and women, as most of the clan do, he is the most loathsome, contemptible, despicable, execrable, abominable and damnable enemy of the human race, and no punishment that could be meted out to him could be too severe, in my opinion. For his special benefit I would restore every torture device of the Middle Ages.

"But we not only grant him immunity; we look with unconcern upon his glorification in the paid advertising sections of a venal press whose palm is greased by the money filched from credulous and gullible members of the human family by these brazen and conscienceless frock-coated hyenas who prey upon human flesh and blood, forever spreading the poison of fear and disease."

One thing is sure: only a publisher who never expected to accept a nickel's worth of advertising from the manufacturers of proprietary internal medicines could have written those words.

My father was so convinced of the evils of patented nostrums that it angered him to see religious journals in his state sell themselves to the medicine fakirs. This indignation led to the penning of the following editorial, titled "In the Name of Christ?"

"Now here is where I am going to bring a storm upon my head, but I can't help it. I'm a born rebel. And when I see a condition that is anything but right I just can't contain myself.

"The subject of this preachment is the *Christian Advocate*, published weekly at Raleigh as the official organ of the North Carolina Conference of the Methodist Episcopal Church.

"The *Advocate* is out to do the work of the great Master; its professed aim is to render spiritual comfort to the lowly, to uplift the weak, to spread the gospel of Christ, to make the world better, to strengthen the morals of mankind; in brief, to do good.

"In the columns of such a paper one would not expect to find painted the dark side of all life; one would not expect indecent utterances; certainly one would not expect to find FRAUD.

"And yet FRAUD is the biggest thing advocated by the Raleigh *Christian Advocate*, and the paper speaks for itself, requiring no accuser other than its own bribed columns— bribed in the interests of quacks and mountebanks who thrive and grow sleek upon the afflictions of the ignorant and the poor.

"In the last issue of the *Advocate* I count 27 advertisements of patent medicines, the bulk of which have been exposed as frauds and as such will not be admitted to the columns of any self-respecting secular newspaper or magazine.

"The entire back page of the *Advocate* is given over to the Chicago quack who professes to give his 'personal attention to the private ailments' of *Advocate* readers. That's a lie and the Rev. Thomas N. Ivey, editor of the *Advocate* knows it's a lie or he is a very ignorant man. But that isn't all.

" 'Cancer cures,' 'Cures for Fits,' 'Cures for Bright's Disease,' every one frauds on their face, are advertised in lurid text with thrilling pictorial illustrations. The Rev. Mr. Ivey knows there is no bottled cure for cancer and knows he is a party to a swindle when he advertises such in his paper. If he doesn't know as much, he doesn't know enough to run a Christian newspaper.

"I say there are 27 patent medicine ads in the last issue of the Raleigh *Christian Advocate*. I say it is an outrageous fact, and I am surprised at the intelligent body of the Methodists in North Carolina who lend their money and prestige to such a fearful propaganda of patent fakes and lies.

"The greatest fraud in America today is patent medicine. Intelligent people know. Quacks thrive on ignorance. They can get the ear of the ignorant only through advertising. They can fool some good people only by advertising in good mediums. A devout old man who regards his religious paper as sacred next to his Bible will pin his faith in 'cancer cures' recommended by the *Advocate* and spend his last dollar for worthless dope that keeps him in a semi-drunken and indifferent state for a while, only to leave him a worse wreck physically afterwards.

"Jesus, in whose name is published the *Advocate*, said 'Come unto me all ye who are sick and weary, and I will give you rest.' The *Advocate* recommends 'Dope your babies on Mrs. Winslow's dangerous soothing syrup' and spend your last cent and wreck your own life experimenting with patent medicine fakes.

"*The Independent* wouldn't dare print a patent medicine advertisement. Some patent medicines may be good. I do know that most are positively dangerous or positively worthless.

"Oh, I know what the Rev. Editor Ivey will say. He will tell you, confidentially, that he can't get enough money from the Methodists to support his paper and he has to take this patent medicine blood money to keep his presses running. And my answer is that if the Methodists of North Carolina, or the communicants of any other denomination, can't support a paper without taking toll from frauds, they shouldn't have any paper at all. Certainly, they will be better off with no paper than with a paper devoted to circulating the fool bait of charlatans and swindlers."

Not one to discriminate as between offending denominations, The Independent Man subsequently tore into the state's Baptist publication in these words:

"I once said that there is this difference between *The Independent* and the *Biblical Recorder:* the *Recorder* lets the sinners off with a promise of Hell in the hereafter, while *The Independent* takes no chances and gives them hell right here and now.

"But I find another difference. *The Independent* prints no fraudulent, vulgar patent medicine ads; the *Biblical Recorder* does indorse and print such frauds.

"And, if anything, the *Biblical Recorder*, the organ of the Baptist State Convention of North Carolina, is worse in this respect than the Raleigh *Christian Advocate,* to which I referred in an article last week.

"I find 17 patent medicine ads in the *Recorder* against

27 in the *Advocate*, but this only means that the fakers prefer the former for cheaper rates or larger circulation. The *Recorder* surely does not draw the line on any fake, for I find in glaring type this awful proposition: '$3.50 Cure for WEAK MEN FREE.' What could be worse?

"Whisky ads are mild in comparison to an offer of drugs for impotent, misspent men. The Rev. W. V. McRae, a pastor of this city, says that between a paper advertising whisky and a paper advertising cures for wrecked manhood, he would choose the first. And Mr. McRae was speaking of Josephus Daniels' *News and Observer* and not the *Biblical Recorder*.

"It speaks ill for the *Recorder's* following that so many men in the Baptist State Convention offer Easy Money for such quacks. The *Recorder* will be doing the work of Christ when it throws these medical sharks out of its columns and preaches God's truth, that the only cure for wrecked manhood is a clean and godlike life.

" 'Cancer cures,' 'cures for Fits' and female fakes fill the columns of the *Recorder* as they do the *Advocate*. And it is true that I find more fakes for women in the *Recorder* than in the *Advocate*, I see such headlines as 'Free to You, My Sister,' 'Women, I know what the trouble is,' and possibly worse. Every one fakers, frauds, traders in human hopes and human lives.

"Can't the Baptists of North Carolina join with the Methodists of North Carolina in putting down this scandalous prostitution of their church papers?

"It is an insult to God Almighty himself for these religious editors, trading on the good will of the Kingdom Come, to stoop to the dirty business of making money out of swindlers who are devoted to swindling the poor with cheap whisky and coal tar dyes called "patent medicines.'

"Dear reader, if you think *The Independent* is doing the

13

right thing in nailing this outrageous business, please mark a copy of this paper and mail it to the Rev. Hight C. Moore, Editor, *Biblical Recorder*, Raleigh, N. C.

"Do it now."

As much as the fraudulent claims in patent medicine advertisements irked Dad, they were not his sole aversion.

What seems new to one generation may be old stuff to another. In the years 1959 and 1960, people were writing magazine articles, newspaper columns and letters to editors deploring the disgusting frankness and grating intimacy of television commercials sponsored by manufacturers of certain laxatives, germicides and other pharmaceuticals. Yet radio listeners and newspaper and magazine readers unquestionably were making the same complaints thirty years ago, as witness the following discourse between the Bank Clerk and the Soda Jerker circa 1930:

"All the worry is over now," mumbled the Soda Jerker, reading from a full-page advertisement in *Liberty* Magazine.

"What trouble?" asked the Bank Clerk.

"I can't figure it out, being as how I ain't a woman," said the Soda Jerker, "But this advertisement for Zonite is telling women not to worry any more, that they have a sure-fire germicide that gets the germ and 'does not desensitize the vaginal tract.' Now just what do they mean by that?"

"Don't be a sap," snapped the Bank Clerk. "It's just another way of saying that here is a new birth control measure that will not take any sensual satisfaction out of the business in mind. It's just another example of the bald and suggestive intimacies permitted in the advertising pages of our gold-digging national magazines and newspapers.

"Why, I'm expecting to pick up a newspaper almost any day with an advertisement telling me in woodpile type to eat Rumble's Beans because there is not a 'corporal's salute in a carload.'

"Or an advertisement for a mineral oil that will not trickle down your leg about the time you are asking your sweetheart for a dance.

"The advertisers of Kotex, Listerine, Zonite and other such products leave nothing to the imagination any more. They flaunt every intimate biological fact pertaining to the female in the faces of readers of popular magazines and newspapers, shamelessly exploiting woman's sex and making vulgar those mysteries that were formerly held personal and sacred.

"I remember the good old days when the purists made it so hot for the makers of Bull Durham tobacco that the company had to send sign painters all over the country to add a board fence to their Bull Durham billboards so as to conceal the sex of their bull. Today I wouldn't be surprised to see a billboard with a picture of a male with his pants down, exposing a posterior that had been deprived of the use of a certain brand of toilet tissue. Indeed I wouldn't."

While patent medicines were one of Dad's principal abominations, he had a profound interest in other facets of the subjects of medicine and hygiene. Accordingly, he waged an unrelenting campaign in the news and editorial columns of *The Independent* for a cleaner and more healthful Elizabeth City.

He kicked off a campaign for cleaner milk with a news story headed "Not a Clean Dairy Near Elizabeth City." The lead paragraph set the stage in these words:

"An inspection of twenty dairies serving milk to Elizabeth City reveals the startling fact that not one of all the dairies serving this city ranks above Grade D, according to standards of the North Carolina State Board of Health. The health of every adult and the lives of hundreds of infants in Elizabeth City are endangered by dirty milk. This is rough stuff, folks, but if we are ever to get a cleaning up of the dairies in and around Elizabeth City and secure anything like a clean and safe milk supply, we might as well face the facts and know where we stand."

There were numerous other stories and editorials on this subject until, finally, the city administration was badgered into adopting a clean milk ordinance and making provision for its enforcement.

Having won that fight, The Independent Man turned his attention to another sanitation matter with this editorial:

"And now that we are in a fair way to get a good supply of clean and wholesome milk from Elizabeth City dairies, it is time we turned attention to another food item that needs inspection. Elizabeth City needs a meat and fish inspector. A stroll through the city market is evidence enough of this need.

"There isn't a meat dealer in Elizabeth City who would wilfully sell meat unfit for human consumption; but the fact is that most of them do it. Meat that becomes otherwise unsalable is worked up into sausage, highly seasoned with much salt and pepper and its unwholesome nature thus disguised. Its disguise is complete when stuffed into a casing.

"I have seen with my own eyes green and slimy meat chopped up into sausage in local butcher stalls. I have seen blood clots and moldy fragments of salt and pickled meats go into the same sausage mixture. Of course, this kind of sausage is not for the better class of trade. It is sold to very poor white people and Negroes who want something cheap. That is the shame of it; it is sold to folks who can't afford drug and doctors' bills; it is sold to make the blood and sinew of the hard-working laboring class who do our hard work, our dirty work.

"And there is no meat inspection here to prevent anything from going into a sausage or to detect and prevent the sale of the flesh of diseased animals.

"It will come as a shock to patrons of meat dealers domiciled in Elizabeth City's markethouse to know that these dealers are permitted to sell meats unfit for human consumption. Patrons of the market are at the mercy of the dealer. There is no serious sanitary inspection of the markethouse. Something ought to be done about that."

This campaign, too, bore fruit with the adoption of an ordinance and the naming of a meat inspector.

In the early 1930s, Elizabeth City's water supply, drawn from nearby Knobb's Creek, became salty and polluted. An application for a loan to improve the situation was turned down by the Public Works Administration, prompting Dad to pen this blast:

". . . We have been in a frightful predicament as regards to city water supply for years. For business reasons, perhaps, we have been restrained from making much of a fuss about it, encouraged from time to time to believe that relief was forthcoming. The time has come when the citizens must take drastic action. Strange, is it not, that in a country that can find billions for the relief of the unemployed, not one dollar can be found for the relief of a city of more than 10,000 people who are slowly dying of an unquenched thirst?

"This newspaper suggests a mass meeting of citizens for Christmas Day. Elizabeth City has lost its faith in Santa Claus; the citizens must play Santa Claus to themselves. It is suicidal to wait upon governmental agencies—municipal, state, or federal—any longer. The citizens themselves must protect themselves. Out of a large and indignant mass meeting, some idea may be born.

"In the meantime, every water consumer in Elizabeth City should withhold payments on his water bills. I for one shall refuse to pay for something I cannot use and which jeopardizes the health and life of myself and my family. I shall pay my sewer bills and I defy the Corporation of Elizabeth City to cut off my water and deprive me of the use of my sewer. If the City attempts to cut off water from my sewer, I shall pray for an injunction and fight my way through the courts as long as I can stand the cost.

"I urge every water consumer in Elizabeth City to join me in refusing to longer pay for water we cannot drink or take a bath in. Let the State ring with our protests against a water problem that no civilized community can longer afford to tolerate."

A subsequent news story told in these words how the battle was at least half won:

"I have referred to Elizabeth City's Public Utility Commission as a Futility Commission. A better name for this municipal appendix would be THE STUPIDITY COMMISSION.

"The Stupidity Commission this week flatly declined to accept the recommendation and polite request of the Board of Aldermen to eliminate all charges for city water unfit for general use. BUT THEY DID GIVE THE PUBLIC HALF A LOAF.

"Stupidity is a kind word when applied to this Commission. By their refusal to comply with the recommendation of the Board of Aldermen and thereby placate an indignant public, the Commission will drive hundreds of households and business units in Elizabeth City to install their own water systems. Once these private water units are installed, the city will be years and years in getting the owners to return to the use of city water. . . .

"The city is pumping into the homes of its water consumers a foul-smelling liquid polluted with salt and hydrogen sulphide, a poisonous gas. . . . The city has no more right to charge for this water than a private corporation would have . . . And this newspaper can confidently say that a lot of people are not going to continue to pay for property-destroying and death-dealing water pumped from a putrid tributary of the Pasquotank River.

"Still, this newspaper has accomplished something. Its blasting of the Commission brought a concession of a reduction of 50 per cent in the water rates for January. The Commission indicates a willingness to continue their reduction until it can produce good water. That's something. . . ."

In another year or so, under steady pressure from *The Independent* and an aroused citizenry, the city abandoned Knobb's Creek and turned to a field of shallow wells as a source for its water supply, and Dad was able to add another notch to his editorial six-shooter.

Dad's writing on health, sanitation and personal hygiene ranged over a wide variety of subjects, including the handling of germ-ridden currency (Filthy Lucre), careless use of the tooth brush (A Dirty Habit), and the custom of shaking hands. On the latter subject he wrote:

"Let's quit shaking hands. It is a filthy and abominable habit inherited from the barbaric past along with capital punishment and a lot of other fool things. Having served its day and purpose, it ought to be relegated to oblivion.

"Many, many years ago some warrior was compelled to show good faith, in seeking an interview with a fellow, by dropping his club, spear and sword and extending the hand in which his instrument of offense and defense had been held. Grasping hands, the adversaries conversed with each other without fear of each other. It became a custom among warriors to clasp hands when they desired to be polite to one another. The custom grew, and today we are slaves to it, often without the remotest thought or knowledge of how the custom originated.

"The human hand is just about the dirtiest thing the human being carries around with him. It carries (in microscopic quantities, it's true) every infection of the human body. The North Carolina State Board of Health says: 'Excrement in minute and invisible amounts soils the hands. It is the general rule to find, the rare exception not to find, intestinal bacteria on the hands of people.' That's what your state health authority says about it. And this excrement of fecal matter, carrying with it the bacteria of typhoid, dysentary and diarrheal diseases, is conveyed from person to person by handshaking . . .

"The soldier, though he may have been the originator of the practice of shaking hands, has abandoned it and has shown us the sensible form of salutation. The military salute is as respectful as the handshake and doesn't pass the microbe.

"The world probably will continue to hang on its handshaking for a good many years to come. The human animal demands the human contact. The child and the savage have this desire satisfied through play; grown-up, civilized men and women, too dignified to play, satisfy the desire for contact by a lot of makeshifts of which handshaking is the most common and dancing the most refined.

"I am in favor of universal repudiation of a silly, useless, positively filthy and altogether dangerous custom. Let's quit shaking hands."

Dad could have been serious when he wrote the above, or he could have been jesting—there was something of the jester in his makeup, after all. But serious or not, one wonders what techniques candidates for public office would be forced to use today had Dad's suggestion been adopted universally.

18. ROUGH STUFF

One of the hallmarks of *The Independent* was its editor's almost unbridled use of forceful language and harsh invective when inveighing against wrongdoing and wrongdoers. He often intended to be shocking and enjoyed more than a modicum of success in that endeavor.

For example, read this lead paragraph about the outcome of a murder trial in another North Carolina county:

"Like an egg-sucking dog that has been caught in the act, the Rev. Thomas F. Pardue, professional evangelist, who violated every sacred tradition of the confessional, must have slunk in the presence of his public when Mrs. Alma Petty Gatlin, whose arrest for murder he caused, was freed by a Rockingham County jury Wednesday night."

And take a look at this headline appearing over a political campaign story in *The Independent:* "Phil Sawyer Indulges in Pediculous Politics—Cheap Political Treachery of Second Ward 'Boss' Disclosed When Candidates Compare Notes—Phil Sawyer's Statement to the Press So Much Bologna."

All the way across the top of the front page in bold face type ran this headline and subhead:

STATE BANK EXAMINATIONS
NOT WORTH A DAMN

J. L. Tucker's Embezzlement of $24,645.43 in Hertford Branch of Carolina Bank Carried on Under Noses of State Bank Examiners, as Bank Embezzlements Always Are.

The story, in part, went as follows:

"N. C. banking laws must be revised; our State Bank Examiners are a joke. Every six months State Bank Examiners walked into the Hertford branch of the Carolina Banking & Trust Co. and examined its books. They slapped its cashier, Joseph L. Tucker, on the back and told him they didn't find better kept books in any bank in the state. The poor saps didn't know how clever a bookkeeper Joe Tucker was. It appears now that Tucker is short in his accounts.

"It is said that the shortage was suspected when auditors found an item credited to savings depositors exceeded the amount of interest due on the deposits actually shown on the books. A search of nooks and corners in the bank then revealed a package of missing sheets from the bank's looseleaf ledger . . .

"And your State Bank Examiners come along and examine only such records as the cashier shows them. How an embezzling cashier must laugh at the bank examiners!"

An editorial titled "Bring This Woman to Book" understandably caused a mild sensation in Elizabeth City. It read:

"I hear myself criticized for reviving the murder of Ernest L. Sawyer in the news columns of *The Independent* last week. I shall keep that murder alive until there is a prosecution. Ernest L. Sawyer was murdered. If his wife didn't actually shoot him down with her own hand, she by her own confession provoked his slaughter.

. . . There is a lot of maudlin sympathy for Mrs. Sawyer. There is too much maudlin sympathy for too many hardboiled women. Married women who play a fast game should be prepared to pay the penalty for their misbehavior. Mrs. Sawyer should be brought to trial . . . The murder of Ernest L. Sawyer should be avenged. Failure upon the part of the Solicitor of the First Judicial District and the Prosecuting Attorney of Pasquotank County to do their work is an invitation to other wild women to play fast and loose with their husbands' affections and kill them when they protest."

"God Damn Lie" Says City's Light Head (this last phrase probably was a play on words) went a headline over the following brief but pungent news item:

"Supt. J. C. Parker of the Elizabeth City Public Utilities Commission resents a news item in this newspaper telling of a neglected electric light on the Primary School grounds.

" 'It was all a God damn lie,' says Mr. Parker.

"For the information of Mr. Parker, this newspaper calls his attention to another street light on Dyer Street, in front of the residence of Caleb Walker, which residents of the neighborhood say hasn't burned since the storm of the night of February 18. Maybe that's what Mr. Parker would call 'another God damn lie'."

And just look at this editorial scalding of one of Elizabeth City's most respected physicians:

"The failure of Dr. Isaiah Fearing, Pasquotank County Coroner, to hold an inquest in the case of the mysterious deaths of Oscar Ames and Nellie and Frank Powell in Knobbs Creek on Saturday, June 8, is probably one of the most flagrant acts of official negligence and stupidity in the history of this county.

"By taking it upon himself to declare those three children accidentally drowned without holding an autopsy is tantamount to setting himself up as one of the most learned diagnosticians in America.

"Dr. Fearing should be recalled from office. If he knows his onions, he will never again be a candidate for the office which he has held without opposition for so many years.

"Dr. Fearing's attitude in the recent triple death mystery has been his attitude in other mysterious deaths in this city and county. If the dead are not in his social set, he loses no time in disposing of them. The trouble with Isaiah Fearing is largely big head and high hat."

At the end of his editorial column one week, Editor Saunders made this terse comment:

"How does *The Independent* get through the mails with some of the stuff it prints?" asks a foolish reader. The reader is called foolish because nothing that would tend to corrupt morals is printed in this newspaper. I may be audacious; I may be shocking; I may border on vulgarity; but the obscene has no place in this newspaper. And with all my harmless fun, I pass along a lot of stuff that makes better men, better women, better boys and girls, and better communities."

Months later, *The Independent* expanded on these views in an editorial titled "Folks Always Like Rough Stuff." It went like this:

"Many good men and women contemplating the rotten, filthy, vicious, lascivious, pornographic literature purveyed by the newsstands and reflected in the moving pictures today think that the tastes of humans are more perverted than ever they were, and that the world is verily going to the devil. It is not so.

"The fact that so many people today deplore the vulgar and indecent in literature and art is the finest evidence in the world that humanity is progressing and that we are working upward and away from that which is vulgar, lewd and insincere.

"Humanity was always vulgar; the human mind always ran to the trashy, the frivolous and the obscene. And no one used to think anything about it. Read the thousand and one tales of the Arabian nights; read the early French and English classics; read your Bible. Shakespeare wrote with the greatest freedom of the rape of Lucrece and the cavortive lustings of Venus after Adonis. Your books of the Old Testament are filled with stories of lust and amativeness that would bring a Federal prison sentence upon any publisher who reprinted them in a modern newspaper. And the world has read the Bible and Shakespeare and the early classics for hundreds of years without a protest.

"The fact that so many humans are protesting against printed indecencies and demanding a more ennobling literature is evidence of a new human appreciation of better and finer things. The world always did run to the vulgar. I prove it from time to time in the columns of my own newspaper."

Obviously, Editor Saunders liked rough stuff, but finally there came a time when he had to admit that *The Independent* had gone too far in the matter of roughness. This was a story in which the inexperienced younger Saunders literally quoted a county judge who, in dismissing a rape case, had described it as "just an old-fashioned friggin' frolic." In an editorial titled "Bang Goes Youth," W. O. Saunders apologized to his readers in these words:

"Depend upon modern youth to go you a step further, if not always a step ahead. Never was this brought more forcibly home to me than when I picked up my own newspaper last week and found a bit of police court reporting that knocked me cold.

"I was out of town last week, leaving most of the writing and editing in younger hands. Every youngster I have ever employed on *The Independent* has made the mistake of trying to pattern after the head man in the show. And I have set them some bad examples. I run occasionally to rough stuff. Bible writers did; so did Shakespeare. But, like Shakespeare and the prophets of old, I have not been shocking merely for the sake of being shocking. I think it will be conceded that my shockers are salty with wholesome humor and horse sense. For instance, when a young bride in Camden rescued her husband from a ferocious jackass that was about to kick him to death, I couldn't resist the temptation to write a headline like this:

BRIDE OF THREE WEEKS
BEATS ASS OFF HUSBAND

"And when a doddering septogenarian married a young wife and boasted after the ceremony that he felt as good as he felt at 25, I couldn't resist the temptation to dress this marriage up with a headline like this:

AN OLD FOOL NEVER
TOO OLD TO FEEL

"I have not run into trouble with the postal authorities in many years, and most people enjoy a little racy phrase when it is pertinent. In fact, most of my readers seem to look for such. But when one of my youngsters reported a police court case last week and quoted a dirty and revolting phrase dropped by Judge P. G. Sawyer, all precedent was broken and no one was more shocked than me.

"I apologize to the readers of *The Independent* and beg them not to condemn the youngster who was guilty of a gross breach of decency and possibly a flagrant violation of the obscenity laws when, of course, I am to blame. I have set a bad example for which youth pays me the compliment of trying to pattern after me and, out of his inexperience, oversteps all bounds. The incident is highly deplorable. I shall try to prevent a recurrence of it by watching my step more closely. And if you say anything to the youngster, just tell him not to pattern too closely after the head man of this show or he'll find himself in hot and deep water. Tell him to be himself.

"And the honorable judge of our County Court could also take a lesson from this and use language more in keeping with the tradition and dignity of the bench. Come to think about it, it's about time we looked around for a more desirable judge anyway."

The point of this editorial was that *The Independent* would never hesitate to be rough when rough language seemed called for, but it did not believe in roughness for roughness' sake. And this credo apparently won not only attention but respect for *The Independent* and its editor.

SHEKEL-GATHERING

19. PULPITEERS

"The Prophet Ham came to Elizabeth City to dynamite Hell out of Elizabeth City. In the course of events it became necessary for me to dynamite a little Hell out of Ham."

In those two succinct sentences, Editor W. O. Saunders summarized the most bitter fight in which he ever engaged and the one which it gave him the greatest satisfaction to win.

Dad's adversary in this particular clash was a high-pressure evangelist and commercial soul-saver known as the Rev. Mordecai F. Ham. This religious bunk-shooter, a onetime lawyer and salesman, had teamed with a business manager and organizer by the name of William Ramsay to run big revival meetings in any and every southern town that appeared to be ripe for such an enterprise.

In the autumn of 1924 Elizabeth City was ready for a big tabernacle meeting. Membership in most of the town's churches was beginning to drop, and there were countless back-sliders among those listed on the rolls of the churches. It was not difficult to persuade the ministers and pillars of the churches that Elizabeth City needed a Ham-Ramsay revival to fill their empty pews with zealous converts and

satiate the townspeople with a new and wonderful religious
fervor.

And so it came to pass that the churches got together
and underwrote the construction of a pineboard and tar-
paper tabernacle seating 4000 and replete with row upon
row of folding chairs, a huge stage and choir loft, an
Inquiry (confessional) Room in which to work over wavering
or reluctant sinners, and a sawdust trail over which they
could walk on their way to salvation. A choir of 200 voices
was organized. The evangelist brought his own pianist,
choir leader and ballyhoo man. And for forty-seven days
and as many nights Elizabeth City went on an emotional
jag such as it had never previously experienced.

Evangelist Ham insisted upon every place of business in
the town being closed during his morning services, and he
prayed God to strike down any merchant who refused to
yield on this point. In another town he had made this threat
and a poor little storekeeper who refused to shut up his
shop for Ham's "holy hour" actually dropped dead. He
had a weak heart anyway, and brooding over the evangelist's
threat plus the taunts and jibes of sanctimonious fellow
townsmen probably finished him off.

It was all but inevitable that a clash would ensue between
Editor Saunders and Evangelist Ham—and one did. Dad
held his fire for two or three weeks, sizing Ham up and
waiting to see if he would make a wrong move. Then it
came. Ham made a vicious attack on Julius Rosenwald,
an enlightened businessman and foremost philanthropist,
then president of Sears, Roebuck & Co., the Chicago mail-
order house.

Ham stood in his pulpit and read rapidly and with
vehemence a lot of stuff purporting to be evidence that Mr.
Rosenwald was party to a vice ring in Chicago that made

14

a business of establishing brothels in which the intermingling of whites and blacks was encouraged, and that Rosenwald had headed a commission which reported no vice in a district which subsequent investigations disclosed as "teeming with dens and dives in which unspeakable evils were taught and practiced."

Dad was to interview Rosenwald for *The American Magazine* a year or so later, but at the time of Ham's scurrilous and defamatory attack he did not personally know the man, although he did know him to be of sterling reputation. At any rate Dad simply refused to swallow Ham's accusations and insinuations, and he sent a telegram to Mr. Rosenwald asking him for a statement of refutation. The philanthropist was out of town at the time but his personal secretary wrote back in part: "We are aware from several other sources of the statements made by Mr. Ham, the Evangelist, about Mr. Rosenwald. While they are false and annoying, and easily disproved, it has seemed the dignified thing to let him say what he pleases . . . To those who know Mr. Rosenwald, the charges are absurd, because his entire life has been devoted to helping humanity. In the fight against commercial vice, he has given a great deal of his time and money, and is continuing in that service. . . ."

Dad published this reply as part of an editorial in which he wrote, by way of conclusion:

"So Mr. Ham may continue to assail Mr. Rosenwald, since he has found a subject who is too big to notice him."

That editorial drew Ham's fire and he assailed W. O. Saunders with all the power of invective at his command, denouncing him as the local anti-Christ and an emissary of hell and the devil. He ended his blast with the declaration that "any man who will whitewash a gang like that (Rosenwald, etc.) in order to prove a preacher a liar needs praying for and needs it bad." The battle was joined.

Dad had fired off a lot of telegrams to Chicago and around the country in seeking evidence to bolster his case against the evangelist, but he had to go to press with his weekly newspaper before the replies arrived, so about all he had to go on was the letter from Rosenwald's secretary plus his own deep-seated conviction that Ham was an infernal liar. This was enough, however, for him to come out with a front page article under a headline boldly proclaiming "I Believe the Prophet Ham Has Lied." The meat of the article was contained in the following passages:

"Now it is not easy for me to produce evidence quickly in reply to Mr. Ham, and I cannot satisfy the intelligence of the community with such flimsy evidence as Mr. Ham can use and get away with; with his gift of oratory, his audacity and his cunning, developed through years of training . . . he can cram almost anything down the throats of the masses and get away with it. Mr. Ham has this advantage, that he claims to be a prophet of God, and has the support of most of the good church people in the town behind him. Out of the goodness of their hearts and the simplicity of their faith, good church people are slow to question anything that parades in the name of Jehovah. The good church people know that there is something wrong with our town and, like drowning men grasping at straw, they think Ham is going to right everything.

"Mr. Ham has the good people of the town with him at present, and he employs this fact to intimidate, bulldoze, damn and destroy every person who doesn't agree with Ham. I say, therefore, that the public will not be satisfied with any sort of evidence I present in defense of any position I must take; I must produce conclusive evidence.

"Now I believe, from what I know about Julius Rosenwald and his works as a citizen, a humanitarian and a philanthropist, that he is a pure and upright citizen and that M. F. Ham has either carelessly or deliberately lied about him.

"I am conscious of the strength of the language I am using. I want to make it plain: I believe that with respect to his charges against Julius Rosenwald, Ham is a careless or malicious liar.

"I am conscious of the fact that failure to justify my belief that Ham is a liar in respect to Rosenwald is going to cost me the loss of friendships and prestige that I now enjoy. But a righteous God speaks to me through my mind, my heart and my soul, and I am helpless to do otherwise than to proclaim what I believe to be the truth.

"I have stated my belief, and I ask all thinking and charitable-minded men and women to withhold judgment upon me until I have had time to sustain my charges or admit that I am wrong. If I am wrong about Rosenwald, I shall be man enough to say so and bow my head in submission to whatever punishment my friends and neighbors— and my enemies in this town—may inflict upon me."

Later in the same article, he wrote:

"When Ham came into this community I received him with an open mind. I have been slow to criticize or condemn him. But since he has snatched off my hat and thrown it into the ring I might as well out with it and say that I believe he is a dangerous fanatic, a shrewd, vicious and uncompromising demagogue, a careless mouth-artist, an irresponsible bunk-shooter, and a stirrer-up of strife, hatred and bigotry."

As they say in the TV westerns, "them's fightin' words, poddner." The effect of this blast at the evangelist was electric. Some of Dad's supposedly best friends withdrew their advertising from *The Independent*. Hundreds cancelled their subscriptions. And Dad was, as he expressed it, "hissed and spat at by human rabbits."

The gauntlet-flinging article appeared in print on November 7, 1924. Within a few days came resounding, irrefutable testimonials as to the character of Julius Rosenwald and the untruth of Ham's charges. Telegrams poured in from such influential individuals as the presidents of Northwestern and Chicago universities, the mayor of Chicago, the editor of the *Chicago Tribune*, the ministers of many of Chicago's leading churches, Oswald Garrison Villard, editor of *The Nation*, and many others. Dad published them all verbatim under the headline: "Did Ham Lie? Read the Evidence." Then he unlimbered his heavy verbal artillery. Some excerpts from this blistering article follow:

"Believing Ham to be a ruthless and menacing liar; believing him to be spreading a gospel of misunderstanding, hate, fury and iniquity in Elizabeth City that would inure to great harm in the city and to the best interests of the churches in Elizabeth City, I saw nothing else to do but to challenge him to a showdown, which I did in last week's issue of this newspaper.

"Ham left every opportunity to retract or modify his statement against Mr. Rosenwald go until Wednesday morning. Having thrown every possible bluff for a week, and having finally convinced himself that this newspaper had nailed him with his lie, Ham told the tabernacle crowd Wednesday morning that he had never said those things about Rosenwald at all, but had simply read what others had said. A flimsier makeshift excuse was never advanced by a cornered liar . . .

"In his first attempt to reply to my statement that he had lied about Rosenwald, Ham told his tabernacle crowd that it wasn't M. F. Ham who had been called a liar, but that Jesus Christ had been called a liar. Ham is not deceiving anyone by such fraud tactics. HE KNOWS THAT I CALLED M. F. HAM A LIAR, and nobody else.

"Ham's only replies to that article last week have been in the nature of hedging, evading and bully-ragging. He has been going to prove great things and he has proved nothing except that he is what I have been representing him to be—a charlatan, a four-flusher and a liar. This language is plain, emphatic, and Ham knows that I am liable before the law for using such language if I can not back it up. Ham is a lawyer himself."

Later on came this passage:

"I say that I have weighed this question thoughtfully and prayerfully, and I am more convinced than ever that Ham should be exposed, and exposed as ruthlessly as he assails those who do not submit to his damnable theology. Ham gives no quarter and admits no middle ground; he invokes the great God of the Universe to bring destruction upon his enemies. I shall give Ham no quarter and I ask the great God of the Universe to have only mercy on Ham for his infamous preachments.

"Instead of defending himself and facing the issue like a man, Ham has resorted to every insidious device within the knowledge of his crafty profession to destroy this newspaper, and it looks as if he is adroitly and insidiously appealing to the basest instincts of the mob in Elizabeth City to bring about my undoing.

"In his pulpit Sunday night he made the remarkable statement that six or seven men who attended the meetings would have killed a prominent man in this town, but that he had dissuaded these men from killing that man. I do not know what citizen Ham's followers would kill, but I insist that his statement to that tabernacle crowd Sunday night was a cowardly suggestion to some of his followers in this town to take someone's life and remove from his path any man who mustered up enough courage to fight a theological hyena and all his infamous works.

"I have said that I believed Ham's theology was debasing and brutalizing and would do more ultimate harm than good. Do I need to submit more proof of Ham's perfidy than his brazen boast that six or seven converts of his meeting are ready to kill some man in this town if he but says the word?

"What kind of religion is it that puts hate and murder into the hearts of so many men who listen to this preacher night after night? I ask you!

"Ham is using the identical tactics that were employed by another preacher in this town fourteen years ago, and which resulted in a riot and the shooting up of my home on a Sunday night. I call upon all good people in Elizabeth City and throughout the State to mark the incendiary utterances of Ham, and if anything happens as a result of his damnably insidious and inflammatory preachments they will know at whose door to place the blame."

"In the meantime," the article continued, "I have no apologies to make for anything I have said about Ham. I am more than ever convinced that he is an insolent mountebank, a ruthless demagogue, a preacher of hate, a joy-killer, a tyrant playing upon the fears, the prejudices and the weaknesses of unthoughtful humans . . . And when anyone disagrees with him, that one is branded as an enemy of God, and all church people are exhorted not to patronize or support in any way the business of that man . . .

"Ham is in a deep hole with the sides soaped, and he will repeat more lies in an effort to extricate himself. I have no doubt that he will read a lot of stuff from government documents that are themselves lies, because there are a lot of liars in Washington and some of them have turned out a lot of lying government documents. I have no doubt that he will say that every testimonial to the character of Julius Rosenwald published in this newspaper is the result

of Russian propaganda. And the regrettable thing is that
there are so many people in Elizabeth City who will be
fools enough to believe Ham and deny authentic proofs
against him.

"I said last week that I believed M. F. Ham to be a liar.
I say now with all emphasis that I know he has lied, and
I am happy to have been the instrument that will forever
discredit him with all thinking men and women in North
Carolina and ultimately drive him out of the state."

That did it. Ham was licked. He kept his revival going
a couple of more weeks and then left town, a much dis-
credited man. Just before his departure, Dad got this editorial comment off his chest:

"The evangelist Ham promises to close his revival in
Elizabeth City Sunday night, after which it is hoped that
God will no longer 'hover like a lowering cloud over Elizabeth City.' Won't it be a grand and glorious feeling to
think of God as smiling once more?"

Dad wound up his anti-Ham campaign on November 21,
1924, with an editorial titled "The Prophet Thoroughly
Repudiated," which started out with these words:

"The battle is over except for a little sniping and bush-
whacking on the part of those who don't know that it is
over, and from this latest and boldest fight in its long career
of fighting for right and truth and justice this newspaper
emerges victorious. My clash with the evangelist Ham has
resulted in a conclusive victory for this newspaper. . . .

"But as is too often the case, only the innocent suffer.
I shall suffer little because I have won: Ham cannot suffer
because he has only to shift his base of operations to some
other state and begin all over again. But Elizabeth City
has suffered, and it is going to require a lot of patience
and tact and hard work to undo the harm that has been
done. In the end Elizabeth City will be blessed and beauti-

fied by an experience that must call into prominence the best, the wisest and the noblest leadership that it can produce.

"Ham came to Elizabeth City to dynamite Hell out of Elizabeth City. In the course of events it became necessary for me to dynamite a little Hell out of Ham. Now that was a lot of dynamite to turn loose on one little town, and it was inevitable that things should be blown to pieces and a lot of people hit by the flying fragments of the explosion. Between the pair of us, Ham and I have blown up a lot of good and a lot of bad. It is the task of those who remain on the battlefield to clear away the debris, bury the dead, patch up the wounded, salvage the good and reconstruct a cleaner, healthier, wiser, friendlier Elizabeth City.

"God helping me, I shall do my part in this reconstruction, and there are others, both in and out of the church, who will do their part. Those who will hinder are those outside the church who have seen in my fight on Ham only a fight against their enemy, and those inside the church who have been falsely led to believe that my fight on Ham was a fight on the churches and on real Christianity. . . .

"It is going to take a lot of love—and a lot of patience and charity—to overcome the seeds of bitterness and hate that Ham has sowed in the hearts of those who have followed him with such zeal. That's our job in Elizabeth City, and the sooner we buckle down to it the sooner the green grass will grow again on the fire-scathed, smoke-blackened, blood-soaked surface of our disordered little corner of earth."

Dad had intended that that editorial should close the Book of Ham, but the experience had moved him so profoundly that he felt a great compulsion to use the Ham episode as the excuse for a stern lecture to his fellow townsmen. And so, under the title "A Peculiar Business," he had this to say in part:

"Now here is where I am going to talk plain to you church people, especially to those of you who stand around the street corners and damn me to hell for not believing just as you believe. The whole truth about you is that you don't believe very much, because you have never thought things through for yourself. You have led an indifferent, thoughtless life for years and years and then, all of a sudden, you listen to a clever salesman like Ham and let him do your thinking for you. In forty minutes or forty days you suddenly get a feeling of great righteousness scared into you or drummed into you, and then you damn me because I don't lose my head and get a mushy heart after your fashion.

"Why did you have to bring this Evangelist M. F. Ham and his crowd to town? I'll tell you, and you can get as mad as hell if you must get mad: BECAUSE YOU HAVE NEGLECTED FOR YEARS TO LIVE THE LIFE YOU PRETEND TO LIVE, THE GREAT RANK AND FILE OF PEOPLE OUTSIDE THE CHURCH HAD LOST RESPECT FOR AND INTEREST IN YOUR CHURCHES. That's why you sent for Ham.

"You sent for Ham for the same reason you send for a doctor; your souls were sick. They were sick for the same reason that your body gets sick, because you hadn't taken care of your souls . . . You are so wrapped up in your business, your family or your worldly pleasures that you do not take time to think lovingly of your fellow man; you rush, you grind or, perchance, you loaf. The attendance at your church falls off; collections are slow; your wives get up suppers and rummage sales to get money to meet the church budget. Your pastor gets discouraged. You all wonder what is wrong. And then you send for Dr. Ham or Dr. Somebody Else to feel your pulse, look at your tongue, listen to your heart, roll you, thump you, pound you and give you a violent physic. The physic begins to work and you feel fine for a season—just like a man who has taken a dose of castor oil and worked off a lot of bad stuff.

"Some of you will behave yourselves for quite a while; a very few will be permanently benefitted by obeying the laws of life after the effects of the purgative have worn off; but most of you will be right back to your old indifferent ways in a very few months. I know you. I know human nature. You can't fool me or make me see you as better or worse than you are. In another five years you will again be wondering what is wrong with the church in Elizabeth City and you will send for another professional evangelist to come in and stir you all up again. Maybe it won't be so long as five years.

"Now let me tell you what you must do—and what I must do—to keep this old town straight, and to win the souls of backward men and women permanently to God. EACH OF US MUST SO LIVE EACH DAY IN OUR RELATIONS TOWARD OUR FELLOW MAN THAT EVERY HUMAN BEING WILL BE INSPIRED BY THE LIFE WE LIVE AND ENCOURAGED TO EMU-LATE THE EXAMPLE WE SET. That is the way and the only way to win the respect of the world for ourselves and for the God we pretend to serve. You see, I include myself in this because I am one of you. Indeed, because I am not a member of one of your churches, I must walk ever straighter than you must walk, because I cannot and will not make the blessed Christ the goat for all of my sins.

"And from now on you must pardon me if I watch you a little more intently and a little more critically; you have told me so much about your religion and sent up so many prayers for my poor soul that I shall be inclined to keep you under surveillance and make notes on you as to just what your religious pretensions really amount to. And in the meantime you are at perfect liberty to make notes on me and spy on my private life if you will. Let's make it a friendly little contest to see who lives right in this town and who doesn't.

"And now, don't worry about my soul; I am not worrying about my soul. God will take care of that. Don't worry because I refuse to pack all my sins off on Jesus. In the final judgment, I shall be judged for the life I have lived, not for the things I have believed or disbelieved. The Great Judge of the Universe will consider not what I believed or what you believe, but the effect of your belief on your character. . . .

"If you are not afraid of the truth and will earnestly seek for the truth, you will discover some day that Ham has played you for a sucker, and you will be verily ashamed of the fact and will hate Ham for the lies and slanders he had preached between those sermons in which he gave us something like a true glimpse of the loving Christ."

It is doubtful that Evangelist Ham ever preached a sermon which, if taken to heart, would do its hearers as much good as that one.

Keeping tabs on professional evangelists, Dad later was prompted to write an editorial titled simply "Hate," in which he exposed how such pulpiteers exploit the human faculty of hating. He wrote:

"There is something elemental in a Billy Sunday revival; he puts on a great show, providing forty days and forty nights of thrilling entertainment for people whose lives are generally starved for entertainment and excitement. To sit with thousands of other mortals on hard pine benches, spit on a sawdust floor, pray, sing and hate like hell is a great relaxation for the masses.

"I say hate like hell, because anything depending upon

human accord and acclaim succeeds best by an appeal to the hate mechanism of the human mind. For instance, we don't vote for candidates; we vote against somebody. The whole country took a violent dislike to Herbert Hoover and Franklin D. Roosevelt was elected president.

"Religion has been in the hands of expert students of human nature for thousands of years; it knows human nature. In their infinite wisdom, the church fathers have long known they could not succeed with an appeal based solely upon the love motif; it is difficult to satisfy men and women with love of God and neighbor; their more primitive nature must be appealed to; they must be given an outlet for hate. And so great emphasis is laid upon sin, the devil, hell and damnation—something to hate. Many evangelists go further than that and provide their hearers greater satisfaction by stirring up hatred of Jews, Catholics, agnostics and heathen foreigners.

"M. F. Ham, the last high-pressure brimstone peddler we built a tabernacle for, was a past master at the art of making folks hate. He could make them hate so hard that they would empty their pockets for him in their blindness and the fury of their hate. Of the two men, Billy Sunday and M. F. Ham, Billy is infinitely more desirable. There is something human and likeable about Billy Sunday. Since our local ministers feel themselves losing their grip every few years and must send for outside help to call the stray sheep back into the fold, I am glad they are sending for Billy Sunday. They could have done much worse."

This was by no means the first time Billy Sunday had merited mention on the editorial page of *The Independent*. Way back in 1913, he had inspired editor Saunders to dash off a highly amusing editorial titled "Solomon for Sunday," the full text of which follows:

The following is given as a verbatim report of the story

of David and Goliath as related from the pulpit by the Rev. Billy Sunday:

Saul and all his sons except David went off to war; they left David at home because he was only a kid. After a while, David's ma got worried. She wondered what had become of his brothers because they hadn't telephoned to her or sent word. So she said to David, "David, you go on down there and see whether they are all right."

So David pikes off to where the War is, and the first morning he was there out comes this Big Goliath, a big strapping fellow about eleven feet tall, who commenced to shoot off his mouth as to what he was going to do. "Who's that big stiff putting up that game of talk?" asked David of his brothers.

"Oh, he's the whole works; he's the head cheese of the Philistines. He does that little stunt every day."

"Say," said David, "you guys make me sick. Why don't some of us go out and sock that gink. You let him get away with that stuff?" He decided to go out and tell Goliath where to head in.

So Saul said: "You'd better take my armour and sword." David put them on, but he felt like a fellow with a hand-me-down suit about four times too big for him, so he took them off and went down to the brook and picked up a half-dozen stones. He put one of them in his sling, threw it, and socked Goliath in the coco between the lamps, and the big guy went down for the count. David drew his sword and chopped off his block, and the rest of the gang skiddoed.

Parson Sunday was a baseball player before he found Jesus and swapped the padded pants for the clerical habiliments, exchanged his leather mitt for a chicken ticket, and quit a diamond to peddle harps and repair halos. He got his vernacular from the ball park and he knows that the average American can understand slang where Queen Eliza-

beth's English can't get an idea across. And so the Rev.
Billy Sunday talks everyday slang to his everyday crowds
and makes otherwise quaint and old-fashioned scriptural
stories over into snappy, slangy, twentieth century Ameri-
canese.

That Sunday's stunt is a howling success is evident if
we judge by the cash he collects and the number of week-end
converts he makes in a year.

I would like to hear Brother Sunday render Solomon's
salacious Song into bleacher English. Wouldn't it be
great? We may presume it would read about like this:

*Solomon had seven hundred wives and three hundred
chickens, and the bunch was about to get his goat when the
Shulamite kid blew in.*

*Say, that kid was the candy. Old Solomonsky fell for it
in a jiffy. "Believe me," said he, "she's some chicken. Oh
you kiddo!"*

*Some shape that. She was built right from the ground
up. And you can bet your block old Sol had a good look,
for there wasn't a piece of her big enough to bite that he
didn't put into poetry. That imperial sheeny was a keen
judge of body.*

*And talk about your bull con—well, that all gazebo was
there with the classiest bunch of chicken feed that was ever
canned. He had the little Shulamite wench drunk on hot
air with the first stanza, and she was limp as a rag and
breathing hard when he made a break for the palm tree in
stanza No. 8 and bit a grape.*

*When you can tell a girlie that her nose smells like an
apple and that the roof of her mouth tastes like wine, you
are safe on third and it's you for a sure score.*

*Old Sol made it all right, all right. But he couldn't stay
around the house with it. The kiddo didn't like the looks of
her thousand rivals, and she asked him to find a nice, quiet*

*little place down in the sticks, where we must now leave them
sniffing mandrakes and swiping pomegranates.*

"But, you say, no preacher could afford to take such a
risque text into his pulpit. You are mistaken. Why, the
foxy old fakers who fixed up the King James version of the
Bible declare that Solomon wasn't making love to a flesh
and blood woman at all; that the song is plainly a symbol
of the mutual love of Christ and the church. And where
Solomon thrust his arm into the cat-hole in the door of
the lady's chamber and gave her such a thrill that she had
to put in a hurry call for the chambermaid, the Bible
makers explain that "Christ awaketh the church with his
calling." (See Chap. 4, verse 5.)

"You will find all this in the chapter headings, put there
by ecclesiastical fakers to dupe the unsophisticated for many
centuries.

"How the first faker must have laughed when he conceived the idea of putting the chaste and anemic Nazarene
into the purple bed of the original dead game sport who
revelled with a thousand mistresses by night and wrote
proverbs in the morning!"

I can only say, after reading that example of Dad's
earlier writing, that I am not sure whether I am more impressed with his biblical knowledge or with his ribald wit.

AN AMERICAN
20. OBERAMMERGAU

Outdoor dramas in recent years have become an established part of the American culture. During July and August of each year, plays telling the story of some colorful or significant era in our nation's history—early colonization attempts, the conflicts of whites vs. Indians, the settling of the West, etc.—are acted out nightly in amphitheaters in picturesque settings in various parts of the country.

Some of these dramas come close to being "good theater"; others are at best mediocre. All depend to a considerable extent on an imaginative setting, interesting lighting effects and colorful costumes for their audience appeal. But all do have a certain appeal, especially for summer vacationers, and thus manage to survive at least for a few seasons.

My father inspired the writing and initial production of the "grandfather" of all these summer dramas on the American scene. "The Lost Colony," a symphonic drama depicting the hopes, the aspirations, the hardships and the ultimate disappearance of a band of English people who sought in the 1580s to plant a permanent colony on Roanoke Island, North Carolina, marked its 25th anniversary in 1962. It has played continuously from about July 1 through Labor Day each summer since 1937, except for a few war years when a blackout on lighting in coastal areas made its performance impossible.

Other outdoor dramas doubtless appeared in this country prior to 1937, but these productions ran only for a few performances or a single season. Only "The Lost Colony" has been able to stay "on the boards" season after season for a quarter of a century.

There are many reasons why "The Lost Colony" has endured where others have failed. For one thing, its amphitheater nestles in a setting of pine-covered sand dunes on the northeast shore of Roanoke Island, on the very spot where the English colonists landed, made friends with the native Indians, planted their maize and other crops, witnessed the birth of Virginia Dare, first white child born of English parentage on this continent, and ultimately disappeared, thus earning the name of "the lost colony."

The very fact of knowing that much of the drama being enacted on the stage occurred more than three hundred and fifty years ago in that exact geographical setting gives the play an appeal that is unique and undeniable.

Also, the lighting effects used in this production are most dramatic and most effective. And the music—an inspired use of old English hymns, carols and ballads, sung to an organ accompaniment by students from the Westminster Choir School—"pulls the lost colonists into the stream of human nobility," to borrow a phrase from a laudatory review of the drama by the *New York Times'* distinguished Brooks Atkinson.

On the financial side, "The Lost Colony" has been able to survive the vicissitudes that beset most outdoor theater because of (1) the employment of native talent, at a very low stipend, for all but a few of the major dramatic roles; (2) the continuing loyalty of several hundred area residents who each year buy season passes; (3) occasional timely emergency support in the way of modest appropriations voted by the North Carolina General Assembly; assistance from the National Park Service, which keeps up the grounds and aids with maintenance and improvement of the amphitheater since Fort Raleigh is a national historical shrine; (5) the generosity of people like Dr. and Mrs. Fred Morrison of Washington, D. C., who in 1961 gave $125,000 to the Roanoke Island Historical Association to help with a badly needed rebuilding of the amphitheater; and (6) the unselfish devotion of such individuals as Alfred Bell, who figured largely in the design of the amphitheater and has nursed it through years of storm damage and financial stress, and of the late Bradford Fearing, who gave unstintingly of his time in attending to the management details of the production.

But—above all else—it is my conviction that the enduring quality of "The Lost Colony" stems from the visionary concept which came from the mind of W. O. Saunders and the brilliant adaptation of that concept by Playwright Paul Green.

My father was possessed of an abundance of vision, a love of his section of the country, and a flair for publicity and showmanship. On an assignment to Europe for *Collier's* magazine in 1930, he attended a performance of the once-in-ten-years production of the Passion Play at Oberammergau, a religious drama enacted by local people. He was enthralled by what he saw, but it was not until months later that he related what he had witnessed at Oberammergau to something that had taken place many years before in Northeastern North Carolina.

In the early 1930s, Dad wrote in *The Independent* an editorial titled "An American Oberammergau," which he persuasively argued that the story of the lost colonists of Roanoke Island was, in its own way, every bit as dramatic as the Passion Play, and that his section might be missing a good bet if it neglected to stage such a drama on Roanoke Island.

This editorial led to the performance of a home-produced drama at Fort Raleigh a year or so later, with Editor Saunders playing the role of the Historian. This was a beginning—but that was all it was.

Not content to let his vision die, Dad wrote to Professor Frederick Koch, director of the drama department and the Carolina Playmakers Workshop at the University of North Carolina, to inquire if he could recommend a Tar Heel playwright capable of writing the story of the Lost Colony. Indeed he did have such a man, said Koch, and that man was Paul Green, recent winner of a Pulitzer prize for a play dealing with sharecroppers in Eastern North Carolina.

Editor Saunders in time was introduced to Green and took an immediate liking to the young professor. As Dad began to explain what he had in mind, Paul Green appeared to be less than enthusiastic. What Dad didn't know just then was that in the early 1920s, while still a student in Professor Koch's department, Paul Green had visited Fort Raleigh and had written an idyllic one-act play about Virginia Dare which had been greeted with something less than critical approbation when read aloud to the Carolina Playmakers.

Unaware of this galling failure in the playwright's life, Dad enthusiastically told Green about the production of the Passion Play which he had seen at Oberammergau.

"Paul," he said, "we've got to have something like that in North Carolina, and I've got an idea. You see, 1937 will soon be here. This will mark the 350th anniversary of the colony and the birth of Virginia Dare also. We ought to have a great exposition, something like the Jamestown Exposition of 1907. We could move a tribe of Indians down on Roanoke Island, let them carry on farming, raise tobacco, set their fishing weirs just the way they did at the time Sir Walter Raleigh sent his colony over. We could have every man on the island grow a beard, and the people could wear the dress of three centuries ago. It would be the biggest thing ever to hit North Carolina. We would get nationwide, even worldwide publicity for it."

The irrepressible editor talked on and on, and Paul Green finally consented to attend an exploratory meeting at Manteo some three weeks later, although he had serious reservations as to the practicability of the proposed project. Saunders made a speech opening the meeting, and Green then made a non-committal speech on the subject of an outdoor drama. The meeting was on the verge of laying an egg. Then pushing forward from the rear of the hall came the late Senator Josiah W. Bailey, who was on a fishing trip in the area and had dropped in unheralded to see what the meeting was all about.

Senator Bailey made an impromptu but exceptionally inspiring speech in which he quoted several excerpts from Shakespeare and asserted the likelihood that descriptions of Roanoke Island sent back to England by the early colonists had inspired the Bard of Avon to write "The Tempest."

"When Shakespeare wrote 'Come unto these yellow sands,' Bailey declared, "he had in mind the sands of Roanoke Island. No doubt about it. The tragedy of the lost colony that happened on this island inspired the pen of the immortal Shakespeare to write one of his finest and most imaginative plays. This is a sacred spot here. Let us put on a drama—our drama—here at this patriotic shrine where those brave pioneers lived, struggled, suffered and died. Yes, let us tell their story to the world."

Interest was spurred and enthusiasm fanned by the Senator's stirring words. The result was that the dormant

Roanoke Island Historical Association was reactivated and plans were laid for the construction of an amphitheater and the production of an outdoor drama at Fort Raleigh. Paul Green, needless to say, had had his interest and imagination stirred anew, and he had consented to write the drama. According to a published report, he resolved this time to redeem his earlier failure to write a moving play about Virginia Dare and the ill-fated Roanoke Island colony, saying:

"This time let me hold true to the stimulation of my subject matter. Let me keep ever before me the sense of homage of this group of tragic, suffering people—more than one hundred and twenty of them, men, women and children—who had fared forth from England on that fateful day in 1587 to brave the turmoil and terror of the vast and raging sea in search of their destiny; these, the keepers of a dream. Away with all the secondhand sources—let it come prime, let it come raw!"

Come it did, and this time Paul Green succeeded wonderfully. The symphonic drama, first produced in 1937, was an immediate success. It inspired Brooks Atkinson, then the nation's leading drama critic, to write in the *New York Times*:

"*The Lost Colony* has made an extraordinarily versatile use of spectacle, sound, pantomime and cadenced speech . . . The dances translate the freshness and wildness of the new world more eloquently than words or scenery could . . . *The Lost Colony* is a simply stated idealization of the adventurous impulse that founded this nation in the restless impulse of Shakespeare's England. Paul Green has written history with a compassion that turns his characters into unconscious symbols of a brave new world . . ."

Since that first year, the drama at Fort Raleigh has gone on and on with a vitality and a durability that no other outdoor production in this country has been able to achieve. Paul Green has made many changes in the script over the years, ever seeking to sharpen an image or strengthen a situation but always retaining the beauty and inspiration of his original words.

President Franklin D. Roosevelt was one of the early viewers of the drama, and since then it has played to a number of ambassadors, governors and other dignitaries and to tens of thousands of ordinary folk who have found inspiration in sitting beneath the stars in a pine-scented forest on the shore of Roanoke Sound and enjoying the stirring words, music and pageantry of "The Lost Colony."

And behind it all, in my humble opinion, lies the imagination and the determination of W. O. Saunders.

21. THE FREE-THINKER

Many individuals with narrow minds, inborn prejudices and the inability or unwillingness to read *The Independent* with discernment drew the conclusion that W. O. Saunders was an irreligious or non-religious man—an atheist, an infidel or, at best, an agnostic.

Dad was, in my opinion, an opinion derived from living with him, talking with him and reading most of what he wrote, a deeply religious man. But his newspaper waged relentless war on religious bigotry, irresponsible pulpiteers and mendicant clerics, and it was from these campaigns that some concluded he was anti-religion. Not so. However, it was from these battles that he derived his greatest satisfactions as a crusading newsman and editor. He touched on this in the Silver Jubilee anniversary edition of *The Independent* in June 1933, saying:

"I have a profound respect for the sincere religious convictions of other people and realize the essential comfort that religion brings to the hearts of common men and women. But I deplore the exploitation of good and simple minded people by charlatans, mountebanks and bunk-peddlers parading under the cloak of religion and engaged in the harrowing of souls for revenue only.

"I have an utter contempt for the gold-digging pulpiteer

and all his tribe and shall voice this contempt so long as I live. The world has suffered much from repressive Puritanism nurtured by selfish, ignorant, lying, conscienceless priests. Elizabeth City has a higher type of ministers than will be found in most Southern communities today because the lower order of theological bunk-shooters just can't thrive in the same town with *The Independent*."

Dad's thinking as a young man was influenced significantly by several of the most noted free-thinkers of the early part of this century—Elbert Hubbard, the Philistine; William Cowper Brann, the Iconoclast, and Robert G. Ingersoll. With these as his mentors, it followed naturally that my father would set down on paper a great many controversial and provocative thoughts, and would express open rebellion against much that he observed of life.

A 1911 editorial titled "Terror of Wisdom" furnished a clear insight into Dad's rebellious nature. It went as follows:

"Moving with the crowd, Col. Harry Skinner, a former North Carolina Congressman, entered the National Theater in Washington to hear Robert G. Ingersoll lecture. Colonel Skinner was just getting into his seat when he heard Ingersoll thunder:

"And where was this God of Moses when these outrages were being perpetrated upon these innocent women and children? Probably he was sneaking around in the bushes burning a lamp for the mystification of some Israelitish ignoramus. I call him a damn brutal God."

"Colonel Skinner, who had never before heard a hint of heresy in all his orthodox career, jumped like a shot cat. 'Great God Almighty!' said he. 'Let me get out of here before the roof falls in.' And Col. Skinner is said to have got out, trampling over the very heads of some of the audience in his mad break for the street.

"Col. Skinner belonged to an age when doubt was proclaimed a most heinous offense that might somehow be accompanied by an instantaneous visitation of divine wrath in the shape of a killing thunderbolt, a tornado or an earthquake.

"And it is surprising how many persons entertain that terror of free thought today. Sh-h-h-h! Not a word! Don't think!

"All this talk of the terror of losing one's faith is bosh and poppycock when it is not the prattle of childish tongues. We don't lose our faiths, we reconstruct them. And there is real pleasure in making new creeds where there is only a sorrowful sentimentality in nursing a dead one.

"There is no such thing as smashing a faith or a delusion. The change from superstition to reason is slow and uncertain. We become skeptics years before we recognize ourselves as such. And then, instead of crying over the rubbish that we long ago lost, we wonder how we managed to carry the imaginary burden of the thing with us so long after we had discarded the thing itself.

"I believe in the efficacy of doubt, of thought, of discontent.

"Only the doubtful may ascertain; only the discontented may realize.

"There is hope for the sweatshop slave when he doubts the justice of the system to which he is bound and begins to manifest his discontent. There is hope for the female sufferers under woefully discriminatory marriage and property laws when they manifest discontent.

"There is hope for the prostitute when she becomes discontented with her way of life.

"Discontent is the stepping stone to freedom.

"If Newton had not doubted, the law of gravitation

might still be waiting for its discoverer and Columbus would not have ventured to sail to a new world.

"Had Martin Luther and John Calvin not doubted the infallibility of the Pope, there would have been no Reformation. And had not others doubted the insufficiency of Protestantism's protest, we would have had no science.

"All life is evolution, a movement onward and upward. The contented rest, sit down, give up and progress is blocked. The discontented keep busy; they move, and the world moves with them.

"My sympathies are with the rebel. I stand on the house-top and wave encouragement to the insurgent, the socialist, the suffragette, the ethical culturist, the raw-foodist, the anti-vivisectionist, the prohibitionist, and to every discontented mortal under the sun. None of them is perfect. They probably never will accomplish the things they think they are fighting for, but they will destroy a great many useless old things and pave the way for more interesting experiments all the while. And if they make mistakes, why mistakes must be made, so let them make them. We will all profit by them bye and bye.

"Life is a game. Let's play it with a vengeance. We accomplish nothing as mere spectators watching the slow procession. Get out and kick the ball. Make a play. If you make a mistake or many mistakes in your short lifetime, take courage; the world will have a million years left in which to rectify them.

"It has been said that Nature wastes a million melons in producing the one prize-taker at a county fair. We do well if once in a million times we do the thing that is worthwhile. What any of us do or think at any given time is of little importance. The important thing is that we keep up the doing and the thinking. Our mistakes will presently be buried forever under two feet of sod or dissipated in the dizzy heights of a crematory chimney."

What many people failed to realize was that Dad knew the Bible as few laymen know it, and probably better than many who wear the cloth. That is why, in his verbal debates and clashes on religious subjects, he frequently confounded his opponents by using the Scripture to prove his point or disprove their contentions.

Typical of Dad's views on the Bible was an editorial he wrote in 1912 under the title "The Word of God." After quoting in full the story of the brutal attack the Israelites made upon the Midianites, as recounted in the Book of Numbers, Dad wrote:

"And this is called the word of God. For nearly two thousand years it has been preached, punched, hammered and burned into us that we must base our conduct, faith and hope of immortality upon this book or be damned. To disbelieve one line of this Holy Writ is heresy, infidelity. To doubt the alleged love and mercy and tenderness of this Jehovah is blasphemy. To repudiate his authority is atheism.

"Two million preachers and more than five hundred billion dollars in property and scenery are employed to propitiate this God and hold humanity in submission to him. But there are a few of us in this world who hurl defiance at the entire infernal, damnable business. We, then, are atheists. We shall surely go to hell. Indeed, the wonder is that God doesn't loose his thunderbolts and kill us with a stroke, as he did Annanias and Sapphira.

"In reply to the direful threats that are made, we simply affirm that we would choose eternal residence in hell with a barb-tailed devil to one year in heaven with a damned, brutal, long-whiskered, grouchy old God who commands the slaughter of babies and pregnant mothers for the sangui-

nary satisfaction of a favorite tribe of barbarians. It is
terrible to think that in that battle said once to have been
waged in heaven, that Lucifer didn't turn the tables and
kick old Jehovah over the parapets.

"When I first began to think for myself, I was asked if
I believed the Bible. I replied that I did not believe all of
it. Orthodoxy threw up its hands in horror and informed
me that if one line of it was the word of God, then every
line of it must be the word of God, and I should not accept
one part of the book without accepting all. I accept Orthodoxy's argument today: I recognize the Book of Numbers
from which I have quoted as the word of the God of priestcraft and churchianity. I will therefore accept nothing that
issues from the book of this God. . . .

"Four hundred millions of Christians accept this book
and base their hopes of paradise and fears of hell upon it.
The greater number who accept this book do so through
sheer ignorance. A lesser number of more intelligent minds
accept it for fear of the prejudice and brute strength of
the majority.

"But lose no hope, all you free-thinkers. The world is
young. It was only yesterday that none could read and
write except the priest. As yet, the organization behind
the church is stronger than that of any government. Better
organized free thought, more liberal education, and we shall
see the god of Israel, borrowed from Egypt, discarded for
God Men drawn from the splendid future of an evolving
world."

Is it not a wonder that The Independent Man was not
tarred and feathered (as he almost was on one occasion)
for daring to print such "blasphemy" in a small, God-fearing town in the South in the Year of our Lord 1912?

I sometimes think Dad may have missed his calling in
not becoming a preacher, a career to which he was greatly

attracted as a teen-age youth. He could quote Holy Writ, thunder against sinners (certain categories) and draw morals with the best of the pulpiteers.

Going back to the question of Dad's religion, I talked with him about this a few years before his death, and he told me:

"I have quit throwing brickbats at Jehovah."

For years, he said, he had thought he hated God, and he held in contempt or pity all who worshipped Him. In the process of time he discovered that his hatred was not a hatred of God at all, but simply a hatred for all bigots, fanatics and simpletons who trade in His name.

In searching out the cruelty, the wickedness and filth of the Bible, he lost sight of its poetry and its higher ethical and spiritual concepts. He eagerly pounced upon the weaknesses, hypocrisies, wickedness and carnality of priestcraft wherever he found it. And it was his conviction that one had but to read and look with a suspicious or sour mind to find enough fault with the ecclesiastical tribe to make the angels weep.

After years of cantankerous doubt, bewilderment and confusion, he attained, by a tedious and circumlocutory route, to something of that harmony and accord with the infinite that the orthodox religionist has found in his unreasoning faith.

Dad's own account of his early unbelief and scorn and the slow but steady awakening of his own concept of deity will doubtless stir feelings of kinship in untold thousands who have had similar experiences but lacked the occasion, the temerity or the rhetoric to set their feelings down on paper. Here is Dad's description of his own personal experience of the soul:

"That wise Frenchman, Voltaire, spoke a profound truth in his oft-quoted assertion that 'If God did not exist, it would be necessary to invent him.' Certainly, out of my own experience of half a century in the valley that lies between the two eternities on either side of us, I can say fervently and emphatically that I have ever felt the need of God. If, long ago, I had only searched in my own heart I would have found Him. But all around me the professional Theocrats had piled the rubbish of their myths, superstitions and dogmas, and I explored the dunghills of ecclesiasticism instead. I explored in vain. For God exists in the hearts and subconscious minds of men or He exists not at all. I am using the word God in a poetic and impersonal sense, as a familiar label for the highest human conception of good.

"Far back in the beginnings of human history, men emerging from jungle life began to sense the fact that the universe was the product of orderly planning and they reasoned, *per se*, that for every plan there must be an architect. The orderly procession of the stars and the planets, sun and moon, day and night, the seasons—everything—seemed to testify to the existence of a master mind at work in the universe. Hundreds of bibles were written and hymns and poems and prayers composed around this Grand Idea.

"So persistent was the idea of omnipotence that a vast theological literature was built up, of which our own Hebrew Bible is an outstanding example. This religious literature was composed largely by dreamers and mystics in possession of few, if any, scientific facts, and whose knowledge of the very earth they lived on was limited in most cases to their local horizons. Many of our so-called religious books were the works of neurotics and fakirs. It is said 'the first priest was the first knave who met the first fool.'

"Upon this ancient literature priestcraft founded religious systems that, by a pretense of divine authority and inculcation of fear in the hearts of ignorant men and women, have persisted down to the present day.

"There is the same obviousness of a master mind, will or spirit at work in the universe today that impressed our primitive ancestors. That obviousness is conceded by science and impresses a higher human intelligence, reinforced by knowledge and education. And today a new religious literature is being written in response to the spiritual needs of men and women who have grown up intellectually and who are no longer impressed by such myths as the Adam and Eve story, the escapades of Samson, Jonah and the whale, a virgin birth, blood atonement and all the mumbo-jumbo of priestcraft.

"In the Twentieth Century, higher intelligences that were driven away from God by a childish theology cooked up in the infancy of the race will find their way back to God through a new and saner and broader concept of duty.

"In my own childhood, I was driven away from God by bumptious, hell-raising pulpiteers in whom I perceived much guile and no humility. In spite of the horror, disgust and resentment with which they scourged my soul, and in spite of the wilderness of doubt into which they drove me, I find my own self, at long last, being drawn nearer and nearer into an intimacy with that divine spirit of love and mercy and beauty and tenderness at work in the hearts of men. I feel myself no longer inclined to hurl barbs of ridicule at a cruel and vindictive myth called Jehovah, but rather to seek the quiet paths and walk humbly before a mystery that offends neither my ignorance nor my intelligence, but fills me with an inward peace and calm that inspires the best that is in me.

"Understand me, I have absolutely no concept of a Personal God who directs in minute detail the petty affairs of men, showering blessings upon this one and that one and sending hurricanes and thunderbolts to discommode or annihilate others. I observe the universe as an orderly mechanism operating in acordance with infinite and immutable laws. If I happen to be standing in the path of a bolt of lightning I shall be struck by lightning; if I built my house on the sands of the seashore, I cannot expect immutable laws to save me from the devastating effect of flood tides and hurricanes.

"In my half-century of living and thinking upon life, I have by both observation and experience perceived a gradual and sure triumph of love and mercy and justice over tooth and fang and claw. It seems to me that there is an unmistakable influence for goodness, truth, mercy, justice and beauty working in nature and in the hearts of men. I have tried to put myself en rapport with this influence, spirit or will. Occasionally I feel the exultation of having achieved such a spiritual triumph. It may be that in such moments I have but discovered and communed with my own better self. Of this thing I am finally and firmly convinced: Men are working ever onward and upward toward God, which is quite contrary to the theology that God created man in his own image and suffered increasing displeasure with his creature ever after.

"But what is the purport of all this writing? It is just this: I apprehend that millions of inquisitive and analytical minds like myself find themselves, quite like myself, hampered in their quest of God by a confusion of tongues. They are still rummaging away among the antiquities of mythology and theology for that resplendent and inspiring light that flames not in the dark and cruel past but ever just ahead of us.

"I should like to convey to these millions, for whom ancient ritualisms and superstitions have no meaning, the thought that in the cleaner recesses of our own consciousness we may find this luxuriant and comforting source of power and light that men call God. And, if I could, I would speed the perfection and compilation of that new literature of religion and morals that is being written out of the larger experience and knowledge of modern men and women.

"This little ball of molten matter encased in a relatively thin and fragile crust of earth—this little planet on which we strut and pose and glorify ourselves—has been rolling for millions of years. It has provided breeding grounds and provender for many species of reptiles and animals now long extinct. Man, a late comer on the scene, has been here for fifty thousand, a hundred thousand or half a million years. Just how long we may only guess.

"For thousands upon thousands of years men lived like beasts of prey, concerned only with their needs of the moment, inert and ambitionless. It was only within the last few thousand years that men learned to think and, thinking, began to dream, aspire and value knowledge. It was only within the last few centuries that men began to collect and coordinate human knowledge. Obviously, it is absurd and unfair to expect a perfect human society or a perfect God to emerge hastily from such ancient, slow and awkard beginning. Man's first concepts of God were necessarily crude.

"The earth is very old; the human race is comparatively very young; evolution is necessarily a slow and tedious process. We have made millions of mistakes and outlived them; maybe we are due to make millions more before we attain to anything approximating perfection.

"And so I pen this thought for all who are disappointed, disgruntled and impatient. The universe is all too big, time all too infinite, for puny man to exaggerate his importance or the importance of disturbances and annoyances affecting his infinitesimally little span of life. Rise above the vexations of the hour, the day, the year and the era in which you move, merge your ego with the infinite, enroll yourself among the immortals, move up with the gods."

To my way of thinking, you'd have to go to a lot of churches on a lot of Sundays to hear a clearer expression of humbleness and reverence than that.

22.   "NIGGER LOVER"

North Carolina over the years has had less racial trouble and fewer lynchings than most Southern states, and Northeastern North Carolina has been singularly free of this blot on the human race. I like to think that The Independent Man contributed in no small measure to this fortuitous situation by repeatedly pleading for racial tolerance, exposing injustices against and exploitation of members of the Negro race, and by publicizing the worthwhile things done by the colored people of our community and section.

Some bigoted individuals in the area even dubbed my father a "nigger lover" because he held out in the columns of his newspaper for a fair break, a chance in life, and an occasional deserved word of encouragement or approbation for members of the Negro race.

It was somewhat to be expected that all of the literate Negroes of the community—the few doctors and dentists, the school teachers and professors, the merchants, the barbers and, yes, even the preachers—respected and admired W. O. Saunders. And this, together with his own inner satisfaction, was regarded by Dad as sufficient reward for any editorial battles he waged on behalf of "the Lord's dark-skinned children."

He told me in later years how much a humble Negro had

comforted him in one of the blackest hours of his bitter fight with Evangelist Ham.

"I was the town's lone pariah and outcast, hateful and damned," said Dad. "I walked the streets of my town with heavy heart. One morning I dropped into a barber shop and a Negro barber beamed upon me. There were a number of customers and loungers in the shop at the time. The barber beamed at me and said in a loud voice: 'Mr. Editor, I'se proud to serve you; you'se a great man. Only a great man could buck Mr. Ham and hold his own fifty-fifty.'

"The words of that Negro barber cheered me and lifted me out of a terrifying slough of despair. For Negroes are a cunning and intuitive race; they don't meddle in white folks' affairs or commit themselves indiscreetly on controversial issues concerning only white people. They are all things to all men. The very fact that this Negro barber was sure of himself in saying out loud in his place of business that I was holding my own was proof enough that I indeed had a fair share of my public squarely behind me. And so it proved."

Although the Albemarle section over the years had been singularly free of lynchings and racial disorders, there was one occasion when Elizabeth City almost had a "necktie party." A Negro man from a neighboring county, charged with the rape of a twelve-year-old white girl, was brought to our county jail for safekeeping. The story that came to Editor Saunders' ears went like this:

The little girl was alone at home with her mother. The father and other members of the family were away. In an outbuilding a little remote from the house lived a Negro man of all work. The little girl was seen playing by the picket fence near the Negro's quarters, and the Negro was seen to enter the shack at about the same time.

A half hour after the two were seen in proximity, the

little girl stumbled into the house bleeding and screaming with pain. She told her mother that Tom, the colored man, had done something dreadful to her. An inspection of the child revealed that she was frightfully lacerated and bore every evidence of having been the victim of a brutal criminal assault. Word of the rape of the beautiful little girl spread through the neighborhood, and the sheriff of the county arrived barely in time to take the Negro away from an angry crowd and get him to the Pasquotank County jail.

This was comparatively early in the day. By mid-afternoon a score or more of outraged citizens in the county in which the alleged crime was committed were organizing to come to Elizabeth City and get the Negro, with full assurance that they would find a host of sympathizers in the town.

The situation was all the more tense, to those who sensed it, because of its sullen, ominous lack of ostentation. Many people think of mobs as howling packs of human hyenas, brandishing sticks and guns and rending the air with blood-curdling shrieks. But Dad knew that mobs do not act in any such manner. His parents were living briefly in Portsmouth, Va., near the county jail, when more than a thousand men marched past their house, took a Negro from jail and burned him at the stake. Dad crouched with his fear-stricken mother at a window and watched the ominous, sullen mob through cracked shutters, and this sight of an ugly mob in action left an indelible impression upon his young mind.

Dad knew that a mob was organizing to come to Elizabeth City and take the alleged rapist from the jail that night, and he knew from boyhood experience about how the mob might be expected to move and act.

In the meantime, he had made a hurried but thoughtful investigation of the alleged crime. The doctor who had examined the child was sure that she had been brutally penetrated, but a microscopic examination of the clothing of the accused Negro showed no tell-tale signs of blood. Still, the Negro had told several conflicting tales, and an alibi that he had hastily given had been completely broken down.

Dad went to the farm house where the alleged assault was committed. He examined the picket fence by the old out-house where the Negro had been domiciled, and a theory evolved in his mind. He went back to the office of the doctor in the case and asked him if the child's wound might not have been inflicted in falling upon the picket fence. The doctor agreed that it could.

Further inquiry revealed that the child had been warned against walking that very fence and had been threatened with a severe whipping if she were ever caught in the act. Dad concluded it was just possible that the child was walking that fence, lost her footing, fell astride one of its sharp pickets, and in her fright and pain, fearful of further punishment, concocted the story that the Negro had assaulted her.

He rushed back to Elizabeth City, hastily wrote the story, speeded up the printing of the paper and had it on the streets of two county seats by nightfall. He told the story as he saw it and predicted that a simple, ignorant, badly frightened Negro who had involved himself by a number of conflicting tales growing out of his stark terror, would probably be proved innocent in the light of later evidence.

There was no lynching in Elizabeth City that night, and a few weeks later the Negro was absolved of guilt.

Dad once wrote that "the race problem in the South is aggravated more by the ignorance of the white cracker than by the ignorance of the profligate Negro. The white Southern cracker has been taught by an ignorant rural clergy that he is a son of God and a brother of Christ, and by the politicians that he was born free and the equal of kings. He doesn't want to know anything else. To him all history is profane, science the work of the devil and his angels, a woman is but a piece of body, and a Negro an accursed brute, a brother of the mule."

Pretty strong stuff, that, to have been published in a country weekly in the South some forty years ago!

In a later year, Editor Saunders was able to document this viewpoint in an editorial titled "Lack of Brains." It went thus:

"I had an automobile accident near Windsor the other night. I needed a wrecking truck to get my car out the mess it was in. I sent word to a nearby filling station for relief. The filling station couldn't help me, but a young Negro in an old rattletrap Ford was at the station and heard of my plight. He came to my rescue with three or four other strapping young Negroes and had me back on the road in a few minutes. I gave him a dollar; fair pay for less than ten minutes' work. It was worth more to me.

"A white man, who had not proffered any help, stepped forward and said to me: 'Giving money to niggers ain't looked upon with favor around here. We hope you won't ever do that again; it puts wrong notions in their heads. They are bumptious enough already.'

"There was an ominous note in the white man's voice and I didn't argue with him. Evidently, paying a Negro to help you out of a hole in Bertie County is a serious offense in the eyes of the lower order of white men in that county. Here is the real crux of the race problem in the South. The white cracker type has been taught to resent the economic advancement of the Negro. And it never occurs to the poor white cracker that in keeping the Negro down he is keeping himself down. To keep another man in the ditch, you've got to stay in the ditch with him.

"In his blind jealousy and contempt for Negro labor that competes with his own unskilled hands, the white cracker type throughout the South insists upon long hours of labor and starvation wages for the black man. And the cracker hasn't brains enough to see that the hours and wages he thinks good enough for the black man determine his own work day and his own wages."

When the Pasquotank County Board of Commissioners refused to vote a small appropriation to help carry out farm demonstration work among the Negro populace of the county, Editor Saunders labeled the commissioners "The Look Backward Club" and blasted their action in these words:

"For hardheadedness, tightfistedness and general cussedness, don't look outside the average Board of County Commissioners. Pasquotank has a representative aggregation of these worthies. The Commissioners of Pasquotank County have one idea, and one idea only, of government, and that is to save money. It has never entered their pates that money is a thing to be spent for the comfort, well being and advancement of folks.

"A month ago it was pointed out to them that they had never contributed a dollar to the support of a county demonstration agent for the colored people. For nearly a year now a colored farm demonstration agent has been doing wonderful work among the Negro farmers of the county. He has been inadequately paid, partly by the Federal Government, partly by the State, and partly by donations from the colored people. And when it was pointed out to the County Commissioners that they ought to do something to help support this farm demonstration work among the Negroes, just as they support such work for the betterment of the white farmers, the Commissioners provided $25 a month for the Negro farm demonstrator by lopping $25 a month off the meager salary of the white farm demonstrator.

"When Mr. Falls, the white demonstrator, refused to stand for the cut in his salary and threatened to quit, the Commissioners this week rescinded their action of a month ago and restored the $25 a month to Mr. Falls but refused to do anything for the Negro. They can't possibly find $300 a year to finance a work that is quite as important to the Negro farmers of the county as to the white farmers. And these same Commissioners are among those who are forever damning the Negro farmer because he isn't as efficient and productive as he ought to be.

"They couldn't be made to see in a thousand years that improved methods of farming introduced among the colored people today will mean better Negro farm lands, better Negro homes, better Negro citizens, and a substantial return to the county in taxes paid by more efficient and more productive Negro farmers in years to come."

On another occasion, when Elizabeth City's most desirable auditorium was denied the sponsors of a proposed series of inter-racial concerts, Editor Saunders wrote:

"How the proposed series of inter-racial musical concerts sponsored by the Young Men's Civic Club found the city's most desirable auditorium barred to them was told in this newspaper last week. No one will ever know how the colored people in Elizabeth City felt about this manifest repulse to their race. Negroes do not wear their hearts on their sleeves. But here is what the Negroes did about it. They got together in Mt. Lebanon Church Sunday night and voted to lend themselves to the programs sponsored by the Civic Club, giving freely of their talent and cooperation, with the understanding that members of their race would seek no admission to the concerts. They would sing their folk songs and their spirituals for the white folks, even though members of their own race would not be permitted even to sit in the galleries.

"Here, then, is a genuine manifestation of the Christ spirit that should make white Christians bow their heads in shame. Blessed indeed are the meek. And there may have been an ominous meaning in the words of Jesus when he said 'for they shall inherit the earth'."

One of the delightful little essays that appeared in the editorial columns of *The Independent* from time to time was one titled "Contrasts," which revealed something of Dad's philosophy about Negroes. It ran as follows:

"I got up at seven o'clock this morning, had a refreshing shower bath, put on cool, clean things, ate an appetizing breakfast, rode down to the office in my sport roadster, turned on an oscillating electric fan in my office and leisurely pursued my work. I quit at five o'clock, locked my office, took a spin in my roadster and then started home. I stopped at the neighborhood grocery and gave an order for some things without leaving the car. I was hot, tired, felt run down and couldn't have smiled for pay.

"And then my attention was arrested by a pair of Negro laborers in hot, greasy, dirty, smelly work clothes, walking briskly, chatting gaily and smiling from ear to ear, showing rows of perfectly sound and white teeth. They had gotten up before six o'clock that morning, had done a lot of chores around their homes and then walked nearly two miles to their jobs in a sawmill on the other side of town. They had worked a ten and a half hour day in that mill, handling heavy green boards and working incessantly to keep up with the machines. And all for $2.00 a day.

"They were walking the two miles back to their homes

now, to a supper of fried catfish, corn pone and warmed over cabbage. And they were smiling, friendly and happy. I wasn't friendly and I wasn't happy.

"Blessed are the poor in spirit, for theirs is the kingdom of heaven. Blessed are the meek, for they shall inherit the earth."

But my favorite Saunders editorial on Negroes was one titled "Just a Little Nigger." Illustrated with a picture of a little colored boy, that editorial provoked scores of cancelled subscriptions and branded Dad indubitably in some quarters as a surenuff "nigger-lover." Here is the editorial that gave so much offense:

"He is just a little Nigger. I do not even know his name; it doesn't matter. I found him driving a team with a gang of day laborers on the race track at our fair grounds the other day. He was laughing and showing his two rows of pearly white teeth. Whirr! went my camera, and I caught the happy image.

"I am printing the picture of that little Nigger here today because I want you to think about him. I think he and his type deserve a great deal of your thought and care.

"This docile, cheerful, smiling, helpful, improvident, indolent, carefree, laughing little Nigger will grow up to be just what you choose to make him. Everything he knows about civilized life and civilized ways he learns from you. He learns quickly from example. He is as plastic as the clay in a potter's hands. What are we doing to make this little Nigger a useful, constructive, provident citizen?

"But a little more than a century ago his forebears were jungle dwellers far remote from civilization. Only yesterday his forebears were chattel slaves to whom the idea of freedom was new, vague, incomprehensible. The little Nigger was born out of his natural environment and it is right much to expect of him to develop into a model citizen at once. It is certainly too much to expect of him when we do not help him as much as we should. A lot of our white people today are quite as indolent, improvident and shallow of intellect as this little Nigger, and we white folks are hundreds and thousands of years remote from slavery. It has been a long time since our kind lived in jungles or were sold on a slave block.

"Be kind to the little Nigger. Do not leave him altogether out of your thoughts and out of your plans. He is going to be a good and useful citizen or he is going to be a criminal and a very undesirable and costly citizen. It is up to us, the stronger, more experienced and more farsighted race, to lend him of our strength and experience and impart to him something of a vision. Whether he is to be a white man's burden or to help the white man carry his burden should be one of our most serious problems and responsibilities."

It may be that the thoughtful, outspoken articles and editorials on racial questions that were written by The Independent Man three and four decades ago helped create the climate that has given North Carolina one of the better records in the South in the segregation/integration struggle of recent years.

SMALL TOWN
23. DOINGS

Your typical American small town has many odd, amusing, embarrassing and scandalous incidents happen within its confines, but your typical American small town weekly, semi-weekly or daily newspaper rarely records these goings-on unless they reach the police court stage.

Not so with *The Independent*. Editor Saunders felt a compulsion to hold up a mirror to almost everything that his fellow townspeople did; he felt that the bad should be reported along with the good, the amusing along with the pathetic, the embarrassing along with the flattering.

Hence, when a prominent young banker went to sleep in the bank after a big evening and his family had the police and fire department looking for him, Dad reported the matter as news. Then, when he was criticized for so doing, he wrote a column suggesting that prominent citizens who indulge in such shenanigans should not holler when publicized. It went:

"That was a funny piece in *The Independent* last week about a prominent young banker going to a party and coming away in such a state that he went to the bank to sleep instead of going to bed, wasn't it?" said the Soda Jerker to the Bank Clerk.

"I think it was darn poor taste on the part of *The Inde-*

pendent to publish a thing like that on a private citizen,"
said the Bank Clerk.

"Well, I don't think so," said the Soda Jerker. "The
conduct of a citizen in private life ceases to be a private
affair when his folks have to call out the fire department
to look for him. And the higher up a man is in the community, the more important it is that the community knows
how he deports himself in his private life."

"But if *The Independent* is going to publish everything
of that sort that happens in this town, then nobody's reputation will be safe," said the Bank Clerk.

"Well, if everybody's reputation in this town is so damn
shaky, then they ought to be published, that's all I got to
say about it," snorted the Soda Jerker.

"In the old days when they went to the corner saloon and
got drunk, they got their names in the papers, but now
that Mr. Volstead and the Anti-Saloon League have abol-
ished the brass rail and the swinging doors and set up
booze parlors in every second or third house on Main Street,
drinking is more than ever a personal and private matter,
and nothing must be said about it.

"There is too darn much home drinking in Elizabeth
City and everywhere else these days. A few folks can't get
together without a fruit jar full of green corn liquor to
play with.

"Instead of going to bed at reasonable hours and leading
the sensible lives most folks used to lead when liquor was
legal, a large proportion of our people think that the greatest fun is gotten out of life now by staying up half the
night drinking corn liquor, eating sandwiches and pigs feet
and dancing to a jazz record on a parlor phonograph.

"The health of hundreds of young people is being under-
mined, their efficiency destroyed and their home life broken
up by too many parties. At one party sometime ago a

couple was missed and the hostess found them in her own bed. I hear of wild parties in private homes in which they get so durned cockeyed before morning that husbands and wives get all mixed up and almost anything goes.

"You're getting to be a regular saint, ain't you?" sneered the Bank Clerk.

"Not a damn bit of it," said the Soda Jerker, "but we folks have got to learn to have a good time without playing hell at it."

Typical of the kind of story *The Independent's* readers seemed to enjoy was one telling how some of the town's flappers had made saps out of a number of footloose married men. Here's how that yarn went:

"Full twoscore married men in Elizabeth City have queered themselves forever in the eyes of certain youth of the town, and they are marked men. And here's how it happened.

"The younger female social set has been hearing things about certain married men in Elizabeth City and they decided to confirm the rumors and their own suspicions. How many married men would steal out at night for a wild party? There was one way to find out.

"And so three devilish young misses went about town last week button-holing this married man and that, asking them if they could get away from their wives for a certain night. 'We are going to stage a little party on the q.t.,' said the devilish young misses. 'We've got five gallons of East Lake moonshine and everything we want for a real party, but the young boys we go with are so silly that we can't trust them and we want to have a little fling with some of you older and settled men who can be trusted.'

"A rendezvous was arranged for, and at the appointed hour a dozen or more of the married men who had explained to their wives that they were going to lodge meetings or out on business were at the meeting place, and others were observed riding by in their cars with furtive looks on their faces. The girls didn't show up.

"And now the married men who fell for the hoax are the laughingstock of the youth of the town. 'We have sure got their number,' said one of the girls to a reporter for this newspaper, 'and we don't want to hear another word from them about the "wild youth" of our town. What it takes for most of them to get wild is just an invitation or an opportunity'."

The ice man has long been the butt of jokes and jests having to do with marital infidelity, but in one story reported in *The Independent* both the ice man and the married woman were innocent of wrongdoing. The story, headed "Husband Finds Ice Tongs in His Bed Room," went thus:

"If you were a newly-wed husband and you came home one morning to find the ice man's tongs on the floor of your wife's bedroom, what would you do about it? You would probably do what this young Elizabeth City groom did, get a new ice man.

"It's a funny story. The young couple in the case occupy an apartment in an old-fashioned residence on East Church Street. The way to their kitchen is through their bedroom. 'Muggsy' Weeks, superintendent of delivery service for the Crystal Ice & Coal Co., happened to be on one of the company's wagons the other morning when it stopped at this particular house. 'Muggsy' wanted to be nice and he delivered the ice himself, obligating to put it in the box.

"The young wife knew Muggsy and not only thought nothing of letting him pass through her bedroom but told him to get the money for the ice from her purse on her chiffonier. And Muggsy laid his tongs on the floor to get the money and walked right off, leaving his tongs right where he had laid them.

17

"When friend husband came home and stumbled over the tongs, he said he had been hearing jokes about icemen all his life, but it ceased to be a joke when the iceman left his tongs in his bridal chamber. Friend husband was satisfied when explanation was made, because the most jealous husband in the world would admit no guile in Muggsy. But all the same, for the looks of things, he asked his wife to get a new iceman and to have the iceman in the future leave the piece of ice outside the door."

Under the headline "They Love Their Wives, But Oh! That Kid," *The Independent* on August 12, 1909, carried this account of a vice raid in Elizabeth City:

"Residents of Ehringhaus Street who have complained for months against an alleged house of ill fame on that reputed quiet and law-abiding thorofare, succeeded at last in lodging a complaint against said naughty house and, incidentally, brought to light such a startling array of chippie-chasers that the police are in a quandary. It is feared that if the women are prosecuted the very exposition of the notorious number of married men involved will fill the courts with divorce proceedings for months to come.

"They do say Judge Sawyer has a list of alleged frequenters of the bawdy house that would fill a side of a newspaper. There were all sorts and conditions of married men and at least two old widowers. There are small boys enough to stock a graded school. . . .

"Judge Sawyer decided it best to stir the stench as little as possible. He ordered the women to leave the neighborhood and continued the case awaiting their removal. . . ."

In 1919, *The Independent* told how an advertisement penned by one of Editor Saunders' best friends almost resulted in violence. The story went like this:

"The editor of *The Independent* came near getting a licking last week, and all on account of the deviltry of

Colonel Isaac M. Meekins. This newspaper published an article dealing with a sale advertised by J. A. Armstrong of Camden, in which it was hinted that those attending the sale would have an opportunity to imbibe Camden County 'Monkey Rum.' When that article came out in this newspaper, Mr. Armstrong came over to look for the editor of *The Independent*. Fortunately, Mr. Saunders was out of office every time Mr. Armstrong called.

"It seems that Mr. Armstrong had nothing to do with the advertising in question. He got Colonel Isaac Meekins to have his bills printed for him, and Colonel Meekins wrote the advertisement. In a spirit of mischief, he tacked the Monkey Rum suggestion onto the advertisement without Mr. Armstrong's knowledge or consent. Of course, this newspaper had no means of knowing that the thing was a joke and cheerfully makes this explanation and apology.

"This isn't the first prank of the kind ever played by Colonel Meekins. On one occasion, J. Q. A. Wood got Colonel Meekins to write a mortgage for him on the personal property of a colored man. Mr. Wood usually takes an all-inclusive mortgage. In writing the mortgage, Colonel Meekins enumerated the Negro's goods and chattels and added, 'and all other goods and chattels whatsoever, including one muzzle-loading shotgun, one picture of Abraham Lincoln, and one yellow hound dog'."

A woman who retained a law firm to demand a retraction of an alleged libel quickly found that she had made a tactical error, as the following news item attests:

"Mrs. Alice Combs, who separated from her husband, Dr. Howard J. Combs of this city, last fall, threatens suit against this newspaper. She has retained Chas. J. Schull of the law firm of Stewart and Schull of Philadelphia.

"Attorney Schull writes to the editor of this newspaper as follows:

" 'I represent Mrs. Alice Combs, who is now in Philadelphia, and there has been brought to our attention the articles contained in your issue of December 20, 1929. Your misstatement of the true facts concerning Mrs. Combs is libelous in my opinion, and in any event should be corrected. There is no question that these articles have caused Mrs. Combs an exceedingly large amount of embarrassment as well as injury to her good name and reputation.'

"To Mr. Schull's letter, the editor of this newspaper replied:

"To use the words of Al Jolson, Mrs. Alice Combs 'ain't heard nothin' yet.' If Mrs. Combs thinks she has an action against this newspaper, let her proceed. I think I am prepared to meet the lady in any tribunal.

"Mrs. Combs' 'good name and reputation' are pretty well known in this city and section and at Virginia Beach where she spent several summer seasons."

"Pluto Water in the Punch—College Boy's Practical Joke Wrecked One Christmas Party." So read the headlines on a story which almost no newspaper other than *The Independent* would have dared to print. The text follows:

"One of the most embarrassing and outrageous practical jokes ever perpetrated in Elizabeth City was pulled off during the holidays, according to an inside report furnished this newspaper by one who 'also ran.'

"At a party given in a certain home popular with the younger set, someone spiked an immense bowl of punch with a quart of Pluto Water, one of the most prompt and powerful physics available. The young people drank freely of the punch and the effects of the concoction began to be apparent in less than twenty minutes. It caught most of them in the midst of a dance and partners suddenly began to break away and desert each other without explanation.

"To add to the dilemma of the guests, there was only one

bathroom in the house and not even all the girls could await their turn there. The party broke up excitedly, some of the boys hurrying away without waiting to take their girls with them. How some of them ever got home is one of those tales that probably never will be told.

"The young man who put the Pluto Water in the punch is said to have left town under the cover of darkness, cutting his Christmas vacation short. It is said he got the idea of putting the physic in the punch at college, which is about as brilliant an idea as some chaps ever get out of a college."

Editor Saunders could find spicy story material in his saunters down Elizabeth City's Main Street almost any day. One such item, headed "Anyway, They Knew What They Wanted," went thus:

"A shy young couple appeared at the registration desk at the Virginia Dare Hotel Wednesday and asked for a room. Head Clerk Hollingsworth handed the man a pen and placed the register before him. The man registered as 'J. W. Rawlings, Berkley, Va.'

"Hollingsworth looked again at the man and again at the woman. 'Did you want a double room?' he asked.

'Yes,' said Mr. Rawlings.

'Well, you will have to register the lady,' said Hollingsworth.

"The lady stepped up and registered. She wrote: 'Mabel Lee Woodington, Brambleton, Va.'

"It is dangerous business for a hotel clerk to ask a couple if they are man and wife, and so, the two having registered separately, Hollingsworth assigned them to separate rooms. Mr. Rawlings to 814, Mabel Lee Woodington to 414.

"A bell boy showed the lady to her room on the fourth floor and then took Mr. Rawlings to his room on the eighth floor. He thought it was a pretty howdy-do that a man and woman just married couldn't have a room together.

The bell boy suggested that they go back and see the clerk.

" 'I want you to understand,' said Mr. Rawlings, 'that I am married and I can prove it. I want one room for both of us.'

" 'Well, for Heaven's sake, mister, why didn't you register as man and wife? How was I to know you were married?' said Hollingsworth.

"Hollingsworth had the register entry properly corrected and then personally showed Mr. Rawlings and his bride to one of the wedding suites on the river front.

"The man looked dolefully at the beautiful twin beds and said: 'This ain't what we want; ain't you got a room with one big bed in it?' He got what he wanted, or at least it may be presumed he did."

When the Bank Clerk one day commented to the Soda Jerker that he hadn't heard of a juicy morsel of scandal in some time, he got this earful:

"I used to hear a lot of scandal around this Volstead swill parlor," said the Bank Clerk to the Soda Jerker, "but I haven't heard a juicy morsel of scandal in several months. Has everybody become decent, or have they lost their virility?"

"From what I hear over the counter, spring is doing her usual stuff," said the Soda Jerker. "For instance, it is common report that one Main Streeter has gone to Reno to get a divorce. It is also a common report that after the national political conventions are over another Main Sreeter is going to the same place and get a divorce.

"In fact, the Reno fancy has taken hold of the imaginations of several unhappily married couples in this town, and there is rumor that a certain young grass widower is also considering a trip to Reno.

"But there are some others in our town who can't afford railroad expenses and a six-weeks stay in Reno, who are just fighting their troubles out at home. Over in the First Ward, one bird and his wife are keeping the neighborhood on edge by accusing each other of all sorts of things. The man employs a detective to trail his wife and another married man; the wife gets onto it and threatens to beat him up.

"Over in the Second Ward, another young business man is having troubles with an irate wife who accuses him of paying too much attention to a blonde frail and is raising the devil so the neighbors can hear it.

"And then there is a buxom widow of fifty years easy, who has taken a notion that life hasn't held enough romance for her, and she is getting herself talked about by her co-quettish ways with every strange man who comes to town and gets introduced to her.

"There is a certain bachelor doctor in town who is ter-ribly afraid of women, and he is being pestered to death by some woman who writes him love notes and sends him senti-mental greeting cards every two or three days.

"The funniest scandal of all has to do with a certain widower who took a transient to ride the other night and parked in the old Fair Grounds. When they got back to his car somebody had stolen all the tires and torn up the ignition. He hasn't said a word about it, but the new tires on his car were so conspicuous that somebody noticed it, and he shopped around until he got some old tires that wouldn't attract attention and call for explanations."

"Stop!" exclaimed the Bank Clerk. "I merely asked for a morsel of scandal and you have served me a barrel full. If half what you tell me is true, our town is morally sick and badly in need of a spiritual purgative. Perhaps it is good that we have religious revivals going strong in two of our leading churches right at this time."

"Hell," said the Soda Jerker, "the folks I was telling you about are all church members."

Many, many columns and news articles similar to the above appeared in the pages of *The Independent* during the approximately 30 years of its publication. They didn't prove that Elizabeth City was more amoral than any other small town in America; they did prove that Elizabeth City had a newspaper that dared hold a mirror of truth to the moral turpitude, the marital shenanigans, the pranks and the salacious gossip that went on in its midst day after day, month after month, year after year.

That was another of the features that made *The Independent* distinctive and entertaining.

IN THE VALLEY
24. OF THE SHADOW

Dad thought he was poor, so poor that he often felt inclined to pity himself. Then, suddenly, he found himself as rich as a Ford or a Rockefeller. How he came to discover the key to what he described as "the greatest gold mine on earth" is related by him in one of his more poignant narratives, titled "In the Valley of the Shadow," which appeared more than thirty years ago in *The American Magazine*.

"I had thought I was a friendless mortal," he began. "I have actually lain awake at night oppressed by the idea of my friendlessness. I would spread my hands upon the coverlet and try to name ten persons whom I could call friends, crooking one digit after another as I named them. I could never name more than six or seven.

"When I started out years ago as a personal journalist, with nothing to lose and everything to gain, and with only my own most unbusinesslike idealism to guide me, my wife never knew when she kissed me good-bye as I set out for the office in the morning whether I would come home that night with a broken head, a blackened eye, or some other disfigurement.

"I printed the news. I exposed every malpractice and every political, financial and social disorder in my little town. I made enemies of almost every important business man in town, and their hostility toward me carried their own large personal following with it. There were years when I didn't print so much as a page of local advertising in my paper.

"I was beaten up time after time, ordered to leave town by a mob of angry citizens gathering unmasked in front of my home, shot at from ambush, sued for libel on numerous occasions, and once barely escaped an application of tar and feathers. Again, I was sentenced to a six-months term to work on the roads of my county with ball and chain, a sentence that in those days was reserved almost exclusively for Negroes convicted of serious crimes. I never served that sentence, and I won almost every one of the numerous libel and slander suits on appeals to the Superior Court of the State, thanks to the high caliber of the upper tribunal of North Carolina.

"I printed things recklessly, but I was always scrupulously truthful. Still, I didn't discover my gold mine; I was covering it up all the time with cinders and brickbats.

"Even the preachers in my town—some of them—assailed me from their pulpits, because they represented the established and highly respectable social order which I so ruthlessly affronted. That brought me into a war with the preachers, and the good reverend brothers had the long end of it for years, because they had discovered that it was fairly easy for them to paint a verbal picture of me as an infidel, an atheist or an Ishmaelite—one of the eternally damned.

"Now, I wasn't an atheist at all, and I think I was just as religious-minded as any of the preachers who attacked me. But it is difficult to live in a small town and publicly expose yourself as differing in your religious views from

most of your neighbors. You can't give greater offense to
a small town than that.

"No matter that some of the leading ministers in the town
believed in my innate goodness and sympathized with me.
No matter that I believed in the brotherhood of man and
reverently accepted the leadership of Jesus. No matter that
I have tried always to deal honorably and truthfully with
my fellow man and live a life so ordered that it would bear
close scrutiny. No matter that I contributed of my time and
means to every worthwhile community enterprise, including
the church. I still found it difficult to live down the attacks
made against me, and I increasingly felt that I was squarely
on the outside in my community.

"My experience with commercialized pulpiteers and
purblind religionists over a period of years had galled and
embittered me. I had a lot of hard thoughts about most of
my neighbors in those days and would have told anyone
that a small town anywhere in America, certainly one in
the South, is no place for an intelligent and independent
spirit to abide.

"But, as is frequently the case, I had been guilty of mis-
judging my fellow townsmen. I was sitting atop a gold
mine that was to yield me fabulous wealth, and I glumly
thought I was sitting on a dross heap.

"Looking back upon those dark days, I perceive how I
fell into such a colossal error and got myself involved in
so much trouble and misunderstanding. I had been mining
human intellects all my life, and had struck little pay dirt.
I had a lot of information that most of my neighbors did
not possess, and I had made the mistake of talking to them
in a language they could not understand about things that
had no meaning for them. I had been wearing myself out
looking for something in the heads of humanity, when I had

only to pause from my strenuous labors to discover that the rare gold of human nature is not in human heads at all but in human hearts."

Then Dad related how finally he came to discover the golden key with which he unlocked "a gold mine of inexhaustible veins that yielded more treasure and revealed newer possibilities of imperishable riches, the more one explored them."

"There was an epidemic of influenza in town, and I thought I had been caught in it," he stated. "But on the third day the doctor sent for a trained nurse from a nearby city. My fever was 104 degrees; there was a frightful pain in my right side, and I was coughing up mucous tinged with blood. Another doctor was called in, and I observed the worried looks of the pair of them as they bent over my chest and back with a stethoscope. I was even then in a sort of stupor, but I knew very well what was going on. The doctors didn't tell me the truth, but they didn't have to. I knew I had pneumonia.

"And when I realized that I had pneumonia, I was sure that would be the end of me. I had been taught to dread pneumonia. Every relative of mine that had ever had it, died of it. And in recent years I had developed a diabetic tendency that kept me on a low carbohydrate diet, and specialists had repeatedly warned me to guard against pneumonia. I just knew that I was going to die.

"But even then I was too weak and ill to give it much thought. I had never thought about death before, but with it confronting me I felt I ought to think about it. My first thoughts, naturally, were of things I had left undone that I would like to do. For years I had intended making a will but had put it off, as most young men do. I worried about that.

"There were many debts I had not paid, and my business

property was still encumbered by a mortgage. My brain was muddled and not functioning very well, but I did a lot of calculating in my head. With the proceeds from my insurance, my wife could pay off all my debts, have the home and a going business intact, and a few thousand dollars in cash besides.

"A few thousand dollars isn't much. But with my other property my wife could carry on, because she had been associated with me in my work for years and in that time had developed into an astute business woman. I was glad then that I had taken her into my business and my business confidence.

"I was happy in these thoughts. What lay before me in some after-world didn't bother me. I had never in my life felt any concern about the hereafter. But on what might be my deathbed, perhaps I should think more upon these things. I dozed off into a feverish, fitful sleep. I felt myself sinking, sinking, sinking. Down, down, down into pitchy blackness I went. There seemed to be no end to the descent. After a long time I landed upon a cold, flat surface that seemed like a rock jutting out over a yawning chasm. I couldn't see much, but I had the feel of it.

"All about me were fluttering creatures excitedly whispering. Their whispers were shrill and tremulous with fright. I wondered why they whispered so much and why they were so frightened. I wished they would quit their fearful whispering. It was cold and cheerless enough down there without these fluttering, excited creatures forever whispering, whispering, whispering.

"And then came a still, warm presence that made itself felt by my side. I did not see it in the inky blackness, nor did I have any contact with it. But I sensed its presence and felt assured thereby. It did not speak in audible words, but it seemed to say to me: 'Behold, there is the Valley of the Shadow of Death; there is nothing in that Valley to fear.'

"Immediately, all the worrisome little whispering voices ceased; there was a great silence, my heart felt at ease, a tired and feverish mind was comforted. I slept in a dreamless sleep. No more did I think or care about what might lie beyond. I have since recalled that I have seen a number of persons die, and of all that I have seen die not one found anything to fear in that approaching shadow of the sable wings of Death.

"Days later, I regained consciousness sufficiently to note in detail the objects about me. The room was filled with flowers, and the air was sweet with the perfume of hyacinths, roses and white narcissus. It was to be several more days before I could understand what all the flowers were about. And still the flowers came. My wife would open them now as they were delivered by the florists and tell me that these were from this friend and those from another. There were flowers from many whom I would never have regarded as friends.

"Flowers and telegrams and letters. They began to let me see the letters and telegrams. I was overwhelmed by the love and tenderness of these messages. And then at last they let me see the newspaper clippings telling of my fight with death, and of my victory. Then, and not until then, did I realize why there were so many flowers and telegrams. For days my pillow was wet with tears of gratitude and appreciation for the goodness and compassion of my neighbors. Men whom I had grossly offended by rudeness or indifference sent me flowers.

"And the churches! The churches that I had scorned and held aloof from, and whose adherents had oft been offended by my outspoken disbelief in their sincerity, had prayed for me in my illness. While the Protestant churches prayed, the Catholics held mass for me, and down in the Negro quarter of the town the good colored people held special prayer services for me in some of their churches in their own fervent way.

"In a few days my wife placed in my hands a little book containing the names of scores and scores of neighbors and fellow townsmen who had come in person or telephoned to my home offering every assistance to my family in my illness and conveying every good and sincere wish for my recovery. With tears trickling down her cheeks, my wife told me that she could not have endured the strain of my terrible illness but for the prayers of the town and the goodness of neighbors from far and near."

This came as an almost unbelievable revelation to my father, and this marked a turning point in his relations with his fellow man. He told the story in these words:

"And then I began to see life in a new and lovelier perspective. I, who had thought the world cold, stupid, indifferent and friendless, came out of a long illness to find that I actually had thousands of friends whom I had never appreciated, and whose inherent goodness I had never discovered.

"Men and women who had never received a favor at my hands in all their lives put themselves out of their way to comfort my wife and children, and sought an opportunity to help me. A humble working man who remembered that I had always spoken to him in passing spent his hard-earned money to buy fruit for me which I could not eat.

"Another rugged soul, who was himself sick with a cold, shouldered his gun and tramped through fields of snow and slush to kill some birds that he thought I would enjoy in my convalescence. One of the few foreigners in town sent me flowers. Some sweet little girls in the primary department of one of the Sunday Schools were moved, by the prayers they heard made for me, to make up a purse of pennies and buy a potted plant for my sick-room.

"A good fellow who had seen his blood relations mercilessly flayed in my iconoclastic editorials, and who must have had many bitter thoughts of me, had two bottles of precious prewar whisky hidden away in his home. He liked his whisky and had high anticipations of enjoying his last two bottles of the old-time stuff some day. You couldn't buy whisky legally in North Carolina at that time, but when he heard one of my physicians say that a little 'pure stuff' would be good for me, he sent me his whisky. I could cite dozens of similar instances of men and women, who had no cause to be friendly to me, putting themselves out to help me when they thought I needed their help.

"And then I thought that all the suffering and inconvenience I had experienced in those dreary weeks in bed were worth all they had cost in physical discomfort and financial loss, because I had discovered the inherent and blessed goodness of humanity. One who will not learn some other way has to suffer greatly to learn that humanity is tender of heart and inherently good, and that he has many friends long unsuspected as such.

"When a fellow is up on his hind legs fighting for himself, and in every way able to take care of himself, no one is likely to pay very much attention to him. Neighbors may pass him by hurriedly with a conventional greeting or a perfunctory nod. He proceeds to hustle for himself, and to carry the impression that no one cares about him very much.

"One forgets that one's neighbors have to hustle for themselves, too, and are so absorbed in their own troubles and afflictions that they really don't have time to be as considerate and sociable as they would like to be. That was my case.

"We are prone to forget that the other fellow has his problems. We may live next door to and have frequent social intercourse with a neighbor who is harassed by financial difficulties, or afflicted with a physical disorder which he nurses in secret. He never tells his troubles, and we never know. Indeed, we often wonder why he seldom smiles. We may even set him down as a grouch when, if we could only know the truth, he may be staggering under some grievous financial, physical or mental handicap that we ourselves could not bear.

"We may condemn him for his unneighborliness, his lack of patriotism, lack of civic-mindedness or indifference to community activities, the while he has just all he can do to keep a roof over his family and send his children to school.

"But beneath the mask of indifference which men appear to wear in the midst of the terrific amount of economic struggle in which they are absorbed beat hearts that are full of warmth and the milk of human kindness. In the mad struggle of life they may cuff and kick one another in their heedlessness, but let one fall or cry for help and a community will rush to his rescue to lift him up, sustain him and comfort him. The fallen one may have been a great transgressor, but his faults are forgiven and forgotten when he is in need of friendship and succor.

"We expect and demand too much of human reason, and human reasoning is therefore often disappointing. It is in the hearts of men that one will find much gold; it is in the subconscious mind or heart of every man where you will surely find a spark of divinity itself, a spark that may be revived into a generous flame of love and sympathy for one who is afflicted.

"Sickness, pain and affliction are, after all, necessary and

18

beneficent phenomena of life. But for distress, perhaps none of the higher human virtues, none of those noble, godlike qualities that distinguish men from brutes, would have been developed.

"Out of much suffering has man evolved those divine attributes of pity, tenderness, love and self-giving. In the presence of sickness and pain, he first learned to pity, then to love. In his ministries to the sick and afflicted, he learned to forget self and made that most wonderful of all human discoveries, that in service to others the greatest joy and satisfaction of life is most surely found."

Dad concluded the narrative of his Great Discovery with these words:

"As I lay convalescing, I thought what a wonderful world to live in this eventually will be when we have found some more ready key than human pain and suffering to unlock the hearts of men. The words of Jesus, assuring His disciples that the Kingdom of God was within them, came to me with a sudden new and vivid meaning. The kingdom of heaven is verily at hand, the brotherhood of man is not a remote ideal!

"Day by day the flowers withered in my room. One by one the vases that had held them in the beauty and glory of their freshness were removed. I knew that I was getting well. My neighbors were back about the business of looking after their own families and their own affairs.

"But by this time I knew that I had found the key to the greatest gold mine on earth, and I knew that I should henceforth and forever have a greater love for my fellow man, feel greater security in his society, and have a greater faith in him and his potentialities.

"I still walk down the streets of Elizabeth City and to all outward appearances I may seem to be the same. But I am not and can never be the same W. O. Saunders. My little excursion into the Valley of the Great Shadow, and the revelation of the beauty of human nature that it brought me, at once softened me and made me a more humble, a more grateful and a more reverent individual.

"There has come back to me a line which I read years and years ago, and which had little meaning for me at the time: 'In a world where death is, I have no time for hate.'

"I am no longer so much interested in yardsticks for measuring the mentality of folks. What they think and don't think doesn't matter so much any more. It is what they feel that matters. God grant me the wisdom and understanding to look yet closer into the hearts of men!"

On another occasion, writing on the subject of friends and friendship, Dad said:

"One's truest friends are those who pay him the compliment of expecting greatness of him. I have had such friends. And as I contemplate the going down of the sun on my life, I realize that they are and ever have been the source of any strength, any courage and any stability that I have ever exhibited."

One such friend, R. A. Lamb, asked permission to write a personal commentary on Editor Saunders for publication in *The Independent's* Silver Jubilee edition on June 8, 1933. In this article Lamb said, among other things:

"To say that he has been and still is a fighting editor is putting it mildly. He has ever been a real hell-raising crusader in behalf of the common people, regardless of color or creed. He has been a wild bull in the public china closet, but a most unusual kind of bull in that he unerringly has smashed only those old pieces of china that were outmoded, unsightly and uselessly cluttering the shelves. Moreover, he has scoured the ancient closet with very hot water, caused it to be put in good order, and fought successfully to preserve the really valuable pieces, not only from less sensible bulls that would destroy the entire collection, but also from others that would help themselves to what they saw displayed. . . .

"A quarter of a century is a long time to suffer hell-fire and damnation in a fight for one's fellow man. But W. O. Saunders has done it with a smile, successfully producing at the same time a delightfully different newspaper. He has taught us many things, especially the joy of independence and the beauty of clean living. He has done much to keep the waters of progress from stagnating, and has proved that a narrow mind is a closed mind. Today he is scarred but not bitter, a little weary but undaunted. For you and me he still carries on. . . ."

Another tried and true friend was W. G. Cox, whose friendship for my Dad never faltered in nearly half a century. When anyone spoke harshly of my father in the presence of Bill Cox, he could be counted upon to respond gently but firmly with words to this effect: "What you say of Will Saunders is not true. I have known him intimately all my life. He is a vigorous personality and a man of many interests. He may make an occasional mistake, *but his heart is right, and was always right, I know.*"

Bill Cox's words bring to mind a paragraph that Dad wrote in his newspaper's 25th anniversary edition, wherein he said:

"I have been thundered at from pulpits, from the bar and from hostile editorial columns as an iconoclast, an assassin of character, a destroyer of reputation and a generally destructive force. In my own heart I know that I have never attacked any man or woman whose life, public or private, did not deserve the light of publicity. And whenever you hear any man or woman inveighing against *The Independent* and calling it bad, you can make a mental note that there is something in the life of that man or woman, or of some blood relation, that will not bear investigation. The enemy of this newspaper, wherever you find him, has a secret if not a known cause to fear a newspaper, that stands as a watchman upon the walls, an ever vigilant sentinel, deeply conscious of its obligations to human welfare and human progress and courageous enough to tell the truth, whether folks like it or not."

A reading of the record would lead one to the conclusion that many a city, county, state and nation today could profit handsomely from having such a "watchman upon the walls" as The Independent Man.

CORN COBS AND
25.   BACKHOUSES

My father held a belief that most of the funnier stories with which humans regale themselves are either sexual or excremental in nature. Accordingly, he was not above using an occasional story in *The Independent* that was perhaps a bit bawdy or risque without being really offensive or vulgar.

In 1931, for example, he wrote an editorial titled "The Corn Cob" which went as follows:

"Why discriminate in the matter of preserving American traditions? Why remember Roanoke Island, Jamestown, Plymouth Rock, Yorktown, Gettysburg: Why preserve Mount Vernon, Monticello and Arlington? Why drag old spinning wheels out of attics and enshrine them in our parlors; resurrect the candlesticks and candle moulds, fire tongs and door knockers of our ancestors; glorify old fashioned samplers and crazy quilts and establish fireside industries to fabricate handmade furniture like our ancestors made? Why so much emphasis upon these things of other years if not to remind us of our humble origins and impress upon us the virtue of the simple ruggedness, worthiness and integrity of these bygones? Why not then do something to preserve the place of the homely corn cob in the great American heritage?

"Think of the part the corn cob played in the life of our ancestors! Toilet tissues had not been perfected; in fact, they didn't even have toilets. Sears, Roebuck catalogs and Lydia E. Pinkham almanacs were not available; the daily newspaper had not come into general circulation. The seldom newspaper was, indeed, cut into strips and twisted into fire lighters and kept in a vase on the mantle. Matches were that scarce even when I was a little boy. Our ancestors used corn cobs, millions of corn cobs. Don't laugh.

"The corn cob was the most sanitary instrument nature ever devised for the use to which it was devoted by our ancestors, and human invention has not improved on it. Nobody's finger ever slipped through a corn cob. And the corn cob was non-skidding. After use, it was thrown on the compost heap to make rich humus for our farms and gardens.

"We hear much said of the decay of modern teeth due to soft living. We eat soft foods and don't give our teeth and gums the exercise nature intended they should have for their welfare and preservation. The result is four out of five have pink tooth brush. Is it unreasonable to suggest that other afflictions to which we moderns are generally subject may be due to the fact that we are denied that luxurious and exhilarating massage that the corn cob gave our ancestors and which brought the blood to now weak and flabby parts, strengthening the muscles, invigorating the cuticle and inducing a post-anal vigor and healthfulness unknown to modern dupes of soft and scented tissues?

"We are constantly reminded of the alarming possibilities of pink tooth brush. More distressing is that pink that the advertising pages of our moron-minded magazines speak not of. This unadvertised pink is due, I am firmly convinced, to the fact that in abandoning the corn cob we sacrificed the stimulating effect of the corn cob on the hemorrhoidal arteries, resulting in the weakening and degeneracy of our organs of elimination.

"Let us not forget the lowly but virtuous corn cob. It was one of the most intimate hand-maidens of our rugged ancestors. It was with Capt. John White at Roanoke Island, with John Smith at Jamestown, with Washington at Valley Forge and with Lee at Appomattox. They say that the first colonists were immediately introduced to tobacco. I say, not so. Search diligently in the archives of the past and I am sure you will find that a thoughtful Indian first fetched Amadas and Barlowe a handful of corn cobs when they landed on Roanoke Island in 1584. They thought about the tobacco later.

"Something should be done to preserve for posterity memories of that early American institution, the corn cob. Think of everything we owe to the corn cob! It was the outstanding sanitary and hygienic instrument of its era. In fact, I don't know how Elizabethan England came to be so fastidious and snooty without corn cobs. I rise to revive and glorify the memory of the corn cob. In fact, I think I shall found a society to be known as the Venerable and Patriotic Knighthood of the Corn Cob, only those who have known their corn cobs to be eligible for membership. The list of eligibles would include nearly all of North Carolina's most distinguished citizens. I should like to have their reactions before proceeding with an organization."

The reaction not only of distinguished Tar Heels but also of distinguished citizens in Washington, New York and many other points was one of great mirth and glee. Of course, Dad had his tongue in his cheek and never intended to found any such organization of onetime corn cob users, but he had a lot of fun in publishing the suggestion.

A mind that could reminisce in the above fashion on a

subject such as the corn cob naturally would find interest in the kindred subject of privies, or backhouses. So it was altogether appropriate that in 1931 the Bank Clerk and Soda Jerker would discuss this subject in a column titled "The Greatest Cultural Influence on Earth." It went thus:

"There ought to be an increase in newspaper subscriptions in Dare County pretty soon," remarked the Bank Clerk to his friend, the Soda Jerker.

"How so?" asked the Bank Clerk.

"Well, I see that the CWA is putting a crew of men to work to build 150 sanitary privies for families that ain't got 'em," said the Soda Jerker.

"I don't see what that's got to do with newspaper circulation," said the Bank Clerk.

"It's got everything to do with it," said the Soda Jerker. "You take folks who never had a backhouse on their farms and, as a rule, they were just that backward they never subscribed to or read a newspaper. Now there ain't anything in the world that promotes the reading habit among folks like having a nice, comfortable privy to settle down in and enjoy a newspaper. You give one hundred and fifty families in Dare County so many nice, comfortable privies and it won't be many weeks before they'll be looking around for something to read. Aunt Meg and Willie and Susie and all the rest of the family will nag and bedevil Ma and Pa until they take a newspaper.

"Yes, sir, I'm telling you that the greatest civilizing and cultural institution that civilized man has ever devised is the little backyard comfort station, commonly called the backhouse. You never heard of a man being self educated in a fence lock or a pine thicket, but give him a backhouse and a mail order catalog and he'll be learning to read in no time."

"I never thought about it before," said the Bank Clerk,

"but by heck I don't know but what you're right. And that reminds me of a yarn that Carl Goerch tells in his weekly, *The State*. He says that one of our lady relief workers was filling in the necessary form for a middle-aged farmer the other day and came to the question relative to house rent, etc.

" 'Do you owe any back house rent?' " she asked.

"There was no answer, so she repeated the question. The old man became sort of restless and fidgety-like but still said nothing. The lady tapped her pencil on her desk and said: 'You know I have to write down these answers for you; Tell me—do you owe any back house rent?'

"The old man eyed her indignantly and also somewhat superciliously. 'Lady,' he finally said, 'we ain't had no backhouse on our farm for nigh onto eight years'."

This dialogue foreshadowed a totally unexpected financial windfall for *The Independent* in the year 1934.

One of the reasons why Dad never made more than a comfortable living from his newspaper business was the fact that he held pronounced and unorthodox views about advertising that didn't lend themselves to money making. For many years a small box at the top of the front page proclaimed to the world that *"The Independent* prints no whiskey, patent medicine or other questionable advertising."

Another kind of advertising which Dad regarded as cheap and degrading was the so-called "co-op page." Every reader of newspapers has seen this type of page, in which the copywriter builds a lot of ballyhoo around any convenient subject, such as the opening of a new bank or hardware store, "Go to Church Next Sunday," National Boy Scout Week, opening of the baseball season or Clean Up-Paint Up Week. With a full page layout or a double page spread, depending on how he gauges the market, the advertising solicitor canvasses the town for suckers. Likely prospects for a "co-op page" with the right kind of appeal are seldom lacking, the chief victims being those advertisers who do not advertise regularly but who buy occasional newspaper space just to see their name in print and to let their fellow townsmen know that they, like all good Congressmen, are wholeheartedly in favor of God, Motherhood and Safety.

Impelled by economic necessity, Dad sold his share of "co-op pages" in *The Independent*, but never relished the business and made no attempt to conceal his contempt for it. A local contemporary, on the other hand, had worked the "co-op" racket to such extremes that no one would have been greatly surprised to see it run a "co-op page" of neatly spaced boxes devoted to cards of condolence upon the passing of some prominent citizen of the town.

One day in the winter of 1934, Dad was in the office of a building supply dealer in Elizabeth City when in walked the ad man from the other newspaper soliciting advertising for a "co-op page" publicizing a Made in Elizabeth City Exhibit. The Chamber of Commerce had persuaded a few local manufacturers to utilize window space in vacant stores to exhibit their products. Vacant store windows on Main Street look bad for a small town. So the local daily newspaper seized upon this incident to work up a "co-op," selling its checkerboard spaces to the manufacturers to call attention to their exhibits.

The building supply dealer took one of the ads with a wry face and then said to the ad solicitor: "I wonder what you'll spring on us next? I honestly expect you fellows to work up a 'co-op' on a backhouse before you're done with it."

This suggestion struck Dad as so ludicrously funny that he laughed aloud, to his own embarrassment and the discomfiture of the ad man from the other paper. He was still chuckling over the incident when he got back to his office.

Dad might have forgotten the matter had he not picked up a copy of the Raleigh (N.C.) *News & Observer* a few days later and had his attention arrested by the following headline:

CWA BUILDS TWENTY-FIVE MILES OF SANITARY PRIVIES IN NORTH CAROLINA.

2,493 New and Modern Pit Privies Replace
Just So Many Insanitary Backhouses in
Rural Sections Throughout the State

There followed an article written by M. F. Trice, Assistant Engineer of the N. C. State Board of Health, describing a pit privy construction program undertaken in ninety-eight of the one hundred counties of North Carolina by the Civil Works Administration. Actually, 21,493 of the new sanitary conveniences had been completed and approximately 15,000 more were planned or under construction.

Dad read on with increasing interest and amazement from the *News & Observer* article:

"The present-day privy is a far cry from the conventional 'backhouse' of a generation ago. The privy of another generation was no more than a crude shelter in which

> All day, fat spiders spun their webs
> To catch the buzzing flies
> That flitted to and from the house,
> Where Ma was baking pies.

"The new-model buildings are identical as two peas in a pod. Whether you find them nestled among the sand dunes of the coastal section or perched upon the craggy eminence of the mountains; whether constructed by the fisherfolk of the east or by the hardy mountaineers of the west—the design is the same. They are the 1934 model privy, and are as standardized as is the production of an automobile factory. And they should be of one design for many reasons, none of which is more potent, perhaps, than that a person may feel at home in one, no matter in what part of the state he may find himself—that is indeed a comfort.

"Each privy that has been erected is a citadel against the spread of disease and death, and as such protects not only the personnel of the household it serves but safeguards the health of the neighbor's household as well. Thus, a series of privies in a community set up an interlocking bulwark against the most insidious and persistent foe of mankind—disease."

Dad learned from our own county CWA Administrator that 400 of the new CWA privies had been built in the county of Pasquotank. Harking back to the incident in the building supply dealer's office, Dad was seized with a devilish impulse, and thus was conceived probably the most unique, most audacious and most hilarious advertising stunt ever staged by a newspaper anywhere in America.

The Independent, with tongue in cheek, devoted a full page to a "co-op" glorifying the CWA's backhouse program in North Carolina. Here follows the full text of that famous satire, including the individual advertisements, all of which were fictional, of course, having been cooked up by Dad with some help from me.

FORWARD PASQUOTANK!

Publicizing an event of Unique Social and Economic
Importance

The construction of 400 sanitary privies in this county under the supervision of the State Board of Health is something of which any county should be tremendously proud. Thanks to the CWA, scores of old-fashioned, un-sanitary backhouses have been replaced by modern privies, built according to the most approved methods as suggested by the State Board of Health. Pasquotank is indeed to be congratulated upon this progressive step.

Some wag might say "Go way back and sit down," but enterprising supply houses in this "co-op" advertisement cannot ignore the suggestion of this newspaper that they take advantage of this unique opportunity to publicize themselves and their respective wares. After all, 400 brand new sanitary privies in our county ought to be as important as a new hotel or a "Made in Elizabeth City Exhibit."

Up to this point, the text had been in a light and breezy vein but was still believeable as an introduction to a bona fide "co-op" page. Then came the advertisements—and the tipoff.

The Pasquotank Chamber of Commerce (with emphasis on Chamber) led off the "advertising" and under the heading "We Point With Pride," gave readers of the page this message:

"The Pasquotank Chamber of Commerce shares Pasquotank County's pride in connection with the 400 new CWA-built privies. After all, the backhouse is something of an educational institution—a seat of culture, so to speak. Many great ideas have been born in them, and thousands of persons have learned to read in them."

Warming up to the subject, the next advertisement advised readers "Don't Use Corn Cobs." It elaborated:

"Are you one of those who still use corn cobs and Sears, Roebuck catalogs? Corn cobs, we admit, have their advantages and are preferable to the ordinary toilet tissue. But you get the same roughage, plus greater comfort and convenience, through the use of BUTT'S TISSUE, the one and only genuine skid-proof tissue on the market today.

Newspapers and catalogs are not printed with medicated inks. Beware of them, too. Be sensible—use BUTT'S TISSUE, 'The Non-Skid Kind'."

Then came an ad urging privy owners to give their sanitary "necessary" a modern note by furnishing it with an inflated rubber cushion. Said the ad: "This commodity not only will be a joy and comfort to Grandad but is supplied in sizes to fit any hole from the slender hole of Sister Sue to the tiny hole of Baby Lou. Ask for this inexpensive Luxury at the Firerock Rubber Co."

The Rumble Radio Co. told readers to "BE MODERN," adding "Don't be content with Sears, Roebuck catalogs and Lydia E. Pinkham almanacs for your privy diversion. Let us install a radio in your Johnny. It will encourage regularity of habit, offset personal static and mitigate the pains of interference."

Under the headline "ODORLESS BACKHOUSES," the Grunt & Strain Drug Co. offered this rather frank message: "There is a carpenter at Nags Head who claims he builds odorless toilets. He builds 'em that way, all right, but they don't stay that way. There is no such thing as an odorless backhouse. But you can assist nature and the olfactory sense by the use of deodorants. We recommend Backus incense burners for every modern privy."

The Eureka Electric Co.'s ad was one which every privy user could readily understand. It reads: "It's nice to own a new privy, but it's no good to you on a dark night if you can't find it. Don't fumble and stumble around in the dark when hastening to heed nature's call. Buy a good flashlight and eliminate this bother. How annoying it is to miss the hole because you can't see it! How much more disconcerting it is if the person who preceded you missed it! It's easy to locate what you are looking for if you have a flashlight."

"We are proud," proclaimed the Backus Hardware Co. (Successors to Piddle Bros. Co.), that "Backus hardware—hinges, nails, etc.—was selected after rigid test for the 400 new sanitary privies for Pasquotank. Both the State Board of Health and CWA are exacting in their specifications for such hardware, with emphasis on its reactions to sodium chloride. It must be rust-resistant. We have the hardware for a bank or a backhouse."

The importance of a good roof to a privy was stressed in the advertising message of the Anti-Alibi Roofing Co., which stated candidly: "You can't help it if you find that the seat has been wetted through human carelessness. But there's no need to let it get wet from rain. Our roofing is weather-proof; that's why it was selected for use on the new CWA privies."

"Enjoy the Luxury of Your Modern Johnny," advised the manufacturers of O. B. Quick, "The Mineral Oil with a Scram," adding: "You couldn't enjoy your old-fashioned Johnny with its flies, drafts and odors. You will want to visit your new State Board of Health model often. To get the most frequent use possible out of your new Rest Room, get the mineral oil habit. And don't let its tastelessness and odorlessness fool you. It's the greatest liquidating agent we know."

A real practical suggestion came from an insecticide maker, who pointed out that: "In even the most sanitary privies, pesky flies and mosquitoes will make their appearance. Despite all the precautions taken by the State Board of Health, you can't keep all the flies and mosquitoes out. And what pests they are—distracting your mind if you are trying to read or, if you fight them, taking energy which you need for your real purpose. Keep a spray gun on hand, and keep it filled with Black Flag."

"EUREKA! Amazing New Discovery," was the exuberant salutation of the next advertiser, who proclaimed: "Throw away your corn cobs, your catalogs and your toilet tissue. We have made a discovery that makes these things unnecessary. CELLOPHANOLAX—The Laxative that Contains Cellophane—A boon to mankind. The greatest forward step in personal sanitation since the bathtub was invented."

And finally, the Three-Holer Lumber Co. concluded the page with an ad congratulating Pasquotank County on "a progressive step of the first magnitude" and asserting its pride at having furnished the lumber for the county's 400 new sanitary privies.

The public demand for this audacious and rollicking satire was tremendous, and it soon prompted this discussion between the loquacious Bank Clerk and Soda Jerker:

"One of the fellows in my boarding house just got back from the World's Fair. He motored up and back. And he tells me that every filling station he stopped at between here and Chicago somebody spotted his Elizabeth City license plate and wanted to know about W. O. Saunders, *The Independent* and North Carolina's twenty-five miles of new-fangled backhouses. That backhouse edition of *The Independent* has certainly spread the fame of Elizabeth City and Pasquotank County." The Bank Clerk speaking.

"Yeah," said the Soda Jerker. "I notice that the Magazine HOOEY lifted *The Independent's* privy 'co-op' page and reproduced it in its September issue without asking *The Independent's* consent or respecting its copyright. But if violations of copyright priviliges don't mean any more than violations of NRA codes, *The Independent* won't get far with a suit against that HOOEY outfit."

"The American sense of humor is funny," mused the Bank Clerk. "Chic Sales wrote a little book called 'The Specialist' dealing with an old jackleg carpenter whose specialty was

19

building backhouses and who was proud of his workmanship. That little book sold into a million copies. And back in 1931 *The Independent* published an editorial deploring the passing of the corn cob as a toilet accessory. That editorial was incorporated in a book of Saunders' editorials and it is about the only thing that made the book sell."

"Speaking of corn cobs," said the Soda Jerker, "I reckon you heard the story they tell on Irving S. Cobb?"

"No, I never heard the story," said the Bank Clerk. "Let's have it."

"It was this way," said the Soda Jerker. "A former North Carolinian went into Irving S. Cobb's office in New York with a friend, introducing himself to Mr. Cobb thusly:

"Mr. Cobb, may I introduce you to my friend George M. Hicks of North Carolina?"

Cobb said: "Hicks, huh. Do you know what we do with 'hicks' in New York?"

The North Carolinian replied slowly: "N-o-o-o, I don't, but I know what we do with cobs in Pasquotank County, North Carolina."

Well, the BC & SJ couldn't let the subject drop there, and a week or so later they were back on it in this discussion:

"Funny how the whole country seems to have gotten a kick out of that CWA Privy Page that appeared in *The Independent* a few weeks ago." said the Bank Clerk. "And they tell me at *The Independent* offices that big New York bankers, stock brokers, Wall Street lawyers, U. S. Senators and executives of big corporations have ordered copies of the paper by the hundreds. You wouldn't think that big men surrounded by every modern convenience and luxury would be interested in a satire on a commonplace thing like backhouses!"

"You forget from what humble beginnings most of the big men of this country came," replied the Soda Jerker.

"I'll bet my shirt that old man John D. Rockefeller, Henry Ford, Will Rogers, Irving S. Cobb and most of the other celebrities you can name have passed many an hour in an old-fashioned backhouse. And you can bet your plus fours that President Roosevelt himself is familiar with them. If he didn't use them in his youth, he certainly formed an acquaintance with them when he found Warm Springs, Ga."

"Our lives are compassed about by memories," continued the Soda Jerker, "and some of the most intimate memories of our childhood are associated with the primitive three-holer back on the farm. We don't discuss these particular memories until some wag breaks out with a wisecrack that opens up the subject, and then we suddenly break into laughter because we've just been waiting for years for someone to drag the subject out into the open. The Saunders tribe did just that thing in the biggest possible way when they publicized the construction of 25 miles of backhouses by the CWA in North Carolina and had a lot of fun with the project. The country was ready for a big belly laugh, and what's funnier than thoughts of an old-fashioned backhouse?"

"It isn't funny when one of the blamed things blows up with you in it," said the Bank Clerk.

"I never did hear of one blowing up!" exclaimed the Soda Jerker. "Tell me, did you ever hear of one blowing up?"

"Yes," said the Bank Clerk. "I have heard the story somewhere. It seems that a certain cautious housewife had bought a gallon of naphtha for use in her spring house cleaning and found she had about half the naphtha on hand when she finished her cleaning. Afraid to leave the stuff in the house and risk a fire or explosion, she took it out back and poured it down a hole in the privy. Her old man had occasion to go out back a few minutes later. He settled on one of the holes, filled his pipe, lit it and prepared to enjoy himself. He lifted the lid from the next hole and dropped the match he had lit his pipe with down the hole. Instantly, there was a terrific explosion, the sides of the Johnny were blown out and the old man was blown bodily into a manure pile fifty feet away. The neighbors dug the old man out of the manure heap and examined him for broken bones or other injuries. Except for being stunned and dazed, the old man seemed to be quite all right. And then someone asked him how it all happened.

"'I dunno,' said the old man: 'It musta been somethin' I et'.'"

In April 1934, Editor Saunders finally told just how he felt about the success of the privy page. In an editorial titled "You May Call It the Irony of Life," he wrote:

"It seems that I have again suddenly leaped into national fame of a sort, on account of a bit of sarcastic and audacious humor perpetrated by my son and myself in the March 2 issue of *The Independent*.

"The CWA was boasting of its major contribution to the health, comfort and sanitary welfare of the State in the building of 25 miles of new sanitary privies in North Carolina. Pasquotank got a half-mile of these nifty new 'field parlors.'

"Now it happens in Elizabeth City that everytime something or somebody does something unusual, the newspapers chase around among local advertisers and hold them up for a whole page 'co-op' ad celebrating or glorifying the event. Why not a 'co-op' ad glorifying the CWA privy project? Why not? And so I passed the idea on to the junior editor and between us we produced the curious results in *The Independent's* issue of March 2.

"Anticipating a demand for extra copies, we printed 500 copies in excess of the needs of our bona fide circulation. The 500 extra copies were snapped up in a few days and we reprinted 1500 more. Reprint has followed reprint until the total circulation of that memorable issue is well in excess of 15,000 copies and promises to run into many thousands more. It seems to have proved the laugh hit of the decade and laid Chic Sales's 'Specialist' in the shade. One day's mail last week brought orders for 700 copies. Orders for 500 copies a day are not unusual. And they come from all parts of the United States. From Washington, Philadelphia, Boston, New York, Pittsburgh, Cleveland, St. Louis, Atlanta, Miami, Memphis, Dallas and Frisco; from Maine to Texas; from the Great Lakes to the Gulf; from the Atlantic to the Pacific.

"Editors of newspapers and magazines of national circulation and big advertisers order them; and executives of big manufacturing establishments and financial institutions; Army and Navy officers; college professors and lawyers. And for this I am famous!

"Back in the summer of 1929 I came out on the streets of Elizabeth City in my pajamas as a challenge to masculine sartorial stuffiness. I finally had to go to New York and let Fifth Avenue and Broadway see my demonstration of hot weather comfort for men. And for that I became famous on both sides of the Atlantic.

"The truly noteworthy things I have done receive scant notice. The fact that I have made a singlehanded fight for religious freedom and intellectual liberty in a Southern rural stronghold of fundamentalist bigotry for more than a quarter of a century has had little acclaim. The fact that I opposed the entry of America into World War I and declared back in 1916 that Woodrow Wilson was not keeping America out of the war, but was secretly mobilizing the resources of the Nation to throw America into the war when and if he was re-elected, brought me only the cordial dislike of the flag idolators. The fact that this newspaper is a pioneer crusader against medical quackery and fraud and has never once admitted an internal patent medicine to its advertising columns gets no notice. But I walk out on the streets in pajamas on a sweltering summer day or print a satire on new-fangled backhouses, and the whole country gives me a big hand. Maybe I don't feel like a poor fish!"

Even so, the privy page did bring in a few bucks at a time when they were much needed, it did bring The Independent Man national fame "of a sort," and it certainly afforded him a lot of fun.

26. THIRTY

The Independent Man rarely was found lacking in opinions
—clear, forthright and often sulphurous opinions—on
almost any subject within the public domain. And he could
express his opinion forcibly and lucidly, so there could be
no mistaking as to where he stood.

One subject on which he was particularly articulate, being
so close to it and so acutely affected by it, was freedom of
the press. I suppose his opinions on this subject had some
roots in the personal experience of seeing a rival newspaper
that openly pandered to the powers that he offended thrive
on advertising that he might have commanded had he
elected to play the newspaper game the way it was supposed
to be played.

Here are some acidulous thoughts Dad penned on freedom of the press after he had been in the business a long
time:

"We boast much of the freedom of the press in this crazy
republic of ours. I can say without fear of successful con-
tradiction, out of an experience of more than a quarter of
a century in writing, editing and publishing, that the freedom of the press is just another big American joke like the
wisdom and integrity of bankers, the sound economic sense

of our business leaders, and the honesty and intelligence of our lawmakers.

"The most dependent, servile, spineless, opinionless and fearstricken thing I know, with the exception of a certain class of ministerial brethren, is the average American daily or weekly newspaper.

"If your big metropolitan daily is owned body and soul by its bankers and big advertisers, just so is the soul of the average small town newspaper owned by its advertisers, the little merchants on Main Street who control the bulk of its advertising patronage and upon whose purchases of advertising space its existence depends.

"No newspaper can succeed without advertising in this age of cheap newspapers. The price of a modern newspaper, even a small town newspaper, probably does not cover the cost of its white paper and postage. Often the publisher spends as much to get circulation as his circulation yields him, if not more—quite a bit more. Your modern newspaper lives by and through its advertising patronage.

"Show me a successful newspaper and I will show you a sycophant and panderer to its sources of advertising. Take the measure of the business leadership of your community and you have the spiritual, moral and intellectual measure of your average newspaper. Great public wrongs must cry to high heaven for correction before the newspaper that might offend some business interest concerned will dare to notice it.

"Your average small town business man and advertiser is himself an opinionless creature who caters to an opinionless public and who takes no stand on any great public or moral issue until public sentiment has crystallized and business expediency demands that he align himself for or against. That is one reason why lying, thieving, grafting politicians have had such an easy time of it in America; the business leaders who should be the great moral and civic leaders in their community are weaseling weaklings playing the game of you-tickle-me-and-I'll-tickle-you.

"Let the Grand Wizard and Boss Mac have their way so long as they and their sons and daughters trade at my store! If a ring of thieving politicians stole both the town hall and the courthouse, the pecuniary loss of his stake in the town and county would not be so great as his personal pecuniary loss of the trade that the ringsters threw his way. Every yardstick for the measurement of moral, social and political values is in most hands but the lengthened shadow of a bank note."

In *The Independent's* twenty-fifth anniversary or Silver Jubilee edition, Dad made this statement:

"It has been a hard, bitter fight bringing this newspaper through twenty-five years in a changing world, often without capital and often without friends in whom one could place all confidence. *The Independent* has never made any money. It has always plowed much of its income back into the business, building up a physical plant requisite to the publishing and printing needs of its community."

As a matter of fact, there were times during the depression years of the Thirties when our family would have suffered financially had it been entirely dependent upon *The Independent's* circulation and advertising revenue. Indeed, there were months when Dad's income from magazine articles exceeded the income from his newspaper.

The job printing plant was another economic boon, and the same Joseph P. Knapp who was instrumental in arranging Dad's entree to magazine writing was enormously helpful on this score, too. Mr. Knapp enjoyed shooting ducks and geese in season at his Mackay Island estate near Elizabeth City and, like many another wealthy sportsman, he became interested in conservation. This interest led to the formation of a non-profit wildfowl conservation group called Ducks Unlimited. Among other things, this organization required a considerable amount of printed matter.

Mr. Knapp, of course, had virtually a printing empire at his disposal, but it occurred to him that it would be a great help to his crusading newspaper friend, W. O. Saunders, if some of this printing could be thrown the way of *The Independent's* job shop. He offered Dad a lucrative job calling for the printing of 50,000 promotional brochures. Dad reluctantly confessed that his printing plant was not equipped to take on a job of such magnitude. Mr. Knapp then went on Dad's note of the purchase of a high-speed automatic job press and made an advance payment on the Ducks Unlimited printing contract that was sufficient to take care of the down payment on the press. Another instance of luck!

There were weeks, too, when the provender at the Saunders home might have been a little on the meager side but for receipts from the Swan Publishing Company. This was a sideline enterprise Dad had set up, with the dissemination of rib-tickling "literature" for mankind's amusement and diversion as one purpose, but the garnering of some much needed extra income as the primary motive.

The job printing business was a little slack in those depression years, and Dad reasoned that if he couldn't keep his presses and his printers busy on letterheads and business forms that tradesmen would buy, perhaps he could keep them busy turning out pamphlets that fun-loving individuals might buy in substantial numbers.

Items published by the Swan Publishing Co. were strictly for laughs or "kicks." One of the funniest of the little booklets was one titled "Runt, the Tale of a Piddlin' Pup, in Ten Piddles and a Puddle," written by Dr. Cy Thompson. This item sold by the thousands.

Another best-seller in the Swan collection was James Whitcomb Riley's "Passing of the Old Backhouse," which sold in great numbers before *The Independent* published its "backhouse" co-op page. Other Swan items included: Benjamin Franklin's "Advice to a Young Man in Love," a letter taken from Franklin's private papers after his death; Eugene Fields' "Little Willie," the "Prospectus of the Aromatic Muffled Bean Co. Ltd.," and a little pamphlet Dad dashed off on the subject of "The Corn Cob."

These little "literary" gems sold by the hundreds and the thousands, and the coins, greenbacks, checks and money orders that came in at the rate of one or two dollars to twenty or thirty dollars a day were economic adrenalin to a newspaper whose advertising revenues were sharply diminished as a result of (1) its independence and iconoclasticism, and (2) the depression that gripped the nation in the 1930's.

But this incidental income did not add up to enough money to enable *The Independent* to continue indefinitely to cope with the competition of its daily contemporary. There just wasn't enough advertising money available in Elizabeth City to support two newspapers at more than a bare subsistence level, and in competing for the lifesaving national advertising of the big automobile, tobacco, gasoline and appliance producers, Dad's newspaper was at a disadvantage because some 20 per cent of its readers lived one hundred to one thousand miles from Elizabeth City, whereas 95 per cent of the other paper's circulation was in its trade territory, which is what the national advertisers wanted.

Finally, and reluctantly, Dad decided to meet the competition head-on and "go for broke" by converting *The Independent* from a weekly to a daily and find out which ultimately would survive. Anyone who knows anything at all about the publishing business knows that this can be a costly and perilous move unless one has access to large financial resources to meet all the heavy expenses of buying new printing machinery, hiring additional mechanical help, waging a circulation campaign, and so on without end.

Dad incorporated the business and floated a stock issue, which he attempted to sell personally and privately to individuals who believed in him and his newspaper. Several Elizabeth City business and professional men put amounts ranging from $100 to $500 into the venture, and several upstate friends sweetened the kitty. One of the latter was Gordon Gray, then a wealthy young newspaper publisher in Winston-Salem, N. C., who later successively became Chancellor of the University of North Carolina, Assistant Secretary of Defense and Special Assistant to President Eisenhower. But the stock purchases collectively amounted to only a few thousand dollars, and it just wasn't sufficient to enable the new daily to hold on long enough to make substantial inroads into the competition's circulation and advertising. *The Daily Independent* was undercapitalized, and only a miracle could have saved it. Nothing miraculous occurred, and Dad finally came to the realization that he had no alternative but to suspend publication and see what he could salvage from the business.

One August night in 1937, the paper was nearly ready to go on the press when Dad walked into the composing room with a heavy heart, handed the linotype operator a piece of copy and announced to the rest of us present that "This is our last edition. I'm having to announce the suspension of publication in a front page editorial. I hope all of you can find something else to do."

Even though we had sensed that this terrible thing might happen some night, the announcement stunned us. No one could find anything to say. We found it hard to look at

Dad's face and into his eyes. We knew that his grief had to be far greater than ours could ever be. This was his lifeblood, and it had ceased to flow; this was his dream, and it was shattered.

Louis Bell sat down at the linotype machine and started setting the fateful announcement. Jimmy Wood went about getting the press ready for its final run. George Haskett, Dad's loyal and hard-working foreman, made the front page ready for the announcement. I put my arm briefly around Dad's shoulders, gave his arm a comforting squeeze and then walked out into the night, choked with emotion. I drove my car to a lonely dirt path beside a railroad siding inside the city limits, switched off the engine and lights, and then loosed the torrent of tears that I had been holding back. I sobbed uncontrollably for many minutes.

The thought kept hammering away incessantly at my conscious mind that a great newspaper had passed from the scene after nearly thirty often hectic, sometimes glorious, ever interesting and challenging years. That a mighty force for righteousness had at last been shackled. That a golden trumpet which had sounded many a clarion call on behalf of tolerance and understanding and enlightenment had been muted. That this was finis—thirty—for *The Independent.*

In due course, Dad returned the new equipment for which he hadn't finished paying, sold off the remainder, and paid off all creditors except the holders of the mortgage on the building, and this could bring enough rent to carry itself. He never tried to go back into the newspaper business and was engaged in trade association work and free lance writing when he met with death in an automobile accident in 1940.

Thousands of individuals in Elizabeth City, the Albemarle section and all over North Carolina still remember W. O. Saunders and his newspaper. There probably will never be another like it, nor another editor like my Dad. He was one of the last and most interesting personal journalists of this country.

He richly deserved, like his newspaper, to be called The Independent, or, perhaps more appropriately, what he often called himself early in his career—The Independent Man.